Oliver Leaman is Professor of Philosophy and Zantker Professor of Judaic Studies at the University of Kentucky. His many books include: *Evil and Suffering in Jewish Philosophy* (1995); *Moses Maimonides* (1997, revised edition); *Averroes and his Philosophy* (1997, second edition), *An Introduction to Classical Islamic Philosophy* (2001); *The Cambridge Companion to Medieval Jewish Philosophy* (edited with D Frank, 2003); and *Jewish Thought: An Introduction* (2006).

'*Judaism: An Introduction* is a balanced and engaging introduction to Judaism and Jewish life. By avoiding tedious academic arguments and going right to the point of the issue, Oliver Leaman engages the general reader as well as college students who are interested in the Jewish journey. In doing so, Leaman presents the ebb and flow of Jewish life, with its issues, arguments and hopes, in a readable form. I highly recommend it.' – *Marc H Ellis, University Professor of Jewish Studies, Baylor University*

'This contemporary introduction to Judaism is well written, engaging, and easily accessible to students. Particularly valuable is Oliver Leaman's treatment of "issues" at the end of the book. He is able to cover a wide range of important and current topics – from Israel to blood libel to the question of race – that any student of the Jewish tradition would find to be of interest. His writing maintains the complexity of the issue while also being straightforward and clear. All in all, the book is a wonderful and welcome addition to the literature.' – *Claire Katz, Associate Professor of Philosophy and Women's Studies, Texas A&M University*

'In *Judaism: An Introduction*, Oliver students and general readers a lively an to understanding the manifold aspe religion. His book is a superb introduc

being Jev dition.' – Susa... *Heschel, Studies, Dartmouth* College

I.B.TAURIS INTRODUCTIONS TO RELIGION

In recent years there has been a surge of interest in religion and in the motivations behind religious belief and commitment. Avoiding over-simplification, jargon or unhelpful stereotypes, I.B.Tauris Introductions to Religion embraces the opportunity to explore religious tradition in a sensitive, objective and nuanced manner. A specially commissioned series for undergraduate students, it offers concise, clearly written overviews, by leading experts in the field, of the world's major religious faiths, and of the challenges posed to all the religions by progress, globalization and diaspora. Covering the fundamentals of history, theology, ritual and worship, these books place an emphasis above all on the modern world, and on the lived faiths of contemporary believers. They explore, in a way that will engage followers and non-believers alike, the fascinating and sometimes difficult contradictions or reconciling ancient tradition with headlong cultural and technological change.

'I.B.Tauris Introductions to Religion offers students of religion something fresh, intelligent and accessible. Without dumbing down the issues, or making complex matters seem more simple than they need to be, the series manages to be both conceptually challenging while also providing beginning undergraduates with the complete portfolio of books that they need to grasp the fundamentals of each tradition. To be religious is in the end to be human. The I.B.Tauris series looks to be an ideal starting point for anyone interested in this vital and often elusive component of all our societies and cultures.' – *John M Hull, Emeritus Professor of Religious Education, University of Birmingham*

'The I.B.Tauris Introductions to Religion series promises to be just what busy teachers and students need: a batch of high-quality, highly accessible books by leading scholars that are thoroughly geared towards pedagogical needs and student course use. Achieving a proper understanding of the role of religion in the world is, more than ever, an urgent necessity. This attractive-looking series will contribute towards that vital task.' – *Christopher Partridge, Professor of Religious Studies, Lancaster University*

'The I.B.Tauris series promises to offer more than the usual kind of humdrum introduction. The volumes will seek to explain and not merely to describe religions, will consider religions as ways of life and not merely as sets of beliefs and practices, and will explore differences as well as similarities among specific communities of adherents worldwide. Strongly recommended.' – *Robert A Segal, Professor of Religious Studies, University of Aberdeen*

Please see the back of the book for the full series list

Judaism

An Introduction

by

Oliver Leaman

I.B. TAURIS

LONDON · NEW YORK

For Renée and Robert

Published in 2011 by I.B. Tauris & Co Ltd
6 Salem Road, London W2 4BU
175 Fifth Avenue, New York NY 10010
www.ibtauris.com

Distributed in the United States and Canada Exclusively by Palgrave Macmillan
175 Fifth Avenue, New York NY 10010

I.B. Tauris Introductions to Religion

ISBN: 978 1 84885 394 2 (HB)
ISBN: 978 1 84885 395 9 (PB)

A full CIP record for this book is available from the British Library
A full CIP record is available from the Library of Congress

Library of Congress Catalog Card Number: available

Designed and Typeset by 4word Ltd, Bristol, UK
Printed and bound by TJ International Ltd, Padstow, Cornwall

Contents

Preface

In many ways I am not a good person to write an introduction to Judaism, or indeed any religion, since I do not think that religions have essences in the sense of beliefs and principles that define them. I think that religions are much looser collections of ideas and practices and can encompass a wide range of doctrines and beliefs, and that makes it tough to write an introduction. It is much easier if one can just specify what the principles of a religion are and then derive the consequences from them. Despite this difficulty, I hope that readers will find something of interest in this account. It is untidy in the sense that I include a whole variety of views and actions as being Jewish which others might exclude, and constantly raise the issue of how we define things as Jewish and what the point of that process really is. I have written several books on religion and in them I do tend to take a much more permissive attitude to what counts as religious, and as part of the religion, than is often the case, which I think has the advantage of reflecting reality, but undoubtedly also has the disadvantage of being messy. I certainly have not included every piece of information on Judaism in this book, though occasionally I have gone into a fair amount of detail to represent something of the richness of the tradition that is involved in these areas of religious life.

I teach a course every year on Judaism at my university and have looked in vain for a book I could use which would serve as an appropriate textbook for the sorts of things I like to talk about, and so in the end I thought I would write one myself. A few years ago I wrote *Jewish Thought: An Introduction*, which covers some of the theoretical issues I discuss in my course. In that book I wrote quite a lot on Judaism's relations with the other religions and with other systems of thought, and thought it would be useful to have a book that looked a bit more closely at the main ideas that arise in Judaism, but that also tried to put them into the context of their historical and cultural environment. This is what I have tried to do here, and yet the emphasis is still very much on those ideas and how they often remain at the forefront of discussions among Jews and between Jews and others even today. I pay especially close attention to the Talmud and the whole commentary tradition in Judaism, since I think it brings out a lot that is interesting about the religion and how it has developed. On the other hand, I am very aware of the problems in using bits of theology to try to make points about a religion, since it is all too easy to select a passage here and there to make almost any point one wants to make, and that is hardly very illuminating about the religion, though rhetorically it may be very effective. I am quite critical in the book about how this technique tends to be employed.

I have started with the Bible and provided a brief, but I hope helpful, account of how it talks about the original leaders of the community that was to become the Jews, their experiences and what these mean for those that followed them. This has very much formed the basis to the substance of debate in Judaism ever since. Then I look at some of the practices of the Jews, both traditional Jews and those who have to a degree sought to reform or adapt the religion to contemporary conditions. The point here is to give something of a flavor of Jewish prayer and law, since that forms the basis of all Jewish life, even of those who do not pray or observe the law. This is what they are reacting against in their decisions about how to live. Finally, I examine a few general statements made about Jews and the religion, which are often expressed and are not as obviously true, or false, as they may initially seem. There is a saying in the American South that it ain't what you don't know that causes problems, it's what you know that ain't so, and in the last section of the book I look at some familiar claims that deserve attention. I particularly want to criticize what often goes under the label of modern Jewish thought, which typically is neither modern nor Jewish – though it *is* thought – and point the reader instead in the direction of the classical texts of Jewish intellectual life. Some of these issues are the ones my students are interested in discussing and I felt they ought to be addressed directly.

One of the stylistic features I have employed that readers should note is that the narrative does not follow a strict chronological order, like many of the traditional Jewish commentaries themselves, but the modern, the medieval and the classical are often intermingled. It is in fact very difficult to distinguish sharply between different periods of

Jewish thought, and often one responds to a very modern piece of thinking with something biblical, Midrashic or Talmudic. When Joseph presents his sons to his father Jacob for a blessing they are greeted with the strange words 'Whose are these?' (*Gen* 48.8). Joseph has been living with his sons in Egypt for 17 years and Jacob seems to have forgotten they are his grandchildren. A couple of verses later we get some sort of explanation, in that he is getting old and his sight is poor. Still, why is this fact not presented before we hear of his confusion at who is standing before him? It could of course be an ironic comment on his fooling his own father Isaac through the latter's poor eyesight to win the blessing over his brother Esau. The commentator Rashi suggests, however, that what happened here is that Jacob foresaw the future – that the descendents of his grandsons Ephraim and Manasseh would be the deplorable kings that were to come. The *Shechinah*, the divine presence, left him with that thought and he did not recognize who was in front of him. It is sometimes argued that Isaac himself was thinking of the future when he gave his blessing to the son who would make better use of it, and so his poor eyesight was more diplomatic than anything else. Whatever we say about this particular case, the blending of the past, present and future, and not necessarily in that order, is very much the Jewish tradition in commentary, and it will be followed here.

I have rarely felt happy at the images that are to be found in books on Judaism. They are often stereotypical and do not represent the variety of Jewish life and practice. I am not sure I have escaped that trap, but at least I know it exists, and I hope readers will find some of the images helpful in their encounter with the religion and culture of Judaism.

I should like to thank Alex Wright, who first suggested that I write this book, and my many different audiences who have heard some parts of it over the last few years. It is impossible to exaggerate the significance of the comments that people make on such occasions, and invidious to thank particular individuals. Lesley Chapman from the Visual Resources Unit at the University of Kentucky was very helpful, as always, with the images. 4word helped a great deal with the style of the book. I am grateful for all their efforts.

OLIVER LEAMAN

Abbreviations and Technical Details

The Jewish Bible consists of three parts: the Five Books of Moses; the Prophets; and the Writings (in Hebrew Torah, Nevi'im and Ketuvim), leading to the acronym Tanakh. This is the Written Law, and there is also the Oral Law, the commentaries on the Bible and on personal and religious Jewish practice, the chief works of which are the Mishnah and the Talmud. In this book, references are often given to these works, and the English terms are used for the books in the Bible. References to the Bible are provided in this form: Book chapter.verse; and for the Qur'an, sura.aya.

References to the Mishnah and Talmud are given in the usual way, but not abbreviated. References to the Talmud are to the Babylonian Talmud except when prefaced JT, which means it comes from the Jerusalem Talmud. References to other Jewish commentaries are also not abbreviated, since I am assuming that many readers will be unfamiliar with them and it is more helpful if they see the full name.

Responsa = *The Responsa Anthology*, compiled by Avraham Finkel.
ES = *Evil and Suffering in Jewish Philosophy*, Oliver Leaman.
JT = *Jewish Thought: An introduction*, Oliver Leaman.

I decided not to add a glossary, but have tried to explain unfamiliar terms as I go along. This occasionally leads to repetition, but means that the reader does not have to flip from the page of text to another page at the end or beginning of the book.

The term 'the Land of Israel' is used to denote what was sometimes called Israel, Palestine and so on before the existence of the State of Israel. Since, in the days of the kingdoms of Israel and Judah, only one part of the country was called Israel, it is better to use the expression 'the Land of Israel' to refer to the whole territory.

CE stands for Common Era, labelled AD (Anno Domini) by Christians; and BCE means Before the Common Era, BC (Before Christ) for Christians.

I have not followed a consistent transliteration system, which I think is only appropriate for books that are written for a specialist audience. I have used the English version of the Hebrew or Aramaic term that I think is most commonly used.

Chapter I

The Bible in Jewish History

The Jews First Appear

There is a great deal of travel in the Jewish Bible, especially in the Five Books of Moses – the first five books in the traditional arrangement of the text, called the Chumash, meaning Five in Hebrew. Sometimes this is referred to as the Torah, which can also mean the whole of the Jewish Bible and can even include the Oral Law, as we shall see. Even when the ancestors of the Jews go to the land of Canaan that God has given them, he says 'you are strangers and sojourners with me' (*Lev* 25.23). Elie Wiesel comments: 'The Jew is in perpetual motion. He is characterized as much by his quest as by his faith' (1970, 214). God tells Abram to go and leave his father's house in what is today Iraq, and travel to a place that God will show him, and from that time onwards Abram, later to become Abraham, is on the move, as are his descendants. He crosses (*avar*) the river – the Euphrates – to enter Canaan and is then called an *ivri*, a Hebrew. He came from Ur and, with his wife Sarai, father Terah and nephew Lot, traveled to Harran in what is today Syria. From there he was told to go to Canaan (equivalent to much of modern Israel), where a famine obliged him to leave for Egypt. From there he moved to the south of Canaan, and then to the Hebron area. There he was told, when he was aged 99 and his wife ninety, that they would have a son, and Isaac was born, after which they were renamed Abraham, meaning 'father of many', and Sarah, meaning 'princess'. When Isaac was born, Abraham, at the urging of his wife, drives away Hagar, the mother of an earlier son, Ishmael. The two almost perish in the desert and are saved by God. Abraham's sons are regarded as the original source of the Jews (Isaac) and Muslims (Ishmael), and the rather difficult relationship between these two communities at different stages of their existence might have something to do with the fraught nature of their origins.

Circumcision became a sign of the covenant between Abraham and God, and later a protracted indication of being a member of the community. In the rabbinic literature, the removal of the foreskin is regarded as an aspect of perfecting humanity, and even the early Christians insisted on circumcision before a male could become a member of that community. Paul later on had a different opinion and this may have been a crucial issue in the rapid success of the new movement that arose out of Judaism. Spinoza, in his *Tractatus Theologico-Politicus*, classified this ritual as the one thing that would establish the distinction between the Jews and everyone else: 'So great importance do I attach to this sign, I am persuaded that it is sufficient by itself to maintain the separate existence of the nation forever' (Spinoza, 1989, 3.53). The Talmudic book of *Nedarim* 3.11 suggests that circumcision has a protective function and we are told that the Temple was destroyed because of a failure to circumcise (*Menachot* 53b). Of course, it is quite a radical step to alter the male anatomy in such a sensitive area, and typifies the dramatic nature of Abraham's relationship with God, culminating in the *akedah*, the potential sacrifice of Isaac. *Akedah* means binding, and is a reference to Abraham's tying up his son and preparing him to be sacrificed. God commanded him to do this (*Gen* 22) and despite what must have been his feelings of love for the child, Abraham set about carrying out the task without argument, which was unusual for Abraham, even to the extent of tying Isaac up and getting him ready for the knife.

There has been much discussion of the morality of this event, in that it is an issue as to whether we should do whatever God tells us to do, or if there are some orders that we should resist, and it has a good deal to do with whether one sees ethics as coming from God, or as independent of him. One of the themes of the Jewish Bible is the practice of many of its main characters of arguing with God. God says he is going to do something drastic and people argue with him, suggesting that he moderate or even entirely reconsider his actions. God tells Abraham that he is going to destroy the cities of the plain and Abraham asks him if he will destroy the innocent with the guilty, and even goes so far as to ask if the God of justice will be unjust (*Gen* 18.25). Later, Moses tries to assuage divine anger at the Israelites' abandonment of God and their disinclination to do what they are told (*Num* 14.13–19). Yet at no stage do Abraham or Moses think they are equal to the God with whom they are arguing, and one wonders if they think they are trying to provide him with information or ideas that he does not possess. Surely not, though there are references in the Jewish Bible to God remembering people, which implies that for a period perhaps he forgot about them. Presumably God has set up these situations to encourage people to argue with him, and the Israelites, and later the Jews, certainly kept up this tradition, with the best example being Job. Job's friends produce the usual religious platitudes to explain his suffering. He must have sinned, we cannot know why God does what he does, there is an ultimately just arrangement of the world of which we are unaware, and we must just be patient and accept quietly the problems that befall us. But Job is not satisfied with this, he rants and raves, and in the end succeeds in drawing God into appearing and responding directly to his complaints. What is most revealing though is God's comment toward the end of the book, in which he condemns the friends who produce the religious formulas 'explaining' the suffering of the innocent. God says he will only forgive them if Job intercedes on their behalf! Only those who argue with God act as he wants, it seems, and those who are meek and mild are criticized for their passivity (Leaman, 1997a, *passim*).

Isaac is married to Rebecca, who is one of Abraham's relatives in the Hebron area, and she produces twins, Esau and Jacob. Like so many brothers in the Bible, these brothers had a difficult relationship. The elder brother, Esau, could expect to receive the birthright from his father, and he does make much more of a contribution to the family through his strength as a hunter, while Jacob seems to have spent a lot more time ingratiating himself with his mother, who helped him eventually to cheat his brother out of his due. Jacob did not fancy his chances fighting with Esau and ran away to Harran, where he worked for a relative, his uncle Laban, and eventually married his two daughters, Leah and Rachel. He returned in some trepidation to Canaan, worried at the reception he would receive at the hands of his brother, but he grappled on the way with a stranger, often taken to be an angel, after which he was called Israel – someone who struggles with God and men, and beats them. God often rewards people for being persistent, like Job or Jonah, even if they are doing or saying questionable things.

Enmity between brothers arises again when Jacob's sons developed a distinct loathing for his favorite son, Joseph. It is not difficult to

imagine the feelings of the brothers at the obvious favoritism in which
Joseph was held by his father, the leader of the family and indeed the
tribe, and their enmity found its target when one day they found him
alone, overwhelmed him and debated what to do to him. Some were
in favor of killing him, others selling him off as a slave – which one
imagines at that time was not much different from being killed. The
latter policy won the day, and Joseph was consigned to be sold in
Egypt, his father being shown his bloody coat, with the obvious
implication that Joseph had suffered a fatal accident. It is perhaps
ironic that Jacob, who fooled his father into giving him Esau's
birthright, should in the end be fooled himself by the sight of
something that was not what it really seemed to be. Joseph succeeded
in Egypt, having the typical (in his case involuntary) immigrant's
range of good and bad experiences, and eventually became the adviser
to the Pharaoh through his ability to interpret the ruler's dreams.

The words a new Pharaoh used reflects many anti-Semitic charges
over the past two millennia – that a significant community now
existed and could be a danger to the host community (*Ex* 1.8–10).
The Israelites needed to be controlled and reduced in both size and
wealth so that they would become more malleable. They became the
Other, a role they were to play for a long time in world civilization
regardless of where they lived or how they behaved. The oppression
they then suffered presumably did much to knit them together as a
distinct community and reduced their assimilation into Egyptian
culture, though some of the Israelites may well have passed as
Egyptians, as we are told that Moses did when he was brought up by
the Pharaoh's daughter. The commentator, and perhaps the greatest
Jewish thinker ever, Moses Maimonides (1138–1204), went on to
speculate that the Jews were to spend 40 years in the desert on their
way to the promised land in order to rid them gradually of their
Egyptian ways of thinking and doing things (Leaman, 1997b). It
would take at least a generation to accomplish this, and a profound
change in living conditions, together with a system of legislation
designed to counter Egyptian culture.

Moses

The name Moses – Moshe in Hebrew – plays on a link with the
word for drawing out of water (*Ex* 2.10). Many Hebrew names in

Leaving Egypt

the Bible are like that, making a reference to something that is going to happen. Moses was born around the thirteenth century BCE to Amram and Jochabed, and had a sister Miriam and brother Aaron. During a time of persecution of Jewish males he was hidden in a basket and placed in the rushes growing in the river, only to be rescued and subsequently drawn out of the water (hence the name) by the Pharaoh's daughter. He was apparently brought up as an Egyptian, but fled to Midian after killing an Egyptian in defense of a fellow Israelite, going on to marry Zipporah and having two sons. Here he again defends the weak, resisting aggression against the daughters of his future father-in-law, Jethro. On Mount Sinai he experienced the presence of God through the burning bush and received the orders to lead the Hebrews from Egypt. Moses protested his unsuitability for the task, especially as he is not a very fluent speaker, so he is told to take his brother Aaron with him to help in his task. Aaron often appears in the rabbinic writings on the Bible as being much milder and more pliable than his brother. The Pharaoh resists Moses' mission, though Moses carries on trying to change his mind, and the Egyptians are punished with the ten plagues. Moses' task is not made any easier by God hardening the Pharaoh's heart, as we are told, which is interpreted by Maimonides as meaning that the Pharaoh has such a wicked personality that whatever he does he has to be punished. In preventing him from agreeing to Moses' proposal, God was intent on having him punished for his fixed evil character. With the last plague, the death of the Egyptian first-born sons, Moses succeeds in leading the Israelites out of Egypt and evading the Egyptians' attempt to recapture them when they change their minds about letting them go. Moses takes the Israelites across the water into the Sinai desert and returns to Mount Sinai, where a detailed covenant is established with God and the whole of the community. His people constantly let him down, yet he persists in caring for them and guiding their route to the promised land. Moses then continues to lead the Israelites to the land of Canaan, but dies at Mount Nebo without himself entering Canaan. This is because he annoyed God in his carrying out of his task, though there is much discussion about how precisely this came about.

A disarming feature of Moses' character is his apparent modesty. He was frightened by the presence of God in the burning bush and refused to look at him, and admitted to not knowing the divine name or being able to carry out the task he was set. When his mission to the Pharaoh is at first unsuccessful and the Israelites turn against him, he complains to God for sending him there (*Ex* 5.22) as the Hebrews complain to him about God's plans for them. These are very human reactions on the part of both Moses and his people. Even when they escape from Egypt and discover the pursuing Egyptian army, the Israelites blame Moses. Moses followed God's instructions throughout the exodus and served as the conduit for divine assistance for the Hebrews throughout this long period when they were threatened by enemies, both human and natural, and the eventual mission was entirely successful. Despite this, the people were often impatient and skeptical about the ultimate success of the mission. When Moses was delayed on Mount Sinai, where he received the details of the law, the people revolted against monotheism and constructed the Golden Calf, an event that caused Moses to smash the tablets he had brought down from the mountain. Eventually, after punishing the leaders of the revolt, he returned to Mount Sinai once more with blank tablets and God dictated the terms of the covenant.

Moses was also involved in constructing the tabernacle that contained the covenant, and continued to intercede on behalf of the Hebrews on the occasions when they were attacked, and the even more frequent occasions when they turned against God and refused to trust in the eventual success of their mission. Even Moses himself, at *Num* 20.10, is shown to be fallible in carrying out an order by God to tell a rock to produce water, when the Israelites were yet again complaining of a lack of sustenance. He struck the rock twice and water did indeed gush out, but the implication was that he had carried out the miracle, not God, and for this he is told, at *Num* 20.12, that he will not be allowed to enter the Land of Israel, though other reasons are also given in the commentatorial tradition. Even when, at 120 years old, he sees the land from Mount Nebo and pleads for admittance, God does not relent. Moses draws up the Israelites and reminds them of their trials in the desert, and summarizes some of the basic principles of the Law they received on Mount Sinai. At the end of the Five Books of Moses, he is referred to as a unique prophet, someone who God knew face to face, and who was engaged in performing the most remarkable actions. Yet, unlike many of the other major figures in Judaism, his burial place is known to no one. In some ways he seems often to have lived under a cloud of suspicion, despite his enormous achievements, and it is worth pointing out that in the prayerbook for the Passover festival, the haggadah, which recounts the events of the exodus in Egypt, his name is not mentioned at all.

Moses, as Musa, figures as a major character in the Qur'an, and is the most frequently mentioned human being (137 references). The account of his life and achievements is broadly in line with the Jewish Bible. He is referred to as both a prophet and a messenger, in accordance with the significance of his role for the Israelites. He is also the most mentioned Old Testament character in the New

Testament, often referred to as representing the Law and prefiguring Jesus. He has frequently become part of modern theological debates, such as whether he was in fact Jewish (Freud thought he was an Egyptian), and what meaning his prophecy has for the three religions that regard him as significant. But, as we shall see, Judaism often treats him often rather suspiciously, and in this he is not regarded very differently from many of the other major figures in the Bible.

The Period in the Desert

The period in the desert reveals a most unflattering side of the Israelites, with their constant wavering in their mission, which was not really something they chose to take on, but were forced to in order to escape from a hostile Egypt – made presumably even more hostile by the plagues the Egyptians suffered at the hands of the God of Israel. How many Israelites actually left Egypt is a moot point in any case. When they left Egypt they helped themselves to the wealth of their former oppressors, which might have done something also to alienate them from their former neighbors, but would not have changed them in any particular way into a distinct people; we have to credit that to the experience of 40 years together in the desert. The Israelites do not seem to be very grateful to God for saving them from slavery, since they on occasion, when things get difficult, complain about their present lives in contrast with how things were in the past – a very human trait indeed. When things change we do often look back fondly on the past, even when there was really nothing good about the past at all, but even a grim past bears comparison with a grimmer present, of course. There is not much in the story of the desert journey to present a picture of an ennobled people; even the theophany, the experience of receiving the Law at the foot of Mount Sinai, is presented as a rather confusing experience for the majority of those present, and of course during the absence of their leader Moses the people promptly rebelled and constructed the Golden Calf. It is hardly surprising that great punishment followed this disobedience, and on a number of other occasions God is very ready to strike those dead who display inappropriate behavior. The laws that the Jews received are in themselves quite harsh in their punishments; almost everything receives a capital punishment, even for not observing the Sabbath (*Ex* 31.15). Yet these laws were to go on to define the Jews as a distinct community for a long time; it seems that there is a real enthusiasm in Judaism to arrive at some defining principles and characteristics that serve to make a distinction between it and others.

There is something about mountains that makes people think about God, and it is hardly surprising that mountains are important in religions such as Judaism. 'God dwells in the mountains', Gershom Scholem suggests in his diary (Robertson, 1999, 192), in the sense that mountains are places that are unpredictable, dangerous and thrilling, just the sort of environment for dramatic religious encounters, for human beings to test themselves and be tested, and for the sublime feelings that arise when contemplating nature in all its wildness and unpredictability.

Mount Sinai and the Chosen People

The Jews are often referred to as the chosen people, and one aspect of this chosenness is related to the receiving of the Torah by Moses and the Israelites at Mount Sinai. For this reason, Jews recite a blessing called the *birkat ha-Torah* before the reading from the Torah during services. One line of the blessing addresses the idea of chosenness in this way: 'Blessed are You, O Lord our God, King of the World, for choosing us from all the nations and giving us the Law.'

Jews are called on to be a 'light to the nations' (*Isa* 42.6), which is sometimes interpreted as doing good in the world through *gemilut chasidim* (acts of loving kindness) and *tikkun olam* (repairing the world). There are certainly problems with the idea of a chosen people if this means that the Jews are taken to be better than anyone else just because they are Jews, and it is worth noticing that Maimonides does not list this in what he takes to be the 13 basic beliefs of Judaism (ch. VI *supra*). This status of being chosen is certainly not limited in time, and at *Deut* 5.2–3 the Israelites say that God made a covenant with them in Horeb; not with their fathers but with *them*, everyone who was there that day. Clearly, the covenant and the status of being chosen are linked, though some covenants are with the whole of humanity (*Gen* 9.8–11). The covenant with the Jews needs to be renewed periodically, reasserted and re-established, and one finds in the Bible and the rabbinic commentaries new ways throughout Jewish history of accomplishing this. After the return from Babylon it comes through the writing down of the Bible, its interpretation in a language that people can understand – namely, Aramaic – and its public recital (*Neh* 8.5–8). In the rabbinic period we have the substitution of the *mitzvot* and prayer for the Temple services and the work of the priests. In modern times it is not clear what we have that is renewing the covenant. For some Jews it is good works – *tikkun*, repairing the world – and this they link with a special Jewish concern for justice (though we shall come to challenge the reality of such a notion in Chapter VI of this book). For others, it is clinging to a literal understanding of their religious obligations, as relayed in the Talmud and similar works. For most Jews now though, it is probably the case that the notion of a special relationship with God has disappeared. The Holocaust certainly destroyed any notion of God looking after his people particularly well, and for many destroyed any possible future relationship with him in any case. It has to be said, however, that it was really the Enlightenment that damaged and perhaps largely extinguished this notion of an ongoing relationship with a God who chose them. Jewish enthusiasm for secularism meant that the ideas of chosenness and covenant became increasingly out of touch with the attitudes of many Jews. What has come to persist is the fact that, since many non-Jews see the Jews are having a special relationship with God, the Jews are thus seen as being to a degree different from everyone else, either in a positive or a negative sense. This has done much to continue to foster a notion of Jewishness, even when it has to survive without any commitment among its practitioners to Judaism.

On some readings of the Torah, the Jews are the chosen people because they have been chosen by God (*Deut* 14.2): 'For you are a holy people to the Lord your God, and God has chosen you to be his treasured people from all the nations that are on the face of the earth.' Though the Torah also says, 'Now therefore, if you will obey my voice indeed, and keep my covenant, then you shall be a peculiar treasure to me above all people,' which makes the chosenness look provisional. God promises that he will never exchange his people. Other Torah verses about chosenness refer to the quality rather than the quantity of the chosen people: 'For all the earth is mine: and you shall be unto me a kingdom of priests, and a holy nation' (*Ex* 19.5– 6); 'The Lord did not set his love upon you, nor choose you, because you were more in number than any people; for you were the fewest of all people; but because the Lord loved you, and because he would keep the oath which he had sworn unto your ancestors' (*Deut* 7.7–8). On the other hand, there are references in the Bible to the enormous size that the Jewish community would reach, as a result of having God's support. It was Abraham's job to broadcast the message of divine monotheism throughout the world, perhaps, but if so he does not seem to have done it. On the other hand, God does not always view his oath as unconditional, nor that the Jews would always maintain their status of chosenness. There are obligations imposed upon the Israelites (*Amos* 3.2): 'You only have I singled out of all the families of the earth: therefore will I visit upon you all your iniquities.' With greater responsibilities go greater sanctions, apparently, so the status of being chosen is not an unalloyed advantage.

There are two aspects of being chosen: one where we need to discuss what it was about the Jews that made God choose them (or was it rather the case that the Jews chose God?). According to one of the accounts, God offered the Torah to everyone, but only the Jews wanted to accept it, and ever since then they have had a special relationship with God. Chosenness creates obligations exclusive to Jews, while non-Jews have fewer tasks that God asks them to perform. The Mishnah book called the 'Ethics of the Fathers', the *Pirkei Avot* 3.14, has this teaching: 'Rabbi Akiva used to say, "Beloved is man, for he was created in God's image; and the fact that God made it known that man was created in his image is indicative of an even greater love." As the verse states (*Gen* 9.6), "In the image of God, man was created.")' The Mishnah goes on to say, 'Beloved are the people Israel, for they are called children of God; it is even a greater love that it was made known to them that they are called children of God, as it is said, "You are the children of the Lord, your God. Beloved are the people Israel, for a precious article [the Torah] was given to them".' The Jews are linked by the covenant which God concluded with the biblical patriarch, Abraham, their ancestor, and again with the entire Jewish nation at Mount Sinai. Of course, this raises the very real question of how far a deal made in the past can create obligations today (*JT* ch.12).

There are many references in the traditional Jewish prayer book to this chosen status. We have already referred to the blessing for reading the Torah, referring to the Jews as a people chosen out of all the nations. In the *kiddush*, a prayer of sanctification in which the

Sabbath is inaugurated over a cup of wine, the text reads: 'For you have chosen us and sanctified us out of all the nations, and have given us the Sabbath as an inheritance in love and favour. Praised are you, Lord, who hallows the Sabbath.' In the *kiddush* recited on festivals, it says, 'Blessed are you ... who have chosen us from among all nations, raised us above all tongues, and made us holy through his commandments.' The *aleynu* prayer refers to the concept of Jews as a chosen people: 'It is our duty to praise the Master of all, to exalt the Creator of the Universe, who has not made us like the nations of the world and has not placed us like the families of the earth; who has not designed our destiny to be like theirs, nor our lot like that of all their multitude. We bend the knee and bow and acknowledge before the Supreme King of Kings, the Holy One, blessed be he, that it is he who stretched forth the heavens and founded the earth. His seat of glory is in the heavens above; his abode of majesty is in the lofty heights.' Like a lot of such passages, chosenness is correlated with duties, so the status has to be earned and by implication can be lost unless the Jews behave in the right sort of way.

Isaiah 45.2 says, 'Come, gather together, Draw nigh, you remnants of the nations! No foreknowledge had they who carry their wooden images and pray to a God who cannot give success.' This used to be the conclusion of the *aleynu*, a significant prayer which is part of the daily ritual, and not unnaturally this caused offense. The chosenness doctrine has caused a lot of problems for the Jews, both now and in the past, but really there is nothing that objectionable in the doctrine, though it can, and sometimes was, taken to an extreme, which is indeed problematic. In his book comparing different competing religions, the *Kuzari*, Yehuda Halevi suggests that there is a qualitative distinction between Jews and Gentiles, something that applies to each group by virtue of their race, though Halevi also seems to accept that once a Gentile converts he is then equal to a Jew. Taking such a view, it is difficult to understand why, for example, God is supposed to have chided the angels who were cheering when the Egyptians drowned in the Sea of Reeds, with the riposte that 'my creatures are drowning and you are celebrating?' (*Sanhedrin* 38b). There are also many references about looking after and respecting the stranger, which are difficult to understand if chosenness means that there is some irrevocable distinction between Jews and Gentiles (*Gen* 23.4, *Ex* 18.3). On the other hand, it is worth acknowledging that minorities who suffer persecution often respond with a theology of inversion, whereby their apparent inferiority is in fact superiority, a superiority that nothing can ever destroy. There are a number of thinkers who do make a sharp distinction between Jews and non-Jews in ways that would be understood by racists and anti-Semites, and this way of thinking has always been very helpful to the latter in particular, but it does have to be said that this is hardly the mainstream Jewish view. It is, however, entirely natural for a community that has been under pressure for a very long time to develop an image of itself that accords in many ways with that of the oppressor, minus its negative features. It is also entirely natural for that community also to accept the negative image.

Early Life in the Land of Israel

Despite his enormous service to the cause, Moses is not allowed by God to enter the land of Canaan, a feat accomplished by Joshua, and for the next few hundred years the country was ruled by judges, the idea being that the Jews did not need anyone else to rule them apart from the (divine) Law and the human interpreters of that Law. This happy state of affairs did not last, however, since the demand arose for a king to be installed, so that the Jewish state would be like every other state in the region at that time, even after the disadvantages of having a king were clearly pointed out. This brings out a common theme in Jewish history – the conflict within the Jewish world between being different from everyone else and being the same, an example of the saying that the Jews are like everyone else, just more so. It is not surprising that there should be such an issue, since it occurs even for the individual, where we often think of ourselves as being distinct from others, and we are after all who we are and not other people, but we also like to think of ourselves as being the same as others in important respects.

The early kings were of questionable quality. Saul was the first king and had difficult relations with many in the kingdom, while his successors, David and Solomon, seemed to take their role rather more seriously than was often good for the kingdom itself. David certainly expanded the state, and is also credited with having produced some major parts of the Bible, in particular the Psalms, and in the Talmud is often said to have combined political authority with a real commitment to religion. However, the biblical account of his life continues the theme from earlier in the Bible of its heroes having a very mixed moral character, to put it no more strongly; and even David is said to have been denied the honor of constructing the Temple because of the blood he had on his hands as a result of his frequent aggression toward his neighbors. The honor was reserved for Solomon – the author traditionally of *Ecclesiastes* and possibly a more cynical individual than his predecessors – perhaps to mark the fact that establishing an institution such as the Temple does involve a passion for working with a variety of different people and persuading them to do what you want, despite their initial ambitions. This political skill was clearly lacking in Solomon's successor, who continued to work the people hard even after the Temple was completed; and this played no small part, the Bible tells us, in the split in the kingdom and the eventual weakening of the grip of the Israelites on the area.

Temple

After Solomon's death the kingdom split into a northern state called Israel and a southern state, including Jerusalem and the Temple, called Judah, and this division was to go on to have dramatic consequences, since it meant that frequent conflicts between the two states became a feature of political life, and made it easier for the powers that surrounded the Jews to interfere in their affairs. The Hebrew people were divided into 12 tribes plus the Levites, a priestly class, and the Kohanim, the priests themselves. Today there is a division into three: the descendants of the priests, who still have priestly status; the descendants of the Levites, who are still Levites; and the descendants of the rest, known as *Am Yisrael*, ordinary Israelites. In the past, different tribes inhabited different parts of the Land of Israel, then stretching far beyond its present borders, even beyond the borders of Israel and the Occupied Territories in the post-1967 period. Presumably, this tribal division also worked against an increase in the notion of solidarity, even at times of danger, between the inhabitants of the region, intent as they often must have been on preserving their own part of the country.

Two Mesopotamian powers invaded and this had a disastrous impact on the two kingdoms in the Land of Israel. First, the Assyrians captured the northern kingdom and destroyed it, carrying away many of its inhabitants into slavery, and then when they were destroyed in turn by the Babylonians, the latter turned their attention to the southern kingdom and destroyed the Temple, also enslaving many of the inhabitants of Judah. Not only were the original inhabitants removed, but other people were encouraged to move into the area. Much of the prophetic literature of this period linked the sufferings of the Jews with the behavior of their monarchs and their turning away from the religion they had accepted in the past, which came to be something of a trope in the theological explanation of negative events in Jewish history. There was a positive development, however, in the eventual domination of the area by Persia, since Cyrus the Great allowed at least some Jews to return to Jerusalem when he conquered Babylon, and to re-establish the Temple, thus building the Second, and, up to the present day, the last Temple. This was organized by Ezra and Nehemiah, and during this period the written Hebrew Bible was put together.

Traditional Jews look back with longing to the Temples, or at least their liturgy does, and even today some prayers call for the building

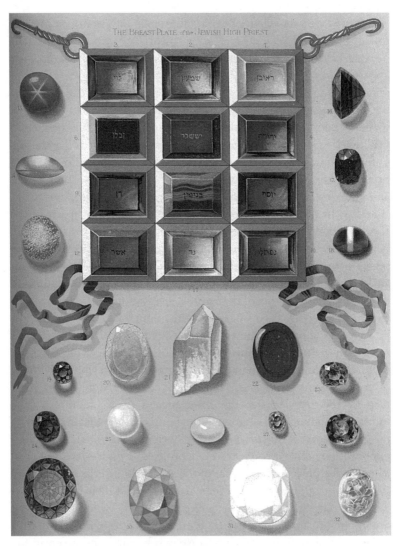

High Priest breastplate

of the Third Temple, but the ceremonies at the time must have been rather gruesome, if their description in the Bible has any accuracy. The slaughtering of animals as an aspect of worship is hardly an ennobling activity, though one should not forget that many of the ceremonies did not involve killing things and must have been more decorous, at least to modern feelings, but the Temple institutions did make two things possible that were surely significant. One was that there was a widespread acceptance of how the Jews ought to behave in relation to what God had told them to do, and a notion about obedience as a virtue and part of a lifestyle. Then there was the fact that an institution existed – the Temples – which embodied directly the nation's turning toward God, so that a number of physical tasks involved in traveling to Jerusalem, presenting animals or, later, money, could constitute a person's religious duties. It is often said that the synagogue did not become established until the Temples were destroyed, since the main site of worship needed to be replaced, but evidence suggests that there were synagogues even while the Temples existed, since people needed somewhere to carry out religious tasks between their trips to Jerusalem, or because they could not, or did not want to, make the journey. And, of course, the frequent dabbling in other religions by the Jews meant that the Temples could be ignored at least temporarily and replaced with something more palatable to the mood of the times. It is important to bear in mind that people need something to inspire them, and when Moses came to rescue the Israelites from Egypt, their 'short spirit' (or disappointment, impatience or broken spirit) and very hard work (*Ex* 6.9; see also *Num* 21.4, *Mic* 2.7, *Prov* 17.29) meant that he received a rough reception. This is very much a theme of the Bible, that the Jews are fickle and need to be kept on course by the right sort of ceremony. One of the institutions designed to change their thinking into a more positive direction was that of the Temple, and it came to take on a vast significance in Judaism.

Jerusalem and Mount Moriah

Jerusalem is replete with sites of sacred significance. We are told that a threshing floor bought by King David from Araunah the Jebusite was the site of the Holy of Holies in the First Temple; and that it was on Mount Moriah where Abraham bound Isaac, literally, and since then all his descendants are linked to the covenant. Some rabbis identify this mountain with the origin of the Creation, and the rock at the summit as a plug holding back the waters of the abyss that is always about to return the world to chaos (2 *Sam* 24.2; 2 *Chron* 3, *Gen* 22; Mishnah *Yoma* 5.2; JT *Sanhedrin* 10.29a). The Jebusites are taken by some Palestinians to be their ancestors, and the reason David chose Jerusalem as his capital was because it belonged to none of the

Israelites and so could perhaps unify them. David is said to be buried on Mount Zion; and this is also the site of the Last Supper, according to many Christians. It is also the place where Jesus is supposed to have reappeared after being dead for three days. This event is commemorated by the Coenaculum or the Cenacle, a small, two-storey structure within a larger complex of buildings on the summit of Mount Zion. The Franciscans built the upper storey in the fourteenth century to commemorate the Last Supper. It is also identified as the 'upper room' in which the Holy Spirit descended upon the Disciples at Pentecost (*Acts* 2.2–3). The ground-floor room beneath the Coenaculum contains a cenotaph that since the twelfth century has been known as the 'Tomb of King David' – even though the recorded burial place of the king was in the 'City of David' on the Ofel Ridge (1 *Kings* 2.10). Beneath the level of the present floor are earlier Crusader, Byzantine and Roman foundations, as occurs so often in Jerusalem. An apse behind the cenotaph is aligned with the Temple Mount, leading to speculation that this part of the building may have been a synagogue.

Former religious buildings have always been incorporated into the structure of newer ones, especially when one religion sees itself as taking over from another. Christian traditions also point to Mount Zion as the place where the Virgin Mary fell asleep for the last time. On that spot, a massive Benedictine basilica was erected. The Franciscans, on their return to Jerusalem, built the present Chapel of the Coenaculum in 1335. The *mihrab*, a Muslim prayer niche, was added in 1523, when the Franciscans were evicted from the building and the room converted into a mosque. The Via Dolorosa commemorates the Passion of Jesus, while the site of the Ascension is on the Mount of Olives. At the Garden of Gethsemane, Jesus prayed for the cup to be taken from him, and the Church of the Holy Sepulchre is yet another site of the Resurrection, a very old church indeed that is possibly built on the foundations of a Roman temple. It is sometimes identified with Golgotha, the place of the Crucifixion, though this was likely to have been some way outside the old walls of the city. The significance of this church means that it is shared by many denominations, who do not always agree on who controls what area, and disputes, which can become violent, do arise. Sometimes they have to be resolved through the intervention of the Israeli police.

The State of Israel came into the full possession of Jerusalem after the 1967 war and regards it as its indivisible capital, though no one else shares its opinion. This means that Israel has control over the religious sites of the three religions, and has dealt with this by generally maintaining an Ottoman-like policy of leaving each community to regulate its own buildings, apart from when conflicts arise. So the two mosques on Temple Mount, along with the other mosques in Jerusalem, come under the authority of the Islamic *waqf*, or foundation, that looks after religious buildings, and Jews are not allowed to go on to the Temple Mount. There is great suspicion on both sides as to the intentions of the other, and some Muslims have denied that Jerusalem has any connection at all with Judaism and the Temple, while some Jews and Christians see it as desirable for a third temple to be built on Temple Mount, presumably after the removal of the mosques. The different Christian denominations are allowed to look after their own property in Jerusalem, but when a dispute arises, as it often does, the State steps in and tries to establish peace. Israel claims, with some plausibility, that there is now more freedom for the three religions than there was during the Jordanian occupation of Jerusalem between 1948 and 1967, since Jews can visit the city and its religious sites freely, which they could not do during that period. On the other hand, there are restrictions on Muslim worshippers, especially during times of tension, which did not exist when Jerusalem was controlled by a Muslim country.

The significance of Jerusalem for Jews cannot be overemphasized. It is mentioned over 600 times in the Bible (but never in the Five Books of Moses) and three times a day in the prayers of traditional Jews, including a wish for the Temple to be rebuilt. Synagogues are aligned so that the direction of prayer is toward Jerusalem, and in particular the Temple, and individuals praying anywhere are directed to pray in that direction. For Muslims, it is the third holiest city (hence its name al-Quds, meaning 'the Holy') and the site of the first *qiblah*, direction of prayer, but now largely significant because of the Prophet's night journey. He rode at night on the horse al-Buraq to Jerusalem, to the top of Mount Moriah, and from there to the heavens to meet the prophets. In fact, the only reference in the Qur'an to Jerusalem is not that direct, but is only to the distant place of worship (*al-aqsa*) (17.1).

For Christians, its significance rests on the life and death of Jesus there, and for some Christians the rebuilding of the Temple plays an eschatological role without which Jesus will not return. According to the Israel Statistical Yearbook for 2000, there were at that time 1,204 synagogues, 158 churches and 73 mosques in the city. Many of the synagogues are very small and belong to ultra-orthodox (*haredi*) communities, who live in the city and spend much of their time involved in religious activities based in particular neighborhoods. While they tend to minimize their links with the State, in recent years these communities have come a little closer to the State of Israel, but in principle they are opposed to the idea of living in a secular state.

Mount Moriah is, according to Jewish tradition, the site of a number of key events in the Jewish Bible, including the Temples, the sacrifice of Isaac and Jacob's dream. It lies between Mount Zion to the west and the Mount of Olives to the east. It is regarded as the navel of the world, as the physical link between God and the Jews. Some Christians believed that the navel stone of the universe lay in the Church of the Holy Sepulchre, where the True Cross had reposed, and the idea of Jerusalem as a particularly close place to heaven persisted in several metaphysical systems, including that of the Freemasons, and their interest in the Temple of Solomon and architectural symbols is based on it. The idea of Jerusalem as an especially religious city has become very much part of the ideology of modern Israel, where it is contrasted with the largely secular and modern city of Tel Aviv, which resembles modern Western cities anywhere (Ram, 2008). Jerusalem remains a city where religious people tend to wish to live, and seek to preserve the religious character of their own areas. So the ultra-orthodox Jews who live in particular parts of the city may try to impose dress and behavior codes even on those passing through their neighborhood, and restrict what can take place on the Sabbath, encouraging or even obliging secular Jews to live in different parts of Israel. In Jerusalem, the disputed nature of the city between Jews and Arabs has made it a natural focus of conflict, which also hardly favors people who wish to live there, unless they have strong religious reasons to do so.

The Temples

King David intended to build a temple, but was told by God that, having shed blood, this would not be appropriate (1 *Chron* 28.3). Solomon constructed it instead in the tenth century BCE (2 *Sam*, 1 *Chron*, 1 *Kings*) and the effort was obviously huge, since he forced his

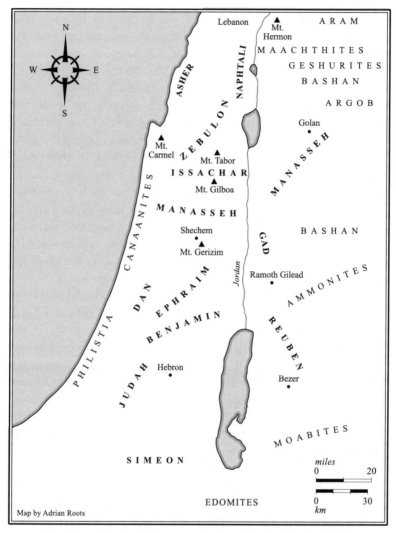

Map of the distribution of the tribes in the Land of Israel at the time of Joshua

subjects to work on the building, and was obliged in the end to cede 20 towns in Galilee to repay King Hiram of Tyre for his material assistance (1 *Kings* 9–11). This is a point often made by religious Jews who are in favor of giving up land for peace. Some argue that it is never acceptable to give up part of the Land of Israel, since the Land had been given by God to the Jews. In fact, it was for being prepared to give up some of the Occupied Territories to the Palestinians in a

peace deal that Prime Minister Rabin was assassinated, by a Jew who
was told that giving up the land ought to be opposed by force. Yet
Solomon gave up land in order to build the Temple.

Prayer, and especially sacrifices, took place in the Temple building
and it lasted for around 400 years until destroyed by the Babylonians
(2 *Kings*, 2 *Chron*), and then a second Temple was built and
subsequently greatly enlarged by King Herod before being destroyed
by the Romans in 70 CE. The first Temple was impressed on the
minds of some of the prophets of the time. Ezekiel, in Babylonian
exile, is told to create a model of Jerusalem and is taken up to heaven
to see the perfect archetype. A great city is on its way to being
reconstituted, and later, when Zechariah sees a man walking around
with a measuring rod and asks where he is going, he is told that he is
going to measure Jerusalem, and that the new city will be so big it
will be as though without walls, apart from the wall of fire that God
will create around it (*Zech* 2.2–5).

In the first Temple, the small area called the Holy of Holies
contained the two tablets of the Law given to Moses on Mount Sinai,
we are told, but these disappeared with its destruction. Only on the
Day of Atonement, the High Priest would enter this room, to carry
out a ritual to atone for the sins of the community as well as for
himself and his family. The Bible commanded Jewish men to appear,
with a sacrifice, in the Temple three times a year – Passover (Pesach),
Pentecost (Shavuot) and Tabernacles (Sukkot) – which came
accordingly to be called the Pilgrim festivals (see Chapter V). One
assumes that this potentially onerous task was often delegated to
others when means made it possible.

During the Muslim occupation of Jerusalem, two mosques were
built on the site of the Temple and only the Western Wall now
remains, widely regarded as being connected to the original building,
though only from the time of King Herod. Many Jews consider
walking on the original Temple site to be forbidden, since it might
involve trespassing on the Holy of Holies, which is strictly forbidden.
The site is now under the political control of the State of Israel, but
they have left the Islamic *waqf* in nominal control and try to prevent
Jews from walking there. Some Muslims deny the existence of any
Temples in Jerusalem, to try to weaken the Jewish claim on the site,
and it has even been suggested that the *kotel*, the Western Wall, is in
fact part of the al-Aqsa mosque and should be known as the Buraq

wall, since Muhammad tethered his mount al-Buraq there while ascending through the heavens on his night journey, according to Islam. On the other hand, the reference in the Qur'an to a *masjid* (mosque) (17.7), in what is often taken to be Jerusalem at a time before there were any mosques, suggests that the most plausible translation is sanctuary or temple. It is also referred to in the account of Sulayman ordering the jinn to build it (34.13), and, of course, in the night journey of the Prophet from Mecca to what is presumably taken to be Jerusalem (17.1), while not named explicitly as such. There is a tendency for religions, especially Islam, to build a symbol of its power and authority on the ruins of a former religion, for obvious symbolic reasons, and it is difficult to believe that the two mosques were not built on that specific site in Jerusalem because it was believed to be the site of a previous Jewish temple. In the same way, a mosque was built on earlier Hindu temples in India, one of which was reverted recently at Ayodya, leading to great controversy, and on important churches in the Middle East. During the Reconquista in Spain, several significant mosques and synagogues were rebuilt as churches. In 2010 there have been reports that, at al-Kifl in Iraq, south of Baghdad and the reputed burial place of the prophet Ezekiel, the Hebrew inscriptions on the tomb have been both erased and covered up, and a mosque is proposed to be built on the site. A large mosque has been proposed next to an important church in Nazareth in the State of Israel, which is no longer a Christian city as far as numbers are concerned, and the obvious symbolism of this is effective in marking the change of status of the city for both the expanding Muslims and the declining Christians.

Orthodox Jews pray three times a day for the restoration of the Temple, and the ceremonies that took place there are still much discussed and remembered even today. It is worth pointing out, though, that just as in the Qur'an, there is no direct reference to Jerusalem in the Five Books of Moses, and this left scope for other groups of Jews, or those closely linked with the Jews, such as the Samaritans, to prioritize other locations – for example, Mount Gerizim.

Mount Gerizim

Mount Gerizim is on the southern side of the valley in which the city of Nablus or Shechem sits, the northern side being Mount Ebal.

It rises to about 2,900 feet above sea level, slightly lower than Mount Ebal. It is the center of worship for the Samaritan community, many of whom live in the vicinity, while the rest live in the Holon area of Tel Aviv-Yafo. They regard Mount Gerizim as the site of Abraham's attempted sacrifice of Isaac, and the location of the Temple, both of which are positioned on Mount Moriah and in Jerusalem for Jews. It was also the direction of the blessings on the restatement of the covenant on the Israelite entry into the land (*Deut* 11.26; 27). This conflict of interpretation developed into a state of great hostility between the Jews and the Samaritans, who came to be regarded as constant enemies.

The mountain became a religious center intended to rival Jerusalem in the mid-fifth century BCE. The Samaritans established their own temple on Mount Gerizim, and in the time of Alexander the Great, according to Josephus, it was increased in size and magnificence. This seems to have aroused considerable antipathy among the Jews in Jerusalem, and both communities sought the support of the rulers of Palestine, whoever they happened to be at the time, for their own community and against the other. The Jews managed to destroy the temple on the mountain, which the Talmud reports with grim satisfaction in *Yoma* 69a. Later, when Christianity became the state religion of the Roman Empire and a church was built on the mountain, this led to a violent Samaritan response which resulted briefly in the recapture of the mount in the sixth century CE and the destruction of churches in Samaria. This response was put down quite quickly, though, and brought about the dispersal of the Samaritan population. Some must have remained, however, since a church was built on the summit of the mountain, which is rather flat, and needed to be protected by a castle. Presumably, if the Samaritans had left completely, that protection would not have been required. Today, the site remains a place where Samaritans live, carry out their rituals and await the coming of the Messiah.

Mount Gerizim plays an enormous part in Samaritan life, and in their version of the Bible the place is mentioned in places where other mountains are mentioned in the Masoretic (i.e. Jewish) text. The many centuries of conflict and rivalry between the Jews and the Samaritans are symbolized by the differences in choice of a holy mountain. For a Samaritan to be recognized as a Jew, he had to renounce any belief in the holiness of Mount Gerizim. There are various interesting remains on the mountain, including some stones that the Samaritans regard as sacred, together with parts of the church of the Virgin Mary and the wall built by Justinian. In the present day, the Samaritan community lives on the slopes and not the summit of the mountain, even though this was the site of their original temple. They use a lower slope, perhaps because of the presence on the summit of a Muslim cemetery, which defiled the original site.

Jerusalem and its Status

There was also a temple at Leontopolis about 200 BCE, north of modern Cairo, and the second is the Temple of Elephantine dating to some 300 years earlier, to about 500 BCE, in Upper Egypt, close to Aswan. These seem to have been set up by Jewish soldiers who were working as mercenaries in the area. A proposal by Hananiah to set up a temple in Babylon at Nahar Peqod was opposed vigorously by the rabbis in the Land of Israel, and it seems that, despite a temple being constructed, the proposal to start a sacrificial cult was abandoned.

The capture of the Old City of Jerusalem in 1967 allowed Jews once again to pray at the Western Wall, and this has become a popular venue. Prayers are often written on paper and placed in a chink in the wall, with the hope that they find their way to heaven and are responded to by God. The whole city has been claimed by the State as its capital, but this status is not really recognized anywhere else; even the USA continually postpones its decision to move its embassy from Tel Aviv to Jerusalem. The plaza in front of the Wall is now hotly contested by different Jewish groups, some disapproving of women mixing with men, or of particular variations in traditional Jewish religious services. The religious status quo is something the State of Israel has tried to preserve in the Temple area. This has led to rather strange consequences. Jews who are in the vicinity of the Temple Mount, and who are seen to move their lips in a way that could be interpreted as a prayer, are sometimes arrested by Israeli police for violating the Muslim nature of the area. Similarly, women who are wearing a *tallit* (prayer shawl) under their clothes at the Western Wall have also been detained by the same police force for violating the traditional interpretation of who can wear a *tallit* (only men) in a place where only traditional forms of worship are tolerated. The government of Israel has been criticized for allowing

only traditional forms of prayer at the Wall, but here they are
following the general Ottoman practice of the State of Israel, which
is not to interfere in local religious practices, in an attempt to
preserve the peace of potentially feuding groups of people passionate
in asserting their rights to the same space.

While the majority of Jews in Israel are secular, there is a
reluctance to relinquish Jerusalem to a Palestinian state, partially
because of the strong attachment by most Jews to what remains of
the Temple and the idea that this should remain as part of the capital
of the State of Israel. On the other hand, there is a growing tendency
for Israelis to contrast Jerusalem with Tel Aviv, the religious with the
secular, the traditional with the modern. For secular Jews, Jerusalem
is an increasingly difficult place in which to live, since so much of the
city and the administration is dominated by the religious community.
The Tel Aviv area, by contrast, is full of factories, company start-ups
and modern buildings, with few restrictions on what people do and
how they dress. Tel Aviv is also far wealthier than Jerusalem, with its
smaller families and big Jewish majority, while the many children
that the traditional Jews, and the Arabs, tend to have in Jerusalem,
along with the absence of industry and the commercial thrust of the
Mediterranean coastal cities, have turned the city into a much poorer
environment as far as national statistics are concerned. It is also a city

Riots in Jerusalem against a car park opening on the Sabbath

where the local traditional Jewish population are frequently in conflict with the local authority, as when a car park that opened on the Sabbath was violently opposed by many Jerusalemites.

The status of Jerusalem will no doubt be a thorny issue in the negotiations between Israel and whatever sort of Palestine may emerge alongside it, if such negotiations ever take place. However, the idea that there are holy places in Judaism is not that easy to accept. A contemporary thinker, Yehoshua Leibowitz, makes the point that a place is holy because certain events took place there; the events did not take place there because it is holy (Leibowitz, 1992, 227). The whole point of Judaism was to do away with the idea that there are holy places or things, and to concentrate holiness on God, a deity who is in every place and all times. Leibowitz compares those religious authorities who call parts of the Land of Israel holy to the 850 prophets of Baal and Asherah, who ate at the table of Queen Jezebel (*Kelim* 1.6). It is worth recalling the criticism that the spies received who visited Canaan and came back reporting that the cities were well fortified and powerful (*Num* 13.28), throwing doubt on the project of conquering them. But God had said that they should be taken and the land was promised to the Israelites through his covenant. The spies were too impressed by what human beings could do and too lacking in faith in what God could do. A belief in the sanctity or significance of particular places could then be seen as antagonistic to the whole monotheistic project.

There is also reason to be a little unsure of this conclusion. It is certainly true that if God is everywhere, then no place is any more significant than any other. Valuing one place more than another is perhaps to think that God is more in one place, or that the place has special powers in some way, as when people put messages in the Western Wall, or in the joke that calling God on the telephone from Jerusalem is free, since it is a local call. While we are told that the Temples were very special places, and the rituals that went on there were highly significant in the relationship between God and the Jews, it is not as though that relationship has come to an end now that the Temples no longer exist. Yet we must also pay some attention to the importance to us as human beings of our imaginative faculty, something that Abraham Kook was very good at describing when he explained what he took to be the Jewish view of how we can come closer to God. Naturally, it is difficult for the finite to come to resemble the infinite, since we know nothing about God and find it difficult even to start to think about him. We also find it difficult to know how to behave, since we are such imperfect creatures and the standards of morality are so far above our capacities and level of existence. God establishes what we ought to do and we try to come closer to him through our actions, but inevitably fall short by a long way.

This is where imagination comes in. We find it tough to be good, and so we help ourselves into this line of behavior by thinking about how much others may admire what we do, or how someone who perhaps is no longer even alive would approve of us. We may find it unpleasant to spend a lot of time praying, and yet if we meet our friends at the synagogue, and if we spend some time before or after, and indeed in between the services, chatting to them, that gives us a motive to keep on praying. It is not a mystery why a *minyan* (quorum) of ten is important in Judaism for prayer, since this is perhaps the smallest size of congregation that can be seen as a community. The Mishnah constantly argues for study not to be private, since more people gathered together makes for a more enjoyable activity, and hence one more likely to persist. Other people may get on our nerves, but they also help us do what is right, and keep us wanting to do it. Certain prayers require a *minyan*, a quorum of ten adult Jews (men only for traditional Jews), perhaps because again it is more interesting to do things in a group of ten than in smaller groups or even alone.

The same may be said of places. The fact that for so many years Jews have prayed at the Western Wall, or had it in their minds while at prayer somewhere else, gives this a resonance when it comes to prayer that other places perhaps do not possess. I wear my father's *tallit* (prayer shawl) and *tefillin* (phylacteries) if I pray in the morning, and they are no different, certainly no better, than any other *tallit* or *tefillin*, but in doing this I think of myself as honoring him to a degree, and I also remember him. I do not think these objects are imbued with some sort of magical power, and surely we should be suspicious of people who think that a message written on paper and placed in a crack in the Western Wall goes straight to God, in the same way that the authoritative Jewish thinker Maimonides disapproved greatly of Jews wearing amulets for protection or indulging in anything superstitious (see, for example, his commentary on Midrash, *Sota* 7.4, and *Guide of the Perplexed* 1, chapters 6 and 3, chapter 37).

Mount Meron

The final mountain to be described is Mount Meron. This is the site of the grave of Shimon bar Yochai, a second-century CE rabbi and official author of the *Zohar*, a major kabbalistic text. The Kabbalah is a system of mystical thought in Judaism, a complex variety of documents that reflect the desire perhaps for a closer personal relationship with God than is possible through ordinary Jewish religious practice and belief. The mountain is a place of pilgrimage for orthodox Jews, who are particularly numerous at the festival of Lag B'Omer, where it is the tradition for their sons at the age of three to have their first haircut. The Aramaic word, *hillula*, meaning 'festivity', was originally used to designate a marriage party. Among Jews originally from Muslim countries, the *hillula* generally commemorates the death of a sage, whose soul is regarded as having been reunited with its Creator. The classic instance of the *hillula* is that marking the traditional anniversary of the death of Rabbi Shimon bar Yochai, which is celebrated at his putative burial place and that of his son Eleazar in Meron, in northern Israel. Crowds as big as 100,000 people attend the festivities, and large bonfires are lit and burn throughout the night. As the political influence of the Moroccan Jewish community has grown in Israel, so has the observance of the various *hillula* ceremonies throughout the year.

Mount Meron is the highest mountain in Galilee, rising to about 4,000 feet, and is also the official burial site of a number of prominent rabbis, in particular the distinguished commentators Hillel and Shammai, and many of their students. There is also a very old synagogue, and the putative burial place of Shimon is now covered with a domed building. The celebration of Lag B'Omer, a festival between Passover and Pentecost (Pesach and Shavuot), has become a significant event for the orthodox community in Israel. The festival itself represents the ending of a great epidemic that killed many Torah students, as well as the death of Shimon bar Yochai himself. He and his son are reputed to have spent 13 years hiding from the Romans in a cave, where they were visited by Elijah and instructed in the mysteries that are hidden in the written Torah, which then became the *Zohar*, or 'glittering'. Though the *Zohar* was undoubtedly written by someone else, and a good deal later, this story has served to make Mount Meron a popular site for those interested in the Kabbalah. It is also much valued by the Mizrachi community in Israel, Jews who originated in the Middle East, and with the growth of the political influence of this community in Israel, their festivals have become far more significant in the State as a whole.

The Importance of Place again

Is it blasphemous in Judaism to value certain places? It certainly is in Wahhabi forms of Islam, and the Saudis have destroyed the sites of the Prophet's family in Mecca and Medina for that very reason. What is important about the Land of Israel is that God promised it to the Jews, and in his covenant the Jews were expected to behave in appropriate ways, both to attain the Land and to keep it. They did the former after a fashion, but certainly did not do the latter, and so lost it.

Some Jewish thinkers are very enthusiastic about the idea of places being important; and perhaps Yehudah Halevi is the best example here, in his poem *Jerusalem*, he starts with, 'Beautiful heights, joy of the world, city of a great king', and ends with the line, 'Your earth will be sweeter than honey to my taste' (Goldstein, 1965, 129). In the *Kuzari*, the Khazar discussant asks quite reasonably why the rabbi thinks the Land of Israel is so important for the Jews, since he says that there were prophets such as Ezekiel, Daniel and Jeremiah who all prophesied in other places. The rabbi replies that the prophets either prophesied in the Land or for its sake. He produces quote after quote from the Bible talking about the significance of the Land and how it is the essential backdrop to the flourishing of its Jewish inhabitants. This is based on a theory that is mentioned, according to which different people have different physical constitutions, and these all find an appropriate environment in a particular place. For the Jews it is the Land of Israel. He blames the collapse of the second Temple on the disinclination of most of the Jews to return from Babylon and support it.

The destruction of the Second Temple encouraged the creation of synagogues as houses of prayer, though there had certainly been such institutions already, even while the Temple existed. In contemporary

America, many Reform Jews call their houses of worship temples. This is to some degree because they see them as replacing the Temples, which will only be rebuilt when the Messiah returns, however that is interpreted. Reform Jews are the followers of a movement that started in nineteenth-century Germany, seeking to modernize Judaism and make it a more appropriate faith for emancipated Jews. The yearning for the Temple to be rebuilt is today only felt among traditional Jews and a number of evangelical Christians, who see it as a precursor of the second coming of Jesus. But Jews should not look forward to this eventuality since they are generally going to come off badly when it happens, not being (the right kind of) Christian, or indeed any sort of Christians at all.

Isaiah Berlin made the remark that the trouble with the Jews was that they had too much history and not enough geography, something which no doubt explained his Zionism. What is important about geography for a community is the sense of place, a place that belongs to the citizens as individuals, and which they have a right to inhabit and enjoy. Ideally it might be feasible for people to accept that all places are the same, since all places were created by God, but if God gives a special status to a particular place and then promises it to a group of people, it is difficult to see how those facts, if they are facts, can be replaced by a general attachment to wherever one happens to find oneself.

Chapter II

Exile

Life in exile has been a familiar experience for Jews for thousands of years, and they often avoided disappearing into the general population. On the other hand, it is probably reasonable to think that the majority of Jews *did* assimilate entirely when they were allowed to do so. It is worth noticing that, even in the past when Jews were able to return to the Land of Israel, they often did not, and do not today either. Before the Jews were expelled from the Land of Israel, they often moved quite voluntarily to other parts of the Mediterranean world and further east. It is difficult, then, to call the period of Jewish life in the diaspora an exile, as though they all wanted to stay in the Land and would have rushed back whenever it was possible. On the other hand, the experience of Jews was often so difficult that they would no doubt have willingly returned if it were possible.

The Babylonians under Nebuchadnezzar conquered the kingdom of Judah and then destroyed Jerusalem and the First Temple. They took back to Babylon as prisoners the royal family and the skilled part of the population of the tribes of Benjamin and Judah. About 130 years earlier, the northern kingdom of Israel had been destroyed by the Persians and their population largely removed to Persia. The prophets provided an explanation for this circumstance as a punishment by God for the sins of the community, and not a permanent cessation of the covenant with God. After all, Jeremiah had argued for a policy of submission to the Babylonians from the rulers of Judah, believing that opposition would end in disaster, as indeed it did, and that a degree of religious independence could survive domination by a foreign power. Now that many of the Jews were in Babylon itself, it follows that the religion could continue in a foreign country, or so Jeremiah suggests, and that the people themselves would return to the Land of Israel at the time God decided it was appropriate.

The eventual outcome would be a return to their original home and the restoration of independence and freedom for the Jews. And indeed, in 539 BCE, the Babylonians were overthrown by the Persians and the new regime allowed some Jews to return to Judah, no doubt with the intention of using them as political allies in their disputes with other powers in the region. The rebuilding of the Temple began, but was disrupted by disputes with the inhabitants of the area, loosely labeled Samaritans, and this was to lead to a great deal of hostility between the Jews and this group, who were linked with them but had different political aspirations and connections with the land. The Temple was completed in 516 BCE and around the same time there was a stricter interpretation of what it meant to be Jewish, rather like the period of the exodus, when rules were suddenly instituted to make a big distinction between Jews and others. After long periods living within a foreign ambit, perhaps, it was necessary to think of some way to make the new community that was emerging from an alien culture really consider itself different. There was an attempt to stress the status of the Law in Judaism, and the priests played a leading role in the State, and yet there also existed a strong diaspora in Babylon, people who perhaps could have returned but felt no need to do so. Despite their absence from the Land of Israel, they in many cases seem to have held fast to their religion and even acknowledged the centrality of the Land of Israel to it, which has become something of a theme in Jewish life ever since.

The Greek Occupation

The wars between the Greeks and the Persians resulted in Greek control of the area, and for a century or so Judah came under Greek rule, a situation that became dire when, in 200 BCE, the Seleucid monarch Antiochus III took over. He was unhappy with the relative autonomy of the region, with its self-governance by priests and a council made up of locals, and he sought to ban the main activities of Judaism, such as circumcision and the Sabbath, and brought many Gentiles in to the region to water down its Jewish character. There is no doubt that a lot of Jews in the country were enthusiastic about the policy of Hellenization, and saw it as the modern way of life that ought to be accepted, and while the religious aspects of it might have seemed a bit strange, the clothes, language and general culture were very attractive. There was a revolt, and like all guerilla wars it no doubt killed more of the locals than Greeks, but Judah Maccabee of the Hasmonean community overcame the Seleucids and in 164 BCE took Jerusalem. The Temple was cleansed of the Greek religion and this is an event celebrated each year by Jews as Chanukah, the inauguration of the Temple. The Hasmoneans were generally successful in establishing the independence of the country, and even expanding it, and no doubt took a grim satisfaction in destroying the Samaritans and their rival temple on Mount Gerizim, but their opposition to Hellenism could not be taken too far. They had Greek names and the leading culture of the day was Greek, and they certainly could not prevent people from participating in that culture. But the main institutions of the State remained thoroughly Jewish, albeit often imbued with Greek ideas and language, without returning to the priests the leading role they had previously had.

There must have been a significant contrast between the Aramaic-speaking and Greek-speaking Jews, and between the growing poverty of the Judaean population and the Babylonian community. A new group of religious experts arose, the sages, and they were divided up neatly into the Pharisees and the Sadducees, and were to continue to play a significant cultural role in the country until the fall of the Second Temple. The Pharisees were enthusiastic about Oral Law and spent a lot of time deriving legislation from the Bible. The Sadducees, by contrast, were mainly committed to the written Torah, and avoided the proliferation of new notions such as those of the afterlife and resurrection of the dead, and the new beings such as demons and angels, something the Pharisees were keen on. In some ways this might have been something of a class struggle, since the Sadducees were linked with the priests and aristocracy, while their opponents were closer to the ordinary people, more sympathetic to their religious requirements in terms of mythology and eschatology, and keen on overturning the existing order of who defined purity for the community. The Pharisees gradually took over, and the absence of the Temple proved perhaps the one factor that was decisive, since without a Temple the role of the priests became rather questionable. Their status remained, but with little solid authority behind it. On the other hand, we know about them through Josephus and references in the Talmud and Mishnah, but it is not clear how accurate these accounts are. There is speculation that some of the negative remarks regarding them in the Talmud are the result of censorship, or self-censorship, when references to heretics or Gentiles were transformed into references to the Sadducees. Their apparent opposition to the new doctrine on the afterlife is plausible as a major point of disagreement with what was becoming the accepted norm in rabbinic Judaism, and was to arise again as a major issue in Jewish thought during the time of Spinoza in the seventeenth century.

The Roman Occupation

The Romans took over in 63 BCE and the Hasmonean dynasty came to an end. A series of rulers took over the running of the country, under the general authority of the Roman Empire. The religious autonomy of Judea, as the province was known, continued, as did the Temple and its services and linked institutions. Jews spread throughout the Roman Empire until the revolt of 66 CE. In Judea itself, though, a number of events occurred that aroused the anger of some Jews, and these were linked to the theft of the wealth of the Temple and the stationing of legions in Jerusalem. The revolt was initially quite successful and it is worth remembering that it succeeded in creating an independent Jewish state for three years, but by 70 CE Jerusalem was captured, the Second Temple destroyed and the country firmly divided into those who were linked with the Romans and those who were defeated and antagonistic to the conquering authorities. Into this confusion, a new and important institution arose – the educational institution that was set up in Javneh and that allowed Jewish learning and commentary to continue outside the structure of the Temple. In fact, this had been very much the norm for the previous hundred years or so, when the competing and collaborating sages had begun to play a major interpretive role in Judaism, and we know that despite the existence of the Temple there were synagogues all over the country representing it, as it were, for those not in its immediate vicinity. A number of revolts took place against Roman rule, which were brutally suppressed, ending with the Bar Kokhba revolt of 135 CE, which led to draconian anti-Jewish measures being taken, both against the population and the practices of the religion. Hadrian was determined to finally bring to an end the perpetual and annoying prevalence of the Jews disrupting the peace of the Roman Empire, and he certainly took no half-measures in this respect. On the other hand, the region of Galilee had not been enthusiastic in the struggle against the Romans during any revolt and so was left alone by the Romans on their return to the area, allowing some Jewish life there to survive and eventually the Romans found it politic to re-establish a Jewish political presence recognized by them in the province that from that time was to be known as Palestine.

The Greek Challenge

Perhaps the greatest challenge that Judaism ever faced, and still faces in a different form, is Greek culture. The military dominance of Alexander the Great over the Middle East brought about a series of rulers committed to that culture which they sought, on traditional Jewish accounts, to impose on the Jews. The reality was probably that the Jews accepted with alacrity this new cultural trend, as they had accepted so many earlier in their history, and it is not difficult to appreciate how the intellectual rigor of Greek thought and the beauty of its material art, plus the fact that it worked in what was at the time very much the international language of world culture, Greek, led many willingly to embrace this new form of thought. For some, no doubt, the Greek religion became part and parcel of a new lifestyle, while for others it was possible to reconcile being Jewish with acting like a Greek, something that became a theme during the next 2,000 years and more. The Hasmonean kingdom established a period of relative independence from the surrounding empires, yet Greek culture was not easy to eradicate from Judaism. It is difficult to overemphasize the significance of the Septuagint, the translation of the Hebrew Bible into Greek, since this made it available to a much wider readership than previously, and it was possible no doubt for Jews who no could longer read the Bible in Hebrew to combine life within a wider culture with a degree of religious faithfulness to their original traditions. The eventual destruction of the Greek empire by the Romans brought about no cessation of enthusiasm for Greek, since the Roman Empire was also culturally in love with Greek culture and language.

The Roman Empire did bring periods of efficient persecution of Judaism, and a violent reaction to it by the Jews. The death of Jesus was not noticed by most people, since crucifixion was such a common event, and messiahs a dime a dozen at that time, but the destruction of the Second Temple in 70 CE certainly was, and it symbolized the end of Jewish life in the Land of Israel in the relatively autonomous state it had previously enjoyed. Jews spread throughout the Roman Empire, and beyond, and were not to return to Israel until almost 2,000 years later. The rapid growth of Christianity was not helpful to Jewish life with respect to the new religion. Religions that emerge out of earlier religions always have a difficult relationship with their predecessors, since the new faith sees the old religion as stubborn, or worse, in its refusal to see 'the truth', and in the case of Christianity the Jews were accused of actually plotting to kill the Christian leader. Jesus was in fact killed by the Romans, but the Jews did seem to be implicated in bringing this about, which was hardly likely to increase feelings of amity between the new religion and the old. In any case, the new religion saw itself as bringing the old religion to its completion, as it were, and it was awkward when the Jews failed to recognize their role in the history of religious progress.

The Jewish Commentaries

While this was a very difficult period for the Jews and their religion, in fact it saw an extraordinary intellectual series of products, the Mishnah and the Talmud, both representing the Oral Law that was the speciality of the sages. The Mishnah was written in Hebrew and the Talmud largely in Aramaic, with both seeking to interpret the Torah, using reasoning (unashamedly Greek in style) to present an understanding of what the Law actually says on a particular topic. The unusual nature of the text lies in the fact that the Talmud at least often presents a variety of potential solutions to legal issues, and invites the reader to participate in the discussion of what the correct solution is, an intriguing feature of the text and perhaps something that was to prove useful later in the development of a particularly Jewish way of tackling intellectual work. There are two Talmuds: a smaller one from Israel, the Jerusalem Talmud; and a much more substantial one from the leading Jewish community of the time, Babylon – the community that had persisted relatively peacefully for hundreds of years despite all the turmoil and destruction that had affected the Jews in the Land of Israel and the Roman Empire itself.

The word *torah* is usually translated as 'the Law', but this is not entirely accurate. Law is linked much more closely with the term *halakhah* and there is plenty in the Torah that has nothing to do directly with law. The word Torah comes from a Hebrew root related to words like teaching and instruction, where the idea is that God is the teacher and the readership are the learners. Sometimes the Torah is described very dramatically as black fire on white fire (*Deuteronomy Rabbah* 3.12, *Song of Songs Rabbah* 5.11, *Zohar* II, 226b). It is worth noting that a good deal of the Torah has nothing directly to do with God, in the sense that God is not its subject, but rather gives advice on how people should live in quite a practical sense. The *Proverbs*, for example, and *Ecclesiastes* from the Written Law, and the *Ethics of the Fathers* from the Oral Law, are replete with hints about how to succeed in life. Similarly, much of the description of events in the Written Law is perhaps directed more to telling us about what we ought to do as human beings rather than what we are obliged to do in our attempt to emulate God.

Rabbinic Judaism had no difficulty in surviving the journey from Palestine in late antiquity to Babylonia, and from the third century CE onwards it experienced a remarkable development. Several generations of rabbinic argument and explanation were collected, mainly in the fifth and sixth centuries, into the books of the Talmud, a huge work that showed the influence of a great deal of editorial work. That editing is to be praised for its inability to throw things out, even though keeping so much material in the volumes made it unwieldy and obscure. As local communities sought to use this work to help them solve their legal problems, they found it less and less convenient to consult the Geonim, who took on the role of experts, in Babylon, and relied more on the local rabbinate. There was also, of course, the Palestinian, or Jerusalem Talmud, which sometimes has a different way of looking at issues, and the most important thing to note about the Babylonian Talmud is that although it is primarily about the Law, it is certainly not entirely so. Much of it consists of reflections on the lives of the rabbis, cosmology, medicine, manners, magic and so on, which sometimes seems like a bit of a distraction, and sometimes gives a degree of background to the more legal parts of the texts, usefully situating it in its time and place. There are also connected to it, but not actually part of it, external (*baraita*) teachings that are external in the sense that they do not refer to the Mishnah. They are also in Hebrew, unlike the mainly Aramaic language of the Talmud. The Tosefta is a series of additional teachings linked but largely added to the Mishnah, produced by the Tannaim, and they, not surprisingly, provide another source of commentary.

The structure of both Talmuds follows the structure of the Mishnah, on which it is a commentary, though it wanders around the topic quite often. It is written in a mixture of Hebrew and Aramaic and is not a work that is easily studied, which has resulted in great enthusiasm in the traditional Jewish world for studying it, since it is so difficult and complex. The commentary of Rashi is included in the printed text, as are comments known as Tosafot, which are thought to have been written by his grandsons, and these are very helpful in understanding what is an often obscure text. In traditional Judaism, the Talmud has immense status and forms the primary subject of study, given its emphasis on Law and how it should be understood and interpreted. Among the Reform movement it is studied and referred to occasionally, but does not have that much status apart from as an important Jewish text that might have something important to say, if one looks carefully enough into it.

A more informal set of commentaries, largely on biblical works, is the Midrash, which was mainly produced in the Land of Israel between the third and eleventh centuries CE, and clearly represents an interpretation (which is what *midrash* means) and an explanation for a wide audience, given the imaginative nature of the stories that are found in this series of books. Sometimes the interpretations presented are very fanciful and often they are conjectural, consisting more of stories and suggestions than a careful and well-grounded argument. They are used quite commonly in Judaism, though, since they have a degree of authority behind them and can be used to illustrate almost any point, provided one looks carefully enough. They also link together a variety of different biblical texts in a very intelligent way, bringing out the implications that are taken to exist in very small differences of expression which have significant implications for our understanding of the meaning of the text as a whole.

Later, a variety of texts were produced, such as Maimonides' *Mishneh Torah* or *Yad Chazakah* (Strong Hand) in the twelfth century, and Joseph Caro's *Shulkhan Arukh* (Prepared Table) in the sixteenth century, which sought to summarize the Law and the commentaries on it. The aim was to provide the gist of the Law so that those who were not themselves able to work through the commentaries, and who did not perhaps have access to a local *beth din* or religious court, could find out how they were supposed to act in particular circumstances (Leaman, 2005). After all, as well as the major systems of commentaries, there were many other forms of discussion of Judaism which added layers of complication, and constantly elaborated the legal basis of conduct. All attempts at codification and simplification merely added another layer of commentary to what it was supposed to be regulating.

Life in Babylon

The Babylon Jewish community was both large and well-organized, and integrated into local society. Initially it looked to the Land of Israel, since the Temple was there as well as the hierarchy of priests, but over time one assumes that the growing chaos in Jerusalem and its environs established an increasingly wide gap between the original home of the Jews and their new life to the east. The Babylonian Jews established distinct *yeshivot*, colleges, and the comparative status of the two Talmuds is instructive here, with the Babylonian version being far more detailed than its Palestinian equivalent, though one must acknowledge that much material has also been lost. The growth of Islam and its rapid expansion helped the Babylonian Talmud to become accepted throughout the Islamic world's Jewish communities, but it also came to be much used in Europe, and the intellectual richness of the eastern community meant that it could respond to questions that arose about practice and ritual. A radical reform movement, the Karaites, arose in the eighth century and based itself on the idea that the Oral Law was entirely unnecessary, since the Bible was clear enough to follow without a commentary. This led to a furious debate in the Jewish world, and the opponents of the Karaites – the Rabbanites – won out, largely because of the influence of Saadya Gaon, the head of one of the big colleges at Sura, or so we are often told. The truth is that we do not know why Karaism came to a virtual end as a significant force in the Jewish world, but one can see why a community that was spread across the world might prefer a centralized idea of what is right and wrong to bind everyone together, rather than leave each separate group (and family?) to work out by itself how to behave. The Karaites developed their own legal system, and it often proved to be much more stringent than that of rabbinic Judaism, which might also have militated against the Karaites' continuing success (*JT* ch.6).

Paul and the Break with Judaism

Paul is often credited with making Christianity a world religion open to Gentiles, and there is some truth in this, since when it started it was largely a Jewish sect. It remained a small Jewish sect but expanded considerably when it was open to everyone, something that became easier once the repression of the Romans had destroyed many of the Jewish communities in the Land of Israel. The Gospels themselves do not make many hostile references to the Jews, but as Christianity developed as a competing religion it sought to distinguish itself strongly from its predecessor. One way of doing this was to blame the Jews for killing Jesus, for not converting to Christianity and recognizing the messianic nature of Jesus. The Christians were then the real chosen people, a role the Jews had forfeited because of their inability to recognize the truth of Jesus' mission. The two Christian empires that emerged – the Roman Catholic based in Rome and the Orthodox in Constantinople – treated the Jews variably while the empires existed, but most were on the whole allowed at least to survive, and the role they should play in a Christian state was much debated. Should not the Christians destroy this community that had dealt so rudely with their leader and denied all their claims for his status? Some Christians certainly took this line, while others argued that the Jews serve as a symbol of continuity with the community out of which Jesus emerged, and while they should certainly not be favored, they could be allowed to live in a subservient state in order to display the consequences of not accepting the significance of Jesus and his role in human salvation.

The role of the Jews as stubborn refusers to see the truth about their Bible and how it pointed to Jesus reserved a dubious role for them in Christian culture. The choice of Jesus as the Messiah was indeed stubbornly resisted for a long time, and only proved tempting to many Jews through extreme pressure. On the other hand, we should acknowledge the great attraction of Christianity for Jews, even before the period of Christian power. As Leo Baeck puts it, 'Paul left Judaism when he preached *sola fide* (by faith alone)' (Baeck, 1958, 177). In his frequent discussions of Paul, he suggests that Christianity was created by him in the form of a romantic religion, full of ecstasy, fantasy, sentiment, mystery and an orientation toward redemptive grace. Judaism, by contrast, the religion from which he came, is the classical faith in which there is a balance between commandment and feeling, faith and duty, a delicate balance that only a Jew such as Paul could initially seek to upset by emphasizing one side at the expense of the other. In many ways it is very annoying to a new religion when the practitioners of the old religion do not acknowledge its truth – rather like people not upgrading to a new computer system when the old one is obsolete. Yet, as we know, there are people who prefer old machines to new ones, old software to new, and who have an argument which often seems quasi-religious to support their preferences.

The accusations against the Jews were legion. A strong distinction was often made between the Bible, which, as the Old Testament, was also valued by Christians, and the commentaries that had led the Jews astray, especially the Talmud. A campaign to convert the Jews through force and disputation was waged for centuries in medieval Europe, with varying levels of success. There were many converts who were ready and able to read Hebrew and Aramaic texts, which they then sought to refute and also to censor. Some of these converts were themselves former rabbis or at least from rabbinic families, and they turned with ferocity against their former religion and its adherents. They sought out what they took to be objectionable passages in the Talmud and excised them in the editions to which they had access, and in public disputations they argued that these showed how corrupt and anti-Christian Judaism was. Not only converts, but a whole category of professional Hebraists, set themselves up in the universities to study Hebrew and to use that knowledge to attack the religion that produced the language. In these 'debates' the Jews were always in a vastly inferior position, but made a decent effort to reply to the accusations against them, often with great skill and lucidity. In particular, a detailed investigation of the Talmud and its references to Jesus and the *Minim* (heretics) does not clearly identify Christianity. The putative hostile actions of the Jews themselves, such as poisoning wells and using Christian blood in their ceremonies, were so wild that it was not easy to know how to refute them. On the other hand, the main theological argument between Judaism and Christianity could proceed at a respectable level, since it runs throughout the New Testament, and the Jews who were involved in these debates did have responses to the criticisms that Christians had been making for many centuries against their religion.

Exile in Christian Europe

When Jews started to settle in large numbers in Christian Europe these tensions sometimes magnified, and sometimes because they were useful to local rulers they were kept under control. The community in the Iberian Peninsula was already established by the first century CE. Sometimes it flourished, but at other times was partially destroyed, before the expulsion of 1492. The center of scholarship moved from the Middle East to Iberia and to Europe, especially France and the Rhineland, despite the very difficult circumstances under which the Jews often had to live. Something of a pattern began to develop. A local ruler would invite Jews to live in his city or country, and for a time used them as part of the economic system to provide capital and to work in certain specialized areas of the craft economy, but when they were no longer required, or it was no longer convenient to pay them for their services, they might be expelled and/or killed by a population that in any case was irretrievably hostile to them. The Crusades were particularly bad times for the Jews, when religious enthusiasm to recover the Holy Land reminded the Christians of the strangers in their midst, and there were many massacres of the entirely defenseless Jewish communities.

One of the remarkable features of a culture is that it often flourishes in difficult circumstances, and withers in comfort. Jewish life in Spain is an excellent example of this, since it was periodically very tough, and in the end impossible, yet produced some of the most impressive and indeed permanent texts and ideas in Jewish culture. Initially, the Christian rulers of Spain were induced by Catholicism to take a harsh line with their Jewish population, leading the latter to welcome the conquest by the Muslims in the eighth century CE, ushering in a regime that was to last for about 500 years. During the first two centuries of this period, Jewish life was able to expand and many positions of political influence were given to Jews, the Umayyad regime being particularly open, it seems, to its minorities in distributing posts and favors. The later regimes that came from North Africa were less open, however, and determined steps were taken by the Almohads either to convert or to drive out their population of unbelievers. During the conflict between Muslim and Christian Spain, the Jews lived in both areas and apparently fought on both sides, and one assumes that they were useful in carrying out negotiations with the other side and gathering information, given the fact that they had co-religionists and contacts spread widely throughout the country. By the thirteenth century, the Christian kingdom was in the ascendant, and the position of the Jews steadily declined, with real religious fervor being devoted to their often forcible conversion or expulsion. When Spain was entirely Christian again, politically the Jews were forced to leave completely, or to remain and be baptized, and it is remarkable that more did not remain, given the incentives to do so. Temporary shelter was found in Portugal, but the Portuguese soon also drove out the Jews, or forced them into becoming (sometimes just token) Christians.

This creation of many new Christians led to suspicion among the old Christians as to the real loyalty of the converts, and the Inquisition was designed to test the genuineness of the conversions that had taken place, with harsh punishments for those who were judged not to be as appropriately enthusiastic as expected about no longer being Jewish. It certainly was the case that a very large number of Jews became Christians, and today many Spaniards and Portuguese are convinced that their ancestors were Jewish, since apparently it is now cool in these countries to have such a background – but, unfortunately for the original Jews, many centuries too late. It is unlikely that all these people really do have Jewish descendants, since for most Jews who genuinely converted they abandoned their connections with their original religion swiftly and totally. For some, however, there was a shadowy and secret existence as Marranos, increasingly cut off from the knowledge of how to practice their Judaism but nonetheless interested in preserving something distinctive about their lifestyle, and in particular religious activities that brought them together to develop their own rituals and symbols. Most of the Jews who left the Iberian Peninsula settled in the Ottoman Empire, which apparently was delighted to receive so many skilled and educated individuals in what was already a largely multicultural empire.

Jews in the rest of medieval Europe were spread out in relatively small but often vibrant communities, where it was possible for them to act as traders and financiers. The Christians were forbidden from being involved in lending money for interest, and indeed so were the Jews according to the Torah, and yet the Jews had good connections across the Continent, and indeed often the world, so they were in a perfect position to facilitate trade by providing travelers and dealers with letters of credit, finance for goods and transport, and introductions to important business people in distant territories. Local rulers took advantage of Jews to borrow money, but also to foster commerce in their territory which, through taxation, no doubt brought in useful amounts of money, and increased general prosperity. The Jews were often legally the property of the ruler and, as one might expect, this was a very fragile relationship, especially when the Church was in dispute with the secular authorities. The Jews were caught in the middle of such disputes, with the Church seeking to gain the allegiance of the population against the ruler by criticizing and persecuting the Jews in their midst. After all, they were excluded from social life and would only be encountered during difficult times in life – when money needed to be borrowed perhaps, or as very visible employees of the king or a local aristocrat. Attacking Jews was a way not only of enriching oneself, but also of gaining the approval of the Church. As one might imagine, while local rulers found the Jews useful, once they became more of a liability than an advantage, they could quickly be abandoned to whatever fate the population had in mind. All sorts of rumors about the Jews found popular acceptance, ranging from the blood libel according to which the Jews kidnapped and killed a Christian in order to use his blood for their unleavened bread, the poisoning of wells and general hostility to the Christian world.

Strangely enough, what brought this long period of persecution to at least a temporary respite was the creation of the reform movement in Christianity, in the form of Protestantism, which directed the attention of the Catholic Church to the new schism in its midst, and away from their traditional enemy. Luther, in the sixteenth century, was at first quite mild in his comments about the Jews, whom he hoped perhaps would prove ready converts to the new version of

Christianity, but when they did not he became far more vitriolic. (Interestingly, exactly the same trend can be seen in the Qur'an, which became progressively more critical of the Jews, perhaps since many of them were resistant to the message the Book presented.) The anomalous status of the Jews in the Christian states continued, with their welfare depending on the ruler, and sometimes they even had to be locked up, often for their own safety, in what came to be called ghettos. In Germany, divided up into many different states, the court Jew who ran the financial side of the administration became quite familiar, and clearly did not arouse warm feelings in the population who were at the taxed end of the state. It is always a prudent strategy by those in charge to set up an intermediary between themselves and those being exploited, since if he is lucky it is the intermediary who is blamed for harsh measures, not the distant but ultimate authority who in fact set in train the whole process.

Anti-Semitism
The European Middle Ages labeled the Jews as the ultimate Other and they were often treated accordingly, and very badly. They were restricted to living in certain areas and following particular trades, trades that made them deeply unpopular among the population as a whole, but very useful to their rulers, who exploited the Jews' financial role to their own advantage. Nothing was easier than to borrow money from the Jews and then decide that they should be expelled or killed, since after all they were Jews, and the money presumably was not repaid. Of course, this strategy could not be employed very often, but a few big frauds of this nature could go a long way to help the economy of the royal household.

One of the great disappointments to the Jews who were involved in the Enlightenment was the continuing existence of anti-Semitism. What was supposed to happen was that, as rationality and science spread through the population, the old prejudices, including hostility to the Jews, would gradually disappear and be replaced instead by a more accurate account of this group of people. In fact, anti-Semitism is often called the most successful political doctrine, since it has existed for many centuries – indeed two millennia – and for a long time the Jews played the role of a people who contrasted with the norm, and every culture needs a notion of what is different from them in order to gain a concept of what the culture actually is.

What made the Jews particularly useful here was the diaspora – even in the earlier parts of their history they were spread out around the world and so served as examples in their locations of a different lifestyle and religion, leading to suspicions of how benign a presence they really were.

Religions often have difficulties with their origins, in the same way as individual people, and Christianity and Islam have these typical issues with Judaism, the religion out of which they both, in a sense, emerged. Both new religions respected the Torah, but suggested it was merely an earlier version of a much more complete and developed truth, the teachings of Jesus and the Qur'an, and the inability of many of the Jews to come over to the new religions led to the familiar doubts about the veracity of the Jews and their motives in refusing to accept what should have been clear to them was the truth. A theme among both Christians and Muslims was the prevalence of the Jews killing their prophets (*Acts* 7) and disobeying God. The early Christians, who were of course themselves Jews, are quite heated in their denunciation of their erstwhile communities, yet we should not be surprised at this, since it is not exactly unfamiliar to us even today that those who convert to a different religion often turn violently against the one they left. They need to persuade themselves that they made the right decision, and to persuade others that they really have moved on. Once Christianity became the state religion it often took measures against the Jews, and indeed the Jews took measures against the Christians who were also Jews, not allowing them to participate in their previous communities and making a sharp distinction between them and 'genuine' Jews.

Once Christians were no longer predominantly Jews, their hostility took on quite extreme forms. The identification of Jews with money has remained a powerful motif even today. In a twentieth century novel, *Light Years*, James Salter calls a Jewish tailor a freak since he has no sense of money. He goes on: 'A Jew without money is like a dog without teeth' (Salter, 1975, 14). A group of North African immigrants in France in 2006 kidnapped and tortured to death a Jew, Ilan Halimi, to extract money from his family whom they assumed, quite wrongly, must have been wealthy.

This narrative continued to build up a negative picture of the evil Jew even after Christian enthusiasm had declined in Europe, and that narrative also had an export potential: it traveled around the world to regions that had never seen a Jew or that had in the past had very different relationships with them. Anti-Semitism should have disappeared along with feudalism and other predecessors of the Industrial Revolution and modernity; it should have been swept away by the Enlightenment and all that it brought with it, as many commentators suggest. The development of new forms of anti-Semitism, out of the ashes of the old religious variety, proceeded rapidly, and of course the Jews were often competitors with others in the general desire to advance in society, so it is perhaps not surprising that there should be a degree of hostility toward them. Given the decline of religion in Europe, a gradual process but quite marked even a hundred years ago, a different rationale had to be found to explain antipathy toward the Jews, and it became largely racial − the idea that the Jews were a particular species that was dangerous to civilization and needed to be dealt with harshly if the latter was to survive. It was very much this sort of approach that provided the intellectual underpinning for the Holocaust; the idea that the Jews are a virus from which Europe needs to be saved, and so every Jew, every aspect of that aggressive 'disease', needs to be destroyed. This hostility is sometimes merely because they are racially antagonistic to the Gentile world, but is sometimes linked with ideas suggesting they are attempting to control that world through evil plots and stratagems. This places the Jews behind a variety of political movements and ideas, which they manipulate in order to further their own interests. Conspiracy theories are often condemned as being patently false, but it does have to be said in their favor that they make the world a much more interesting place, peopling it with monsters, hidden strategies and the need to interpret what happens constantly in terms of the conspiracy that is taken to represent the dominant power. They also to a degree excuse and explain the impotence of those being conspired against, since the narrative often sees the conspirators as being all-powerful.

Anti-Semitism provided a critique of Judaism and the Jews that was taken seriously by many Jews in Europe, who tried to discard as many of the traditional features of the religion as possible, including sometimes the religion itself. The prevalence of anti-Semitism, and the serious implications it had for Jews in Western Europe, as signified by the Dreyfus Affair, and in Eastern Europe, the pogroms and massacres in the Russian Empire, was not lost on the Jews themselves, of course, and led to a debate about what the best counter-strategy would be. Zionism started to look a bit more plausible, though it was still in the nineteenth century and for most of the early twentieth century very much a minority enthusiasm for Jews. Many accepted the premises of anti-Semitism that the Jews had lived an unusual life up to then and needed to change, to become more like everyone else, and once this happened, so the reasoning went, there would be no more reason to hate them. Some thought this could come about through socialism and the participation of the Jews in their native countries; others thought it should happen through the Jews setting up their own country where they could, like the new countries of Italy, Greece and Germany, re-establish their former links with their roots and be accepted as one nation among many others, no better perhaps but certainly no worse. This debate still continues in that many Jews are not happy with the activities of the State of Israel and blame it for the antipathy that is sometimes directed against Jews. Others see the success of Israel as the best answer to anti-Semitism, since the Jews have shown that they can defend themselves and will no longer go to the slaughter like animals. Whether the eventual outcome will be any different is, of course, something that has yet to be seen, but in a sense it is not the most important issue here, since no one in the heyday of nationalism in the nineteenth century expected it to be easy to establish a new country out of the ruins of the old, nor was it expected that the old colonial masters would suddenly cave in to the demands of the new nation. Many in the country would still identify with the previous authorities, and so their loyalty would be in question, but these are all quite normal aspects of the creation of a new country. So the fact that the State of Israel is not universally loved, and sometimes has difficulties with some of its citizens, is hardly untypical of nation-building, even when this is a widespread activity. The idea that anti-Semitism would end once people saw that Jews could run their own affairs in an ordinary state – which Israel is to a degree – has turned out to be wildly optimistic, but then countering prejudice was never likely to be a simple matter of confronting the bigoted with a bit of evidence.

The prevalence of anti-Semitism has created an interesting Jewish reaction: the self-hating Jew. There is a tendency for people who are treated poorly to regard themselves in a similar way, and the notion of the self-hating Jew is the result: someone who is ashamed of his or her Jewish heritage, and as a result tries to hide it or does not identify with the Jewish people. There is no doubt that this Jewish attitude exists and yet it has become a bit of an easy label with which to describe any Jew who is critical of Judaism and/or the State of Israel; this is unfortunate, to put it mildly. It does have to be said that it is not clear how one ought to react to prejudice. A muscular reaction may seem the noblest move, but it can also result in amplifying the very behavior it seeks to counter. Those hostile to the Jews may find the attention they are paid as a result of their attitude very gratifying. People who are seeking attention, like children in a classroom, find that saying certain shocking things can bring them into the public eye and make them the center of discussion, something they might very much enjoy. One cannot help thinking that President Ahmadinajad of Iran made so many remarks questioning the existence of the Holocaust and threatening to exterminate Israel because it immediately brought him into the public eye, both in the West and in the Islamic world. In the West, these remarks caused shock and horror, which only increased his status in the Middle East, whose leaders were not brave enough, in the opinion of many, to tell the truth about the Jews and their history. Even without this favorable Islamic reaction, Ahmadinajad clearly enjoyed the media attention that occurred after he had said these things about the Jews, and the fact that they were felt to be so shocking vindicated the general thesis that the Jews control everything, since otherwise why would such a fuss be made?

The Enlightenment

The Enlightenment in Europe is often said to have had a huge impact on the Jewish world. In fact, it had a huge impact on the whole of European civilization. There are many ways of understanding the Enlightenment, and many ways of defining it, but here we mean the advocacy of the use of reason as an ultimate guide on how to act and understand the world. This obviously has implications for religion, as the Enlightenment seeks to dethrone it from its previous position of influence and, indeed, superiority. To a certain extent the Enlightenment is connected with the growth in Europe of two types of Christianity, often at odds with each other, but after the Thirty Years' War a degree of exhaustion set in as far as religious conflict was concerned, and exhaustion is a good motivation for looking in a new direction. The notion of toleration arose, again not unconnected to the feeling of exhaustion, since if you cannot destroy your enemy, you have to live with him or her, presumably, and that means finding a good reason to act in this way. A concept of natural religion arose, according to which all genuine religions share certain basic and rational religious principles, and the implication is that all religions ought to be allowed to exist, since they all embody the truth to some degree. Judaism was often felt to be at odds here, since its dependence on tradition and ritual made it seem far from rational, and the lifestyle which Jews had been obliged to adopt seriously challenged the idea that they could adhere to rational moral rules. The Jews were the largest non-Christian minority in Europe, and how they should be treated became very much a touchstone of how the Enlightenment would deal with communities with different lifestyles, languages and customs – precisely the situation of the Jews. Some suggested that there was something very different about Judaism, which meant that the Jews were incorrigible, and so could never really be part of the modern state. If this is accepted, there is then no necessity to enable them to become such a part. On the other hand, it was also argued that the Jews were only as distinct as they were because of the role they were obliged to play in Western culture, and once this was changed, they would also change.

Moses Mendelssohn

The symbol of the Jewish Enlightenment and reaction to the Enlightenment was Moses Mendelssohn. Born in 1729, he was educated both in Jewish subjects such as the Talmud and in secular philosophy. In this he was not unusual, but he was unusually gifted as a writer, and his books and essays won him a wide readership, perhaps sometimes because their author was a Jew, and so had at that time rarity value. He remained a practicing Jew, and defended the religion to others, unlike some of his Jewish contemporaries, who were intent on disappearing into the larger Christian German world as soon as they could. His staunch defense of Judaism confused many German Christians, who could not see why someone would stick with the old religion when a new and improved model was available and could easily be adopted. Mendelssohn became very much the representative of enlightened Jewry in Germany, and was obliged to

Moses Mendelssohn

explain constantly why he had remained a Jew. If, as he said, and as the Enlightenment argued, all the main religions were merely different versions of the truth, why not switch from one to the other when it was convenient to do so? In fact, many German Jews did this when it became possible to do so, and Mendelssohn's reply was that, if Judaism is no better than any other religion, then it is also no worse, so why bother converting? The riposte is, why not convert if it is advantageous to do so, and here the argument begins to go in quite interesting directions, since Mendelssohn had no objections to Christianity apart from the fact that it was not his religion. Rather in the way that one owns a particular house, and that is the house one lives in, without necessarily saying that it is the best house in the world, Mendelssohn declared he would remain faithful to Judaism. His critics pointed out that this is perhaps like saying that if a better house were to become available, one would stick with the house one happened to be brought up in, which seems irrational. But Mendelssohn replied that, in fact, if all the houses were more or less the same, then there is no reason to move. One theme in his work which became standard is his argument for the separation of the state

and religion, where the former is the appropriate coercive organiza-
tion, since its citizens agree to subject themselves to it, while a religion does not have the agreement of all the citizens, since there are a
variety of religions available, and should restrict itself to trying to
persuade rather than to force people to act in appropriate ways. Here
he could point to Judaism as basing itself more on actions than on
beliefs, so the legislation it prescribes can be seen as linked with the
principles of rational religion. He hits on a very real difference
between Judaism and the other religions such as Christianity and
Islam here, which is that the latter two are intent on converting
others and showing them how to achieve salvation because they see
those outside of their religion as being seriously in the dark. This is
not the standard Jewish view, and if it were, then heaven would be a
rather empty place, in whatever way we interpret it. For Christians
and Muslims, it is important that people convert to their faiths, but
for Jews the reverse is the case, as conversion is generally discouraged
and made far from easy. This is because it is not important for people
to be Jews to be good or to obey God, and if it were then there
would be very few good or obedient people in the world. In his
famous play *Nathan the Wise*, Lessing presents, in true Enlightenment
style, the three Abrahamic faiths as being similar to each other,
almost interchangeable, but this is certainly not how they generally
see themselves (*ES* ch. 7).

One of the features of Mendelssohn's approach that is worth
noting is that he was not only writing for the Gentile community but
also for the Jews; he was trying to persuade the latter that they should
seek to enter modern society and leave behind their very restrictive
and, in his opinion, narrow life. Hence his German translation of the
Hebrew Bible, produced in Hebrew characters, and with a
commentary designed to explain in modern rational ways the ancient
text. One of the tasks that the emancipation took on itself was to
control the understanding of the Hebrew language, which had until
not long before been very much the prerogative of the Jewish
religious authorities, and the attempt was made to wrest it from the
old centers of power. Once Hebrew was widely understood, it was
argued, then the ordinary Jew could hope to understand his holy
texts by himself rather than relying on the version provided for him
by the rabbis and the organizations they represented.

The French Revolution

It was the French Revolution that really moved the treatment of the Jews into the forefront of the way an enlightened country behaves. Most of the Jews in France lived in Alsace, a part of the country taken over in the previous century, and living very much apart from the rest of the (Alsatian) population. These Ashkenazi Jews were keen to involve themselves in a broader range of work, but they wanted to preserve their relative autonomy. A debate arose about whether it is possible for a community to remain separate and yet also be full citizens of the state, a debate that continues today. There was also a degree of realism which suggested that, if the Jews were to become full citizens and yet continue to restrict their activities to the money lending sector – which brought them constantly into unhappy relationships with the majority French population – they would be at the mercy of that population. There were indeed disturbances, but in 1791 the Jews were granted legal equality with other French people, and as French armies spread throughout Europe they announced that the Jews would be regarded as citizens with an equal status to the rest of the population. But Jewish emancipation did not resolve all the issues that were outstanding – in particular, how to reconcile the existence of Jewish institutions that had grown up over many centuries and that allowed the Jews to run their own affairs to a degree, with the idea of all citizens living in a state that had a monopoly of power to punish and tax, and so on.

The significance of the status of the Jews became evident when Napoleon took a great deal of trouble to make clear what he wanted to happen, and set up a series of consultancy measures to involve the whole Jewish population, through its representatives, in what he wanted done. He was interested in offering the Jews French citizenship, but wanted to know what they would give up for this to be feasible. The assumption was that the Jews held a number of unreasonable and objectionable ideas, such as that they were superior to Christians, that they would only obey their own laws and their own leaders. This was not at all the case, he was told by the Jews he consulted, and they would be delighted to accept French citizenship, forgoing their previous status as a largely self-governed community. However, it turned out that Napoleon had plans to make greater demands on them, and in 1808 he made it clear that he expected the Jews of Alsace to comply with his demands that they submit to special residential and employment rules, rather going against the idea that they were equal citizens. On the other hand, after ten years, these rules were not renewed and the Jews did become recognized as citizens of France.

The situation in the rest of Europe was more varied. In the states that made up Germany, some reacted to the emancipation of the Jews by Napoleon's armies by seeking to confine their activities once more, when those armies had been defeated. Some took the opposite approach, regarding emancipation as going hand-in-hand with modernity, something that was necessary if Germany was to resist France successfully. The reaction to the French Revolution could have taken the line that the inferior position of the Jews was a policy that ought to be respected and continued, in contrast to the revolution, but this was not what in fact happened. While progress on this issue was uneven, many states did gradually find scope to allow their Jewish population to feel at home in their civil society, and opened up to them a range of careers and possibilities. Along with this, however, often came demands, sometimes for money, a familiar demand to be made of local Jewish communities, but also that the Jews should change their way of life, which of course was not an easy thing to accomplish rapidly, given the restricted roles that up to that point they had been allowed to play. What became a firm part of the agenda, though, was the idea that a deal would be struck, the state would give Jews the ability to be full citizens, and the Jews would give up their very distinctive practices, language and appearance. And here we reach the nub of the problem of the transaction. How much would the state give, and how much would the Jews relinquish? Would the state really give the Jews equal rights, or would these rights merely be formal and not something widely accepted by society in general? This distinction is an important one and was to become vitally important when European society came to turn its back on the Jews and their rights.

The other side of the Enlightenment was its radical effects on the culture of the Jews themselves, and in particular their relationship with their religion. The whole approach to Judaism was called into question, and the Hebrew language became an aspect of that controversy. Who was to control the understanding of that language – the establishment of the traditional rabbis, or anyone able to under-stand the language and its grammar? A great deal of commentary had built up since the days of the Mishnah and the Talmud and how they were interpreted in Europe, and this had much more to do with the hermeneutical approach of the leading rabbinic authorities than with the basic religious texts of Judaism, the Torah as narrowly conceived in terms of the Five Books of Moses, or the wider Tanakh, including also the Prophets and the Writings. A reform movement arose in Germany and questioned the rigid nature of Jewish law and the necessity to follow it, on the grounds that this had more to do with tradition than with rationality, and so contravened the principles of the Enlightenment. The process started with the introduction of secular subjects into the curriculum, and in particular the German language, and along with this went a whole new understanding of Judaism itself, which came to be recognized as one religion among many others, and a religion that could and should be studied with reference to other faiths. That in itself is a big step, since once a religion sees itself as just one religion among others, an immediate distancing takes place and objectivity comes into the analysis.

Wissenschaft des Judentums

It is this sort of approach that led to the *Wissenschaft des Judentums* school in the early nineteenth century, a movement that thought an academic approach to Judaism would prove that it was just as sound and rational as any other religion. They also wanted to reform the religion, by stripping it of its inessential elements, the features that had accrued to it over the centuries, and getting back to the basics. It was these superficial elements, it was argued, that aroused the ire of the Gentile world, and once Judaism was cleansed of these unfortunate accretions it would be respected, as would its practitioners. One of the main targets was the Talmud, which in fact had often been attacked by those critical of the Jews in the past, as though it was the main cause of what was wrong with Judaism. The rabbis were to be replaced, the suggestion went, with a new class of modern clergymen much more like Christian ministers, educated in secular as well as religious subjects, and the legal aspects of the Talmud were no longer that relevant to them since the Law was now to be the prerogative of the state, not the Jewish community. Even some of the traditional communities saw the necessity of embodying some modern principles in their organizations and systems of thought, and argued that there was no problem in linking science with religion, as indeed on one level there is not. There also existed communities who sought to reject everything they associated with modernity; their strategy was to turn their backs on the developments that were taking place all around them.

Jews began to involve themselves in the affairs of the state, since they were recognized increasingly as citizens or quasi-citizens, and felt able to pursue their interests in the public sphere for the first time. They campaigned for equal rights for themselves, and participated in the struggles for independence of their various countries. The late nineteenth century saw the establishment of a number of new countries, with new constitutions, and the Jews were involved in all these struggles. They often played a large part too in the new radical movements that developed into socialist and communist parties, and by the twentieth century the early identification of Jews with money and property became mixed with another stereotype: the Jewish revolutionary, intent on overturning the state and totally changing society. Combining these two ideas into one concept of the Jew took some nifty thinking, but was manageable, and, after all, revolutionaries were known to plot and conspire, like financiers, so that at least common characteristics could be established quite easily, and the principle that Jews act in concert is helpful whatever cause they are supporting. In fact, of course, Jews rarely do anything in concert, and one of the many stories that has become almost undeniable in the Islamic world is that on the Sabbath before 9/11 the Jews in New York were told in synagogue not to go into work on Monday because of what was going to take place. What is amusing about this story is not that it is false, but that the idea that the Jews on Wall Street would be in a synagogue on any Sabbath, in large numbers, would be miraculous. Most Jews in the USA would not know where their local synagogue was, if there was one, and certainly would not go to it. But the idea of the Jew as the implacable and committed enemy of everyone else, someone who only achieves power and influence through the ruthless manipulation of the media and the power that money can provide, really needs the associated idea of their being in it altogether, since otherwise the very small numbers of Jews worldwide would make them seem rather puny as enemies. One needs the notion of them as a race, and this was the achievement of Nazism, emphasizing Jews not as a religious group but as an ethnic group. Even an enlightened world appreciates the necessity to disband enemies and resist occupation by alien forces. Since the Jews were often at the forefront of social and economic change, anyone fearful of that change could easily identify what seemed to be their main antagonists, the Jews. In many ways, then, the Enlightenment was a mixed blessing for the Jews.

Can Jews be Good Citizens?

The way in which a group such as the Jews is often used to represent something else has always been a problem for their public perception. For a great defender of the Enlightenment like Voltaire, the Jews were a problem, since he associated them with the Bible and so linked them with everything he hated about Christianity. On the other hand, for Nietzsche, the Jews were to be praised since this was, in his mind, another way of attacking Christianity. Voltaire regarded the Jews as part and parcel of traditional Europe, incapable of making the leap to the new era of progress and rationality, since they were so benighted by their traditions and their inability to enter fully into modern society. At the very least, the only way of accomplishing this leap would be for them to abandon their Jewishness. It is certainly true that at the time Voltaire was writing in the eighteenth century, the tiny French Jewish community was barely visible and restricted to specific areas and professions, though there is some evidence that the even smaller Sefardi community did succeed in making some legal inroads into ordinary French society. That community had after all been living for some time in France proper, not just in the newly acquired province of Alsace. What particularly offended Voltaire, and so many others, about the Jews was a particular understanding of the concept of chosenness, the idea that they are a particular community and so are unable to merge into the universal notion of what it is to be a citizen in an enlightened state. This is something that Feuerbach also refers to, claiming that the miracles in the Bible are taken to be 'purely at the command of Jehovah, who troubles himself about nothing but Israel, who is nothing but the personified selfishness of the Israelitish people, to the exclusion of all other nations' (Feuerbach, 1881, 113–14). He argues that monotheism is egoism taking a religious form. The trouble with the Jews is that they seem to operate outside of history, not changing their practices and beliefs, and carrying out a great deal of their commercial life between themselves rather than as part of society in general, or so Voltaire charges. Again, it is the egoism charge, the idea that they are a people who live separately from others. As such, they are surely unfit to be members of a new modern France or Europe, where a common reason operates and determines the actions and institutions of daily life. A couple of years after the Holocaust ended, President Truman wrote in his diary (21 July, 1947):

> The Jews, I find, are very, very selfish. They care not how many Estonians, Latvians, Finns, Poles, Yugoslavs or Greeks get murdered or mistreated as D[isplaced] P[erson]s as long as the Jews get special treatment. Yet when they have power, physical, financial or political neither Hitler nor Stalin has anything on them for cruelty or mistreatment to the underdog.

As we know from what in fact happened, Voltaire's concerns were unduly pessimistic, on the one hand, but to a certain extent they were quite accurate. The Jews in Europe played a large and enthusiastic role in promoting the Enlightenment and became very well integrated in modern societies, to the extent that in some ways they came to represent science and modernity, progress and change, and they saw themselves reflected in the Enlightenment. Like many converts, they became highly enthusiastic about their new way of thinking.

This was to be their undoing, however, since on the one hand they started gradually to disappear as a distinct group into the mass of ordinary citizens in Europe, becoming largely indistinguishable from everyone else. But on the other hand, they came to be resented by those forces of reaction and tradition that saw in the Jews everything they most hated and feared, in particular that desire to move on, to employ modern ideas to resolve problems and settle disputes. The rise of fascism and racism in Europe in the twentieth century almost succeeded in destroying the whole Jewish community there through systematic murder and expropriation. In the twenty-first century, religion is making something of a comeback among some groups in Europe, and the Jews are seen rightly as being predominantly secular and, through their perceived links with Israel, as separating themselves from the rest of the world and its aspirations for that region. Voltaire was dubious about the ability of the Jews to become proper citizens and to become part of the Enlightenment, yet now the concept of the Jew is often the concept of a citizen and an

ברכות וזמירות

A 'modern' family gathered around the table, singing traditional songs

enlightened individual, and it is for this very reason that new doubts are raised about them and their role in any future society.

The trouble with these generalizations about Judaism, as with generalizations about religion as an entity (of course, that is also a generalization), is that they are not accurate. The God of the Bible is not just concerned with the Jews; in fact, many of the events recorded take place before the notion of the Jews makes any sense at all. And even after the Jews become some sort of separate community, the rest of the literature in Judaism becomes relevant, although not so easy to fit into a nice neat category, and the rest of humanity becomes very much a topic for discussion. It is certainly true that this literature is mainly concerned with the Jews, since it deals largely with Jewish law, so why would anyone else be interested in it? Yet there is also material on Gentiles, and the Noahide laws are included, plus a good deal on relationships between Jews and Gentiles; and there is no doubt that the God referred to in Judaism is, of course, concerned about all his Creation, not just the very limited number of Jews in it.

Chapter III

Conflict and Survival

Eastern Europe

The part of Europe where Jews initially found a friendlier reception on the whole was in Eastern Europe, in particular in Poland and the linked territories of Lithuania and Ukraine. In the thirteenth century the political situation there calmed down considerably, and Jews were encouraged to settle and develop the forests and open spaces which the Polish Crown was interested in colonizing. The Jews who had had problems in other parts of Europe to the west found this a tempting prospect and took up the invitation, though to a degree they were yet again acting as intermediaries between the king for whom they were often working and the aristocracy who sought to take charge of the land. The rapid expansion of Jewish life and wealth in this region also led to a growth of learning, and the academies of Eastern Europe came to be so well known that even after they were totally destroyed by the Nazis, their influence survives throughout the Jewish world. Despite this success, there was opposition to the Jews from other settlers in the region, and certainly from the aristocracy, who resented the way that the royal prerogative reserved some key economic activities for the Jews, who were expected to funnel the wealth back to the Crown. The Jews were often asked to work for local aristocrats, though, handling their business affairs, which of course put them in touch with the ordinary people, and between the latter and their employers. They often lived in their own communities, speaking their own language – Yiddish – and of course following their own religion, and thus no doubt attracted some suspicion from the local population, for whom they must have been a significant alien import. In 1648, a large number of Jews were killed by the revolt of the Ukrainian Chmelnitski against the Poles, and it is interesting that they were identified with the Polish authorities, showing how well integrated they were into the power structure of the country. Over the next few centuries there were a variety of attacks against the Jews, leading to a great deal of movement in the nineteenth century and later, out of the region entirely and westward to Western Europe and the USA, and later to Israel.

The break-up of Poland in the eighteenth century resulted in most Jews living in what was then Russia. This was not a positive step, since most of the Russian rulers were antagonistic and keen on limiting the occupations and areas of residence of the Jews, and encouraging them to convert to Orthodox Christianity. In part, a policy of forcing Jewish boys to enter the army for 25 years was aimed at ridding them of their Jewish links and obliging them to adopt Christianity. Despite these measures, their distinct community survived, and was eventually allowed to move, in limited numbers, into the big Russian cities as well as into some of the professions. However, after the assassination of Alexander II in 1881, a variety of pogroms occurred in the Ukraine, Jews were expelled from Moscow, and over the next few decades violent outbursts against the Jews took place at various times throughout Eastern Europe, particularly in what was then the Russian Empire, and there is no doubt that many of the leaders of that empire were hostile, to put it no more strongly, to their Jewish population. This was no longer the occasional hostility to a community who seemed to be privileged and who had different styles of living from the majority, but had become an organized system of murder and expulsion, which left the Jewish population with little choice except to flee if they could.

There is something of a theme of Jewish life in Eastern Europe: the more the political disruption, the tougher life was for the Jewish population. The three partitions of Poland in the eighteenth century certainly put their lives on the line, and the incorporation of most of them into Russia was very difficult, since Russia had until then had a very small Jewish population, one that the state officially discouraged. Catherine the Great was not unaware of the advantages the Jews could bring to her empire, and initially quietly encouraged Jews to move into Russia proper, especially to the new territories in the south that had been captured from the Ottomans. She also granted them minority rights in what had been Poland, since there were other minorities, such as the Catholic Poles and other ethnic groups, who came to resent the fact that the Jews were for a period regarded as being legally equivalent to them. They were restricted to living and working in certain areas, like most Russians, but for most of the Russians the restrictions were placed with respect to them as individuals, and not as members of a group. It has to be said that, over time, wealthier and more influential Jews – the people who could, for example, pay to avoid their children being conscripted – were able to move out of what came to be known as the Pale of Settlement and into the capital and other large cities in the main part of Russia. Some Jews got into the universities and became physicians and lawyers, and the new industries and financial structure of the country had a significant number of Jews working in it. But the Pale only came to an end during the First World War, when there was so much disruption of Jewish life in the area because of forced expulsions by the Russian army operating in this area in its confrontation with the invading German armies. There was no alternative but to allow the Jews to live elsewhere if they could not live there, an issue that was dealt with rather differently when the Nazis came to control the same area a few decades later. The protracted war and its disastrous conduct had much to do with the downfall of the Tzarist regime in 1917, and the Jews were often enthusiastic about the freedoms that were contemplated which would result in an end to the regime of discriminatory treatment with which they were so familiar. There were also two significant political Jewish movements that were both on the left politically: the Bund, a socialist party working to integrate the Jewish working class with their non-Jewish peers; and the Zionists, who also saw in the new state a socialist opportunity for a new form of Jewish life. There was no reason at the start for either of these groups, or indeed the many Jews who were connected to less radical parties, not to acknowledge the improvement in their situation represented by the end of the Tzarist regime.

One of the significant differences that occurred after the end of the First World War was the creation of many smaller states out of the Russian Empire, and most Jews then became citizens of Poland, Lithuania, Latvia and Estonia. An unstable new state, Ukraine, massacred many Jews, whom they saw as being allied with the Russians, and the revolt against the Bolsheviks often took the form of attacking the Jews, who were always, of course, a popular source of persecution among the local population. Yet the Bolsheviks were unenthusiastic about the Bund and the Zionists, as they were worried by groups splitting up into their own communities in a country they were trying to unify, and of course the Bolsheviks were basically very hostile ideologically to religion as a whole. The eventual triumph of Stalin was not a positive step for the Jews, since he seems to have been personally antagonistic to Jews in any case, and saw those in the government and the Party as antagonistic to him. He was also given to believing in conspiracies against him, and Jews often figured large in his imagination here. However, many Jews moved to the large cities and achieved reasonable careers in the new sectors of the growing industrial state, and apart from those who were involved in the worlds of Jewish culture and politics, life was far superior to the situation under the previous regime.

The Nazis

Much to the amazement of everyone, probably including the victors, the German Republic came in 1933 under the control of the National Socialist German Workers' Party, often abbreviated as the Nazi Party, and its leader Adolf Hitler. This party had come out of nowhere to win a large public vote, and serves as an inspiration to many subsequent extreme racist parties. It based itself on a variety of principles, but of interest to us here is its militant anti-Semitism, a genuinely held passion for the view that the Jews were intent on harming Germany and the Aryan population of the nation.

The Aryans were supposedly the original inhabitants of Germany, and their control of their destiny was threatened by the growing influence not only of Jews, but also of other races such as Slavs, Roma (gypsies) and types of people such as socialists, the disabled and the homosexual community. In 1933, the Nazis swiftly took total control of the country and the outlook for the Jewish population rapidly became very difficult, if not immediately impossible. The 1935 Nuremberg Laws validated a radical separation of Jews from everyone else, and they were excluded from the organs of the state, the professions and cultural institutions. But many Jews were optimistic that things could not get much worse, and there were difficulties for anyone wishing to emigrate, since many other countries that would have been appropriate havens, such as the USA, had quotas they were unwilling to relax. In any case, few Jews wanted to emigrate; they felt themselves to be Germans and hoped

Der Stürmer: *Nazi newspaper, with the border declaring 'The Jews are our misfortune'*

the difficult situation would resolve itself in time, as had often happened in the past when the Jews in Europe were threatened by negative forces.

Of huge significance was Kristallnacht, 9 November 1938, when a nationwide pogrom occurred for the first time. A German diplomat in Paris was shot by a Jewish teenager, whose parents had been deported from Germany and ended up in difficult circumstances in the border area, since Poland did not want them either, nor the other

18,000 Jews who were in a similar situation. The decision was taken by the German government to treat this as an attack on Germany by world Jewry, and to exact revenge on the German Jewish population. The date on which the diplomat died, 9 November, was by chance the fifteenth anniversary of the beer hall putsch in which Hitler first tried to overthrow the Weimar Republic, and was thus highly auspicious for a violent reaction by the forces of those who had in the past been so few in number and with little support, but now had control of the whole German state. Orders went out to burn down synagogues and attack Jewish property, though no one was supposed to be killed. However, many were, and others died because of the rough treatment they received from the gangs who attacked them. About 30,000 Jews were sent to concentration camps, a grim forewarning of what was to happen over the next few years; private property was seized by non-Jewish Germans and every effort was made over a 24-hour period to harass and humiliate the local Jewish population. The fire brigade was withdrawn and only intervened when the properties of non-Jews were at risk. This event had huge significance, since it boosted the desire of Jews to emigrate, and finally brought to their attention that there was no longer any future for them in Germany.

When the Second World War began the position of the Jews only got worse, and their living conditions were rapidly downgraded, their property progressively expropriated and, as the German control of Europe expanded, yet more Jewish communities came under the control of those who seemed intent on making their lives as difficult as possible. At first the intention seems to have been to move the Jews to a part of Poland and there work them to death, with the desirable outcomes, from a Nazi point of view, of increasing war production and gradually ridding the nation of the Jewish enemy. Once the Soviet Union was attacked, such large numbers of Jews fell into the Nazi area of control that it was felt that the project of getting them to work themselves to death would be too slow a process, and it would be better to think of some way of destroying them more efficiently. To a certain extent this was always part of the process of dealing with the Jews, since communities were often taken out of town and forced to dig pits into which they were thrown after being shot, and random murders of Jews were, in any case, commonplace.

Even these pervasive acts of murder proved to be too slow for the ambitions of the Nazis, and the decision was made to construct some major camps in central Europe which would destroy Jews, and others, on an industrial scale, using gas to kill them, and then the bodies would be burnt afterwards. Trains from all over Europe took the victims to the centers where they were killed, until by the end of the war around six million Jews had been dispatched, some directly in the gas chambers or other killing processes, and some by hunger and disease. The Nazis were successful for a long time in keeping the process a secret, since otherwise their victims would not have been so willing to cooperate, not that there was much scope for resistance. From what is known about Jewish ideas about what awaited them in the east at that time, there was a good deal of incredulity at the idea that the Nazis would murder people who otherwise could have been forced to work for them. It was also still difficult to believe that a center of culture such as Germany could really set out to murder such a large and innocent group of people with such barbarity, though experience soon disabused the Jews of this illusion. The idea that, at a time when Germany was fighting for its life against enemies from the east, the west and the south, enemies who had purposefully landed on the continent of Europe to confront them, resources would be taken from the war effort to convey Jews to be murdered in the east is difficult to understand even now. There was some resistance to the Nazis by the Jews, but since most of them were in family groups, and the local population was almost always even more hostile than the Germans, resistance was not a plausible strategy.

In the new countries of Eastern Europe the situation was in some ways even more dire, since there was continuing hostility by much of the local population toward the Jews, despite the rights for minorities that existed in the official constitutions. At least before the war cultural life was able to exist because of the degrees of relative separation between the different communities, since, unlike the situation in the Soviet Union, there was no policy of trying to create a unitary ideology for everyone in the country. Yet the basic hostility of the local population was to prove costly when the Nazis rapidly conquered the countries of Eastern Europe and found very enthusiastic allies in their policy of murder and theft of the Jewish communities in their area. Most of the victims of the Holocaust came from Eastern Europe – about 4.75 million of the six million. Poland was particularly badly hit, and many of the major extermination camps were situated there. The Germans made a good choice of Poland, since it was entirely under their control, already contained a large number of their intended victims, and many Poles were hugely antagonistic toward their Jewish citizens; so even those Jews who managed to escape from the rounds of executions, concentration in camps, systematic murder and so on were often killed or captured by the local population. Despite this, there was in Eastern Europe a degree of Jewish violent resistance, most famously in the Warsaw ghetto in 1942, and this often took place when a large numbers of family members had been killed. A young survivor could then go off and was no longer responsible for helping those close to him.

What is often regarded as remarkable is that in Poland the defeat of the Nazis did not mean the end of the problems for Polish Jews. Several hundred Jews, or more, were killed after the war by Poles in pogroms when they returned to their home areas. The vigorous local level of anti-Semitism survived the war unscathed: the Jews were often identified with the Russians who were taking over the country and were still very unpopular. Many Poles had helped themselves to Jewish property when the Jews were deported and were reluctant to hand it back. In any case, since the Nazis had cleansed Poland of the Jews, the locals were not going to welcome the Jews back, or even to allow them to return. There was more safety in the large cities, but in the small towns and the countryside, the murder of returning Jews had a predictable effect on those thinking of returning. This phenomenon was not limited to Poland, as many countries were not exactly upset by the removal of the Jews from their villages, towns and cities. For one thing, it meant the disappearance of a minority who had been regarded at best with neutrality, but more often with hostility. It meant the removal of competitors in work and business, and also opened up a lot of property to the local Gentile population, who often happily looted the possessions and land of their absent neighbors. When those neighbors looked as though they might be about to return, it is not difficult to imagine the concern that was evoked. The influence of this feeling of guilt was not limited to the immediate post-war period. It has been argued, for example, that anti-Semitic events in Greece in 2009–10, where today there are only 5,000 Jews, has a lot to do with the widespread knowledge that many of the homes in the area, especially in modern Thessaloniki, used to belong to the Jews who were deported and murdered, and who used to live in what was called Salonica. As the Jews were taken away, reports from the time describe how readily the local population helped themselves to the property that immediately became available. It is not difficult to imagine the feelings of entitlement, guilt and self-justification that made this sort of appropriation feasible, and how it affects relationships today between Gentiles and the tiny remnant of the Jewish community that used to live in parts of Europe. Despite the fact that some very impressive examples of assistance by European Gentiles to Jews took place during the Nazi times, they were usually heavily outweighed by those who were ready, and indeed eager, to profit from the new state of affairs.

The Soviet Union

The attack on the Soviet Union by the Germans led to a certain softening in relations between the state and its Jewish population, as the former was aware of the need to portray itself sympathetically to the West. But after the war the mood changed and the hostility of the West was no longer significant, so familiar prejudices and suspicions arose once again. The creation of the State of Israel was initially supported both diplomatically and materially by the Soviet bloc, since it was seen presumably as giving the Russians a way of disrupting what had been a Western-dominated Middle East. Yet the idea that the Soviet Jewish populations could identify themselves with Israel was totally rejected, and the label of Zionist and rootless cosmopolitan came to be shorthand terms meaning Jew in much of the Communist press. Continuing repression of Judaism and Jewish institutions reached its height in 1953 in the Doctors Plot, when it was 'discovered' that six Jewish physicians were intent on murdering important Communist functionaries. Only Stalin's death in the same year prevented a show trial that could have resulted in dire consequences for the Jewish population of the Soviet Union as a whole. The situation was not much better in the other Warsaw Pact countries, where Jews had often been among the early Communist leaders and so drew the opprobrium of the local population for being not only Communists, and faithful to Moscow, but also Jews, so they were even more dependent on Russia for their position. Emigration to the West and Israel became popular and caused a radical reduction in the size of the local Jewish populations, until the situation arose that the Jews were nothing more than a distant memory, and so became an appropriate object of nostalgia (*JT* ch. 13).

America

The year in which Christopher Columbus discovered America, 1492, is notorious in Jewish history as the date the Jews were expelled from Spain. While some Jews did move to the parts of the American continent then under Spanish control, it was as Marranos or crypto-Jews, and they found the New World to be no more hospitable than Spain had been to their beliefs and practices. Only those Jews who escaped from Spain and Portugal managed to practice their religion openly. An important community developed in the Netherlands at the time when that colony of Spain separated from Spain itself, a move that was linked with opposition to the Catholicism of the Spanish regime. It participated in the financing of the colonization of America and a significant number of Jews moved with the Dutch to America. New Amsterdam, later called New York, had a small community even in the seventeenth century, a situation that was not changed by the new British rulers. The absence of any significant hostility toward the Jews encouraged immigration to the British-run part of the land, up and down the coastline and into what is today called the West Indies. The encouraging news of the tolerant character of the territory produced ever more Jewish immigrants. Their enthusiasm was put to the test during the War of Independence in 1776, when several Jews rose to prominence in the fighting of the war and the prosecution of the cause. In the Civil War of the next century, there was no common Jewish position on the conflict; those living in the North tended to support the Unionists, and those in the South sided with the Confederacy.

The rapid growth of the American economy benefitted the Jews living there, who identified themselves increasingly with their country. One aspect of this identification was the growing popularity of the Reform variety of Judaism, which found a natural home in the German Jewish population. But this group was quickly outnumbered by the rapid immigration of Jews from Eastern Europe, seeking to escape the hostility of the general population. This new community did not identify closely with the rather formal Reform, and they were also often unenthusiastic about orthodoxy and religious tradition as a whole. Many Jews were aligned with socialist or Zionist groups, and their links with any religion were very weak or non-existent. Those who remained connected with Judaism had a wide range of choices before them. A variety of different traditional groups existed, who often stemmed from parts of Eastern Europe, together with what came to be known as modern orthodoxy, built on the persona of Rav Soloveitchik, a considerable intellectual presence with a commitment to both orthodoxy and secular knowledge. Then there was the creation of what became the Conservative movement, which remained close to the traditional forms of Judaism but sought to represent a more modern position, with some adjustments to take into account modernity, in particular in its understanding of the point of ritual rather than in anything different in the ritual. So, for example, the Conservative movement accepted that the Torah might not have been given to Moses on Mount Sinai in both its written and oral forms in quite the way that more traditional interpretations have it. The Reform movement sought to create a more American form of Judaism, which came much closer to the ways of prayer customary in churches, and a more egalitarian approach to the participation of women in the rabbinate, the services and the administration. Finally, the small Reconstructionist movement had a huge effect on non-traditional Jewish synagogues in the USA, though in itself it never became very large. Through emphasizing the social and cultural role of Judaism, its creator Mordechai Kaplan brought out what had always been a crucial aspect of Jewish identity, but not one that had generally been acknowledged explicitly in the ritual.

The expansion of the American Jewish community led to its becoming, until recently, the largest Jewish community in the world, especially after the destruction of European Jewry in the Holocaust. With the rise in wealth and influence of the USA, after the Second World War it also became the most powerful force in the Jewish world. It took some time for Jews in America to play a full part in political life, but when they did after 1945 it became effective in advocating a State of Israel and defending the rights of Jews elsewhere.

The American community is no longer as significant in the Jewish world as it was in the past. In 2005, amid the celebrations of 350 years of American Jewish life, it was announced that, according to Israel's Central Bureau of Statistics, the country's population of self-identifying Jews had reached a total of 5,550,000. The closest parallel number for Jews in the USA (where the figures are probably less precise and collected in a different way) is 5,290,000. With this news, an era that began following the Holocaust, when America emerged as the undisputed center of world Jewry, came to a close as Israel overtook the USA as the largest Jewish population center in the world. It is also the case that, at the start of the third millennium, the majority of Jewish children in the world spoke Hebrew, since most of them were in Israel.

The Jewish community in the USA is, in fact, shrinking. There are several reasons for this. Jews outside the orthodox communities have small families. Also, there is a growing enthusiasm for intermarriage that seems to expand all the time, and this results in many families with Jews in them no longer regarding themselves as Jewish, or bringing up their children as Jewish. Synagogue membership is declining and many synagogues have literally run out of congregations. On the other hand, the traditional communities have continued to flourish, at least as far as numbers go, and there has also been a growth in the creation of more informal prayer communities such as the Chavurah movement, and the growth in the early twenty-first century of small *minyan*s – prayer groups of the minimum size – based in workplaces and houses rather than in formal institutions. It also has to be said that as Jews often regard their Jewishness as more of a cultural than a religious category, they may continue to regard themselves as Jews despite a lack of enthusiasm for religion, and pass this feeling on to others also.

Zionism and the Return to the Land of Israel

After the creation of the State of Israel, Jews in the Arab world found themselves in a difficult situation. Their loyalties were widely suspected as being divided between their own country and Israel, and it proved much easier for local Arab governments to dispossess and drive out their Jewish citizens than it was to overcome the nascent Jewish state. Jews have lived in what is today Israel for thousands of years, though in varying numbers, and for long periods there were hardly any Jews there at all, as a result of the draconian measures carried out by the Romans and other invaders. There are halakhic suggestions that living in the Land is meritorious, but Jews did not return in large numbers until the nineteenth century, when persecution in the parts of Europe controlled by Russia, and Russia itself, led to some resettlement in agricultural communities, often financed by Jewish philanthropists in Europe. Small groups of religious Jews have always moved to the Land, but they were largely ignored by the local inhabitants. However, the larger-scale immigration of European Jews and their attempts to control sizeable chunks of territory led to considerable antagonism with the local Arab population, who saw this as an alien invasion designed to change the ethnic balance of the country, at that time under Ottoman rule. Attempts were made by the Zionists to persuade the Ottomans to allow more Jewish immigration, but hardly surprisingly this was not met with a warm reception. They had more luck with the British, and Chaim Weizmann (1874–1952) managed to extract from them the Balfour Declaration, in which the British looked to a Middle East when Turkey, Germany's ally, had been defeated and what would be done with the spoils. Palestine was indeed occupied by the British army, and the Turkish forces driven out and defeated. According to the Declaration, the Jews were to have a homeland there, though it also stated that nothing should be done to harm the rights of existing communities in Palestine. The British received the country from the League of Nations in 1922 and set out to prepare it for independence at some stage, despite the significant anti-Jewish riots that took place. Weizmann's role in obtaining the Balfour Declaration led to his election as the movement's leader. He remained in that role until 1948.

The British Mandate led to greater Jewish migration to Palestine and significant Jewish land purchases from the existing Arab feudal landlords. There were riots as a result, often involving Arabs who were now without land or employment, in 1920, 1921 and 1929, sometimes accompanied by massacres of Jews. The victims were occasionally local non-Zionist orthodox Jewish communities, such as the community in Hebron destroyed in 1929. Britain supported Jewish immigration in principle, but in reaction to Arab violence imposed restrictions on it in practice. During the Second World War, the British controlled Jewish immigration and tried to do so again after the war, but the sight of concentration camp survivors being arrested by British soldiers when they tried to enter Palestine brought scorn on the mandatory power, especially in the USA, which for the first time threw itself enthusiastically into the Zionist camp. The British presence was challenged by militant Jewish groups who used terror to drive them out, and the creation of a state for the Jews was approved by the United Nations, but this was rejected by the Arab countries in the area. There have been a number of subsequent wars in which the Arabs have not so far succeeded in dislodging the Jews from the country, despite the revulsion with which Zionism is regarded in much of the world.

It is difficult to understand why Zionism has been condemned as racism or attracted such widespread criticism. There have been many ethnic conflicts in which one group wins and one group loses, and eventually they reconcile themselves to the situation, or work out some way of tolerating the state of affairs that has come about. Israel does call itself a Jewish State, yet many non-Jews live there as citizens, and most of the Arab countries say in their constitution that the religion of the state is Islam. So the idea of a state being linked with a particular religion or, indeed, group is hardly novel in the region. It is also difficult to classify all such opposition to Zionism as anti-Semitic, since some opponents are very committed Jews, and others certainly are not anti-Semitic. On the other hand, there clearly seem to be anti-Semitic tropes in the quite specific hostility with which Israel has been regarded, and the idea of the rapacious, violent and bloodthirsty Jew has played a part in the demonization of the Jewish State. This places critics of Israel in a difficult position, in that it is often difficult to avoid an anti-Semitic stance or associating with anti-Semites in attacking the State. Yet such criticisms may in themselves be quite reasonable and unassociated with classical anti-Semitism and, indeed, Jewish critics of Israel in the diaspora are inhibited from expressing criticisms with which Israeli Jews themselves have no difficulty.

Zionism has a variety of forms, but there are two main Jewish doctrines: one secular and one religious. The creator of the modern Zionist movement, Theodor Herzl (1860–1904), was a secular Viennese journalist, though originally from Hungary, who, it is said, was persuaded by the Dreyfus Affair to think that the Jews had no long-term future in Europe. Dreyfus was an officer in the French army who, like many French Jews, came from Alsace, and was suspected of having spied for the Germans. A period of imprisonment was imposed on him and this led to a campaign to vindicate him, with those opposed to Jews being full citizens arguing that he was guilty. The implication was that, even if Jews abandoned their traditional isolation and specialized professions and sought to enter mainstream European society, they would ultimately be rejected. Herzl took from this that Jews required a national home, and in the nineteenth century many nationalities such as the Italians, Greeks, Germans and so on campaigned for and won a national home of some kind. It was in line with this desire that Zionism was established, and for Herzl that home did not have to be in Palestine – he was prepared to countenance anywhere that was available, even seriously considering parts of East Africa when this was proposed by the British, or even Argentina. The Zionist movement encouraged Jewish migration to the Land of Israel and was eventually successful in establishing Israel in 1948 as the homeland for the Jewish people. Its proponents regard its aim as self-determination for the Jewish people. The proportion of the Jewish world living in Israel has grown steadily since the movement came into existence. In 2010, roughly 40 per cent of the world's Jews, and a majority of Jewish children, live in Israel.

In Herzl's book, *Altneuland*, he argued that once the Jews had their own country they would be able to lead normal lives and would be regarded as a normal community by the Gentile world. The other part of the title, *Der Judenstaat*, is interesting, since it does not mean the Jewish State, it means the State of the Jews. It is as though he was acknowledging that a variety of different sorts of Jews would be living in the same state, and that they would have to find some sort of modus vivendi if this was to be pleasant, or at least possible.

Religious Zionism is the doctrine that the Land of Israel was promised to the Jews by God, as recounted in the Torah, and so they have a right to live there, and indeed a duty to settle the land. The language is expressive here; someone who goes to Israel is said to go up (*alah*) to Israel, and in Israel, to go up to Jerusalem. Clearly, the reference here is to going up spiritually, though the location of Jerusalem is quite high compared to much of the surrounding countryside. Leaving Israel is often described as *yeridah*, going down. There is a vast literature in Judaism describing the significance of Israel, and in particular Jerusalem, perhaps surprisingly in a religion that managed to survive quite happily out of its original location. Zionism has a variety of meanings, but is linked with the doctrine that the Jewish people should have a homeland in their former location in Palestine. Religious Jews concentrate on the fact that this land was promised to

them by God in the Bible, and since he made the whole world he can
say who ought to live where. Secular Jews refer to the historical links
between this area of the Middle East and long periods of settled
Jewish history. The term comes from the Hebrew reference to Mount
Zion in Jerusalem, which came to represent the city and finally the
nation. There is no essential connection with Palestine; other home-
lands have been contemplated and even accepted by a number of
Zionists, but most Zionists in the past, and all today, focus on parts of
Palestine as the location of the State.

Many Jews regard whatever diasporic country they live in as their
homeland, and may even argue that it is the best place for Jews to
live. The first three decades of the State of Israel were dominated
politically by a form of socialist Zionism, led by Ashkenazi Jews who
advocated Jews becoming producers and active participants in all
aspects of the economic life of the new country. Often rather skeptical of religion, they sought to forge a secular modern country in
which Jews could throw off their diaspora mentality of subservience
to others and take charge of their own future. In recent years this
approach has been overshadowed by what might be called liberal
Zionism, a belief in the free market and individualism, and the principle that Israel should be a modern, highly technological and entre-
preneurial country firmly in the Western camp, which in fact in
many ways it has become. Nationalist Zionism is based on the party
established by Jabotinsky, and developed into the Likud party with a
less sympathetic attitude to Israel's Arab neighbors and inhabitants.
The party took over as a major governing group after 1977, but was
later rocked by its abandonment by its leader and the creation of the
Kadima party, which had a definite line on peace that went very
much against the uncompromising approach of the Likud. There has
been a steady decline of the parties on the left in Israel in recent
years, which perhaps reflects a change in the aspirations of many of
its citizens against the prospect of a socialist Zionism.

The religious parties have problems in reconciling themselves with
a state which, to all intents and purposes, is secular, although parts of
Jewish Law have become the personal law for the Jewish citizens of
the State. Some parties will have nothing at all to do with the State
and ignore it, or do their best to oppose it, but most have effected
some form of conciliation with it – in particular to extract resources
and influence from political deals, and because the increasingly large

numbers of religious Jews in Israel has widened their political influence. In the view of many traditional Jews, Israel should be a Jewish State, not just in the sense of having a Jewish majority, but also in that its character is Jewish. This means that Jewish religious Law should be the Law of the State (for Jews at least) and the State should be infused with Jewish values based on Torah observance. Some religious Zionists see the settling of the land as an important stage in the messianic future of the world, a view that is shared by some Christian Zionists, who see the return of the Jews to Israel as a preliminary to the second coming of Jesus, which has led them to support Israel against its enemies. On the other hand, some religious Jews are totally opposed to Zionism, seeing it as pre-empting God's decision as to when to send the Messiah and lead the Jews back to Israel. Secular Jews have often opposed Zionism, seeing it sometimes as a narrow form of nationalism, and viewing a national home for the Jews as a poor alternative to integration in the countries with Gentile majorities.

For most Israelis, Zionism is an abstract notion that has little to do with their life in the land in which they were born and still live, and, like most people, they think they have a right to live where they do. However, some Israelis reject the Zionist idea that there should be something exclusively Jewish about the country, arguing that a state in which both Jews and Gentiles could live as equals would be preferable to the existing situation. Most Israelis are secular, even though the religious Jewish community is rapidly growing in number and so also in influence, and they accept Herzl's view of Zionism, where Israel is seen as the national home of the Jews as a people, but not necessarily with any requirement to institute a religious lifestyle for its Jewish citizens.

Zionism has been pilloried by its enemies as racist and as a particularly evil idea, and Israel as an especially problematic country. The fact that it is the only state with a non-Muslim majority in the Middle East has perhaps had something to do with this, since the states around it do on the whole, like Israel, recognize a major religion in a state as the religion of the state, in their case usually Islam. They are not generally so well-disposed toward the religious minorities in their states as is Israel, and have, ever since Zionism became effective in their region, opposed it violently. Even within the Islamic communities themselves there is often a great deal of violence, especially between the Sunnis and the Shi'ites, where intolerance is at such a high level on occasion that people are prepared to kill themselves if it means that they can kill many of the other group at the same time. The Arab countries do not on the whole have democratic values as strong as Israel's either, and it is difficult to see why Zionism has aroused such universal ire, apart from the fact that it stands in the way of a total Islamicization of the Middle East. On the other hand, opponents of Zionism sometimes argue that it was the creation of the State of Israel that has led to all the present-day problems in the Middle East, including the expulsion of the Jews from the Arab world and the growing hostility between Islam and the other two Abrahamic religions. Regarding Israel as a pariah state is seen by many as an appropriate reaction to Zionism, since the doctrine is similar to the apartheid doctrine of South Africa in the days of white supremacy, in giving preferential treatment to one racial group over others.

Despite what many say about Israel, it is in fact a very ordinary sort of state, a member of the modern technologically-sophisticated world economy, largely indistinguishable from many parts of the USA and Europe. It is annoying that in many books on religions such as Judaism and Islam, or on countries such as Egypt and Israel, we are often offered stereotypical images of men on camels, traditional Jews praying at the Western Wall and so on, as though this is what the country or the religion is all about. Israel is seen as a country dominated by the desire for Jews to pray at the Western Wall, whereas in reality most Israeli Jews would not know how to pray at the Western Wall or anywhere else, and even if they did would have no interest in doing so. The riots that take place in Jerusalem when a car park stays open on the Sabbath or when a popular rabbi is arrested for some crime are events that involve a thoroughly isolated and quite limited proportion of the population.

Similarly, on the Arab side of Israeli citizens, there are some who identify completely with the Palestinians in the wider world, and wish to bring about the end of the State of Israel. There are even some who are prepared to use violence to bring about this end, and whose commitment to Arab nationalism or the idea of Palestine as an Islamic state is very strong. Yet most Israeli Arabs are far from sharing these views, and get on with their ordinary lives within the context of the State of Israel. Even those who are opposed to the State in the Arab community locally perceive they are far better off both materially and legally in a country that is law-abiding and employs efficient economic practices than they would be a few miles to the east in the Occupied Territories or in Jordan, or in the other surrounding countries that have large Palestinian communities. In those places Palestinians have often been treated very poorly, far worse than in Israel, and it is telling that this has even been the case in what are today called the Palestinian territories.

This is the very undramatic news that is so boring it is hardly worth reporting, and therefore is not generally reported. It suggests that Israel is in many ways the sort of ordinary state its creators had in mind, though, of course, they had a variety of opinions about what Israel ought to become. Had Israel remained the vaguely socialist state of its first three decades, or if it ever becomes a far more religious state, then it would be really rather unusual as a country in comparison with many other countries in the West. But it will be said that Israel is in the Middle East and not in the West, and the fact that it identifies itself and is identified with the West is a further indication of its unusual status. Yet the West is no longer a geographical description; there are many countries in the East, and even in the Middle East, that are aligned with the West, and the increasing globalization that affects every country makes these sorts of distinctions increasingly irrelevant.

Here we need to acknowledge the point that it is not only Israel that has existential issues about the sort of state it is, but many other countries do too, including many of Israel's neighbors. It is worth remembering that these countries were on the whole created by earlier colonialists and have borders and include communities that are not necessarily in accord with any other reality. Despite the strain on the independent states in the Arab world in reconciling themselves to those borders, it is remarkable how quickly a notion of what it means to be an Iraqi citizen, say, or a Syrian, have developed. There are certainly problems here, especially since many Syrians think that their borders are far wider than anyone else believes, but often individuals do relate to their own country, even in conflicts with those who are otherwise close to them ethnically or in religious terms over the border. What is worth bearing in mind, though this has hardly been noticed, is that in the Arab world exactly the same sorts of issues about national and religious identity arise as are seen in Israel, and not necessarily as a result of Israel's presence. Many of these issues arose in the nineteenth century when discussions about what to do about the Ottoman empire were under way, and how the Arab world should organize itself should that empire be overthrown.

Even more prosaically, this sort of discussion is not at all limited to the newer independent countries of the Middle East. The nature of the country in which one lives is often regarded as an essentially contested concept in the USA and in the countries of Europe. One of the issues that has arisen in recent discussions about whether Turkey should enter the European Union is whether it is European or not. This raises all the sorts of issues about what is Europe, how do the individual European countries fit into a general union, and what the nature of that union ought to be, which to a degree also energizes the Middle-Eastern political debate. Certainly, Europe is now post-Christian, as enthusiasm for Christianity is very much on the decline, but far from being totally absent in defining what countries see as their essential character. As we know from the ways in which Jews can be Jews without being religious or even theists, Christians in Europe can see Christianity as an important part of their identity – not in the sense that they are believers or go to church, but because they are not something else, nowadays increasingly Muslim. Whether this sort of identity is strong enough to provide a real basis to distinguish Christians from others remains to be seen, but perhaps the constituents from which we can construct a social identity are rather limited, so we have to make do with what is available. If all that is available are some distant memories of a previous religious form of life, then perhaps that will do.

Jewish Experiences of Islam

After the creation of the State of Israel, Jews in the Arab world found themselves in a difficult situation. Their loyalties were widely suspected as being divided between their own country and Israel, and it proved much easier for local Arab governments to dispossess and drive out their Jewish citizens than it was to overcome the nascent Jewish state. Xenophobia is rarely an unsuccessful political strategy and it worked well, at least temporarily, to shore up the position of the Arab governments, who could at least offer their citizens the property of the departing Jews, such as it was. The arrival of those Jews from the Arab states altered the demographic balance in Israel from Ashkenazi to Sefardi or Mizrachi, from Jews primarily from

Europe to those mainly from the Middle East, though the elites did not change for a considerable period, and even today do not reflect the demographic changes accurately. These expulsions do not represent the general experience of Jews in the Islamic world, which was on the whole much more positive than it was in Christian Europe. On the other hand, they do represent the arbitrary nature of what can happen to minorities in any part of the world, and in the past, Jewish life in the land of Islam was often insecure and sometimes impossible. Apart from in Morocco, the numbers of Jews left in the Arab world today is almost imperceptible, in some countries actually consisting of single numbers, which is remarkable considering the longevity of those former communities and their considerable numbers until recently. Much of the Arab world has become *judenrein*, in a manner that confirms the fears of those who see the world as in constant conflict with the Jews. For those opposed to Zionism it is regarded as the inevitable effect of the creation of the Jewish State.

The only Islamic countries in the Middle East that still have sizeable Jewish minorities today are Turkey and Iran, and apart from occasional problems they live peacefully without much hindrance affecting their way of life. Iranian Jews do not find it difficult to move to other countries from Iran, since they are widely regarded as having a difficult time there, despite the evidence, and have many powerful advocates in other countries. Attitudes to Jews in Iran, even among those supportive of the Ahmadinajad regime, are fairly mild, and people do distinguish between Jews and Israel, a point that the government crudely makes by inviting to its conferences ultra-orthodox Jews such as Neturei Karta (The Guardians of the City), who reject Zionism, and who, it has to be said, are a tiny minority in the Jewish world. Those who in 2009 supported the opposition to Ahmadinajad are quietly rather supportive of Israel, not out of any particular love for Israel but because they see the government as opposed to Israel, and so the assumption is that there must be something good about the State. It is difficult to know how to assess things such as attitude in a closed society like Iran, and especially one that is very suspicious of Israel, not surprisingly, given its frequent threats against the State, but many people have suggested there is very little anti-Semitism in the country. Sometimes this apparent philosemitism is taken rather too far, as when in 2009 the *New York Times* writer Roger Cohen visited Iran and discovered that the Jewish community was free to protest along with everyone else against Israel

(*New York Times*, 22 February 2009). It would have been more interesting to have discovered that they were free to support Israel. The Jewish member of parliament, Mohamed Motamedh, whose seat is reserved for the Jewish community, admitted that he was an Iranian first and a Jew second, and one wondered whether it would have been possible to have reversed the order and still remained in public life in Iran. It has to be said, though, that opponents of the regime, and there are many, identify countries which the regime constantly criticizes, such as the USA and Israel, quite positively.

Turkey

Compare Iran, however, with Turkey, one of the first countries in the world to recognize Israel and its closest official ally in the Islamic world. In 2009, the government of Turkey distanced itself firmly from Israel after the Gaza war, and Erdoğan made several interesting remarks which seemed to contrast radically the behavior of Jews and Muslims. The President of Sudan was said not to be a possible war criminal because he was a Muslim, but the Jews were labeled as being very good at killing people. This taps into a history in Turkey of great suspicion of the Jews and anyone connected with them, even the Dönmeh Muslim sect, who have been Muslims for centuries, yet which are regarded as fantastically powerful in Turkey and highly conspiratorial in nature. The bookshops in Turkey are full of books on how Jews control everything everywhere, and how many leaders are in fact Jews or crypto-Jews, all acting in concert with other Jews against the Gentile world. The Prime Minister of Turkey, Recep Erdoğan, a passionate critic of Israel, plus the creator of the secular Turkish Republic, Kemal Atatürk, have both been falsely identified as Dönmeh. It is true that Atatürk went to one of their schools, but so did many Muslims, and the Dönmeh are today thoroughgoing Muslims, with a few family connections between them, but nothing else to link them even with the deviant kind of Judaism they represented in the past. The Dönmeh are descended from the Jews who accompanied Shabetai Zvi, the false Messiah, on his journey to the Land of Israel, a journey that was brought to an end in Turkey by the conversion of Shabetai Zvi in 1666 in order to save his life in the Islamic Ottoman empire.

Most of his followers abandoned Zvi once he converted, and it is difficult to maintain the status of a Jewish messiah if he converts to a different religion. Some, however, argued that this was part of the messianic project, and that his conversion was only nominal, and the mission remained on course. This small group remained in the Ottoman territories, basing itself eventually on Salonica, where it was obliged to relocate to Turkey after the founding of the Turkish Republic and the wars with Greece – fortunately, in this case, since otherwise they would have been wiped out by the Nazis along with the Greek Jews in the city. The Dönmeh did represent a distinct group in Turkey for some time, being enthusiastic participants in the Young Turk movement and advocates for reform, yet today they have almost totally disappeared into the general Turkish Muslim population. But in the public imagination they are immensely powerful, working with each other and with Jews elsewhere to frame a world in accordance with their wishes. The request by Herzl for a Jewish national home in Palestine was rejected by the Sultan Abdulhamid II, and in revenge the Jews are said to have decided to depose him. So when the Jewish Emmanuel Carasso went to inform the Sultan later of his exile in Salonica, this all fits in, as does his residence there in the house of the Jewish Allatini family. The Young Turk movement that initiated the end of the caliphate, and Kemal Atatürk who brought it directly to an end, are both linked with the Jews, and any connection with Salonica and its large Jewish population is tantamount to proving the connection. Mustafa Kemal came from Salonica. What is interesting about this idea is that it is held so widely in Turkey that, despite any evidence, even a group of Jews who converted hundreds of years ago to Islam is suspected of still being really Jewish in some sense, and of acting in concert with other Jews. One of the entertaining factors here is that, of course, any followers of Shabetai Zvi have for a long time been strenuously rejected by the rest of the Jewish world as following a version of Judaism that is unacceptable to any mainstream Jew, whether Ashkenazi or Sefardi.

In fact, the greater friendliness by Turkey to the Jews and Israel in recent years was very much a reflection of a view that might be called anti-Semitic. It was felt that the Jews are powerful and so when Turkey had hopes, now rapidly diminishing, of entering the European Union, they thought it would be helpful to recruit Jews, in the USA and elsewhere, to advocate for them. They were also worried about the prospects of a military coup against them and thought that if they could get the Jews on their side, with their enormous power throughout the world, as they saw it, this might prevent such a coup. The previous religious government in Turkey, led by Erbaken, was brought to an end by the military, and if Jews are seen as being behind everything that happens, it is not difficult to project them as bringing about this Turkish military intervention on behalf of secularism. The *Protocols of the Elders of Zion* is widely read in Turkey, as is *Mein Kampf*, and this further encourages belief in all-powerful Jewish conspiracies. This placed the Jews in a dilemma, since they felt pressured to downplay or even to deny the Holocaust-like massacres of the Armenians in Turkey at the start of the twentieth century. The idea was that, by being nice to the Jews in America who have such enormous influence over everything else, Turkey would gain an important ally in its European ambitions. Indeed, it did succeed in recruiting significant support among Jewish organizations in the USA, but the effect this was supposed to have had on Europe is obscure, since despite the anti-Semitic assumptions of a global Jewry pursuing its own goals, the view of anyone in America, Jew or otherwise, has limited significance for anyone in Europe. Of course, the turning away from Israel is linked with other events, such as the perception of there being less of a threat from Turkey's neighbors, such as Iraq and Syria, and the religious party in power in Turkey, the AKP, has naturally good relations with similar parties in Islamic countries. But it might also be said that the rejection of the Dönmeh as real Muslims, and the refusal to regard the actions of Muslims as possible genocide, represents a significant misunderstanding of Islam. Once one has converted to Islam one ought to be regarded as just as good, or bad, a Muslim as the next person, and Muslims certainly can go awry, as they have in the past – and in the present on occasion. What the Turkish Prime Minister in 2009–10 was doing was acknowledging a warmer relationship with Muslims than with the followers of other religions, whatever their respective actions, and what the Turkish public was doing was distinguishing between those who have converted from Judaism to Islam and everyone else in the Muslim community. Yet one of the virtues of Islam is to disregard, at least formally, the racial and ethnic distinctions between different people and to accept as Muslims everyone who genuinely becomes a Muslim. Perhaps the assumption is that the Dönmeh are not really Muslims. Yet the evidence is that they are, and they did not convert in recent years but, in fact, four centuries ago. Presumably, at the present time, when it might have been in their interests to identify themselves as Jews and emigrate to Israel, or the USA, they could have done so, yet they did not. We can therefore see what they genuinely thought they were – Muslims – and the suspicion in which they are held in modern Turkey is a significant indication of the attitude toward Jews in that country, even though the object of the prejudice is not in fact Jewish at all.

It is worth pointing out, though, that an anti-Semitic atmosphere in a country can provide a very potent ingredient in that country's foreign policy. Visitors to Turkey are often told of the multicultural nature of the Ottoman Empire, of the Christian and Jewish minorities that flourished during that time, and of the many churches and synagogues that still exist in the cities of Turkey. It is true that some of these institutions still exist, though hardly flourish, but they exist within a broadly hostile atmosphere of suspicion about the minorities in a country that is overwhelmingly Muslim. Many of these buildings are no more than that – just buildings – with no worshippers, or some thoroughly cowed worshippers who realize that their role in a country that seems, despite its immense Muslim majority, to be unsettled by any non-Muslim presence is very limited and perhaps temporary. Here we need to point to an important aspect of anti-Semitism – it is a potent idea that is easily stimulated but, once aroused, is only restrained with great difficulty. The idea that the world is run by a group of conspirators makes politics exciting, a case of good versus evil, and the idea that they are Jews fits in with centuries, indeed millennia, of suspicions about the traditional Other, the stubborn Jews who are seen to persist in their obstinacy and continue as a witness to the non-truth of the revelations by Jesus and through Muhammad.

From the Islamist point of view, in Turkey the Jews are linked with secularism and Kemalism, and several important Jews in the past were in those movements. Jews do tend to be secularists, since they do better in states that have no particular religious affiliation. The fact that there is no evidence of conspiracies to prevent Turkey from becoming an Islamic state is not evidence that such conspiracies do not exist, since of course there would be no such evidence: conspirators do their conspiring in secret. There is plenty of evidence, though, that Jews prefer to live in a secular society, and this can be taken as prima facie evidence that they oppose an Islamic state, and

because of their enormous power and influence prevent it from coming about. This strong criticism of the Jews has not only come from
the Islamists, but also prevails on the left and among the nationalists,
angry at the behavior of Israel in its dealings with the Arabs, and
often entirely hostile to the very idea of a Jewish country existing in
the Middle East at all. The secularists might have been expected to
have supported the Jews, who are themselves largely secularists, but
they feared losing out to the xenophobia of the Islamists in their
denunciation of the Jews, and wanted to show that they also rejected
the idea of a Jewish state and were dubious about the influence of the
Jews on Turkish affairs. Since Israel is so closely linked in the public's
mind with the USA, the unpopularity of the latter is often linked
with hostility to the former, and since Israel is so much less formida-
ble an enemy compared with the USA, it is also so much safer. The
Turkish left threw Israel into the anti-American mix, and in itself
that is perfectly acceptable, since to be opposed to Israel and its policies is not to be in itself anti-Semitic. It depends largely on the language that is used. But the language that is used is largely
anti-Semitic, resting on the evil designs of international Jewry, the
power of the Jews in the West, and the utterly unbalanced treatment
of the actions of Israel as not only being as bad as the Nazis, but in
fact worse. So the Israeli onslaught on Gaza was said to have been
worse than Auschwitz, and the treatment of the Palestinians in Gaza
worse than the treatment of the Jews by the Nazis in the concentration camps. One has to allow for a degree of hyperbole in politics,
but it is difficult to accept these as serious claims. Would they have
been made against any target apart from the Jews, one wonders?

Tolerance and its Limitations

Despite these contemporary problems, there is no doubt that until
recently the history of the Jews in the Islamic world was very different from their experience of the Christian territories. In the original
centers of Islam, such as the Arabian peninsula, the Jewish minority
was either swiftly murdered or forced to convert, and no doubt there
was also much voluntary conversion. On the other hand, they also
managed to exist quite happily for extended periods within parts of
the Islamic world, especially if they were linked with particular rulers
who found them useful, such as the Ottomans, or if they were helpful in the balance of power between Jews, Christians and Muslims, as

in Iberia. Legally they were classified as *ahl al-kitab*, 'People of the Book', and as such had certain privileges, in contrast to complete polytheists, for example, but this status varied and continues to vary as local conditions vary. There is a good deal of rhetoric today on how tolerant the Islamic world was to its minorities, but this is far from the truth, largely because the concept of tolerance is a very modern one. Feuerbach, thinking of Judaism, suggests that 'Absolute intolerance [is] the secret essence of monotheism' (Feuerbach, 1881, 113–14). There were periods of peaceful coexistence, and periods when the Jews were either murdered, or forced to convert or emigrate, but the Jews usually managed to survive when there was a general lack of hostility from the host population, and when that attitude changed, the position of the Jews changed. It was not just the creation of the State of Israel that brought this about; throughout the Muslim world, Jews were often treated poorly and, even when they were not, they existed at the whim of either the ruler or the mob, not a very desirable situation. However, it was nevertheless often better than the situation under Christian rule, and it is important to acknowledge this difference. It is equally important not to posit the existence of some putative 'Golden Age' in which the different Abrahamic faiths coexisted in total harmony, since such a state of affairs never really existed.

The difficulties that Jewish communities often had in living with their host communities did nothing to hinder Jewish cultural life, or so it seems, since a huge amount of intellectual creativity took place throughout what came to be called 'the exile'. There seems to be something of a crude generalization that culture flourishes in more inhospitable conditions, like some plants that do poorly when they are treated well. In some ways one can see why this might be the case. A degree of disjointedness from the society in which one lives encourages the thinker to consider clearly and urgently how his or her principles, or what might turn out to be his/her principles, relate to those of the wider community, and how well they stand up on their own. Jews have often been good at discussing the culture they live in, since they often are slightly outside of that culture, and share the enthusiasm but also sometimes the antagonism toward it of the outsider. They have also had some experience of trying to link that culture with what they might take to be their own culture, and in contexts in which they are invited, gently or otherwise, to convert the link between one culture and the next is an important issue. After all, if the culture one may take up is in fact at the very least no worse than one's own, then why not convert? In modern times the issue is more one of assimilation than conversion, but just as significant.

It is often said that the experience of Jews in the Islamic world was quite different from that in the Christian world, but this is not really the case. The rapid expansion of the Islamic empire soon took over the main Jewish centers in the Middle East and North Africa, and this might have been a problematic state of affairs for the local Jews. After all, the Prophet had dealt very roughly with the Jews of Arabia, who were largely massacred and enslaved by him when they opposed his progress. The Qur'an takes a variety of approaches to the Jews, sometimes being sympathetic, perhaps reflecting a period of hope that there would be many willing converts, to being quite sharp, when the majority of the Jewish community refused to fall in with the message of Islam. So, initially, the direction of prayer was Jerusalem, and then it became Mecca. The Jewish communities in Arabia were swiftly reduced in importance and became subservient to the growing power of Islam, and, indeed, those Jews who remained in the Arabian peninsula never recovered any sort of polit-ical influence (*JT* ch. 5). The conquest of further areas with signifi-cant Jewish minorities obliged the new power to work out how to treat these groups, not only the Jews of course, and as they them-selves were a small minority once they had left Arabia, it was politic for the Arabs to compromise with these groups, at least until the Muslims had established themselves as being firmly in charge of every aspect of the state. After all, in the beginning, the languages, system of taxation and structure of society were almost totally unknown to the conquering Arabs, and they needed time to absorb such a vast territory and so many different kinds of people. The rapid Islamicization of this area should be regarded as one of the many suc-cesses of the Islamic conquest, and the People of the Book, as the Qur'an calls the Jews and Christians, were expected to pay a special tax as non-Muslims, and accept an inferior status in society, but apart from that they were often allowed to continue doing their work and celebrating their faith. In fact, there was legally a range of disabilities under which the Jews suffered, although these were not always actu-ally applied, yet in some ways they were quite mild compared to what they might have been had the law always been strictly applied.

On Muslim relations with Jews, there are some mild, peaceful and tolerant verses such as 29.46: 'Do not argue with the People of the Book [Christians and Jews] unless in a fair way.' Similar injunctions are found in, among others, 2.62, 2.136, 2.256, and the second part of 5.82, though the first part of the passage is more belligerent. It is certainly the case that Islam reveres Christian and Jewish prophets and messengers, and that the Qur'an is full of references to many Jewish prophets.

The main Jewish center in Babylon was now part of the Islamic world, and the Jews were given a degree of institutional independence, first under the head of the exiled community – the *rosh galuta* – who was believed to be related to David, and then increasingly under the heads of the academies, who were also the legal experts – the Geonim. The growing wealth of the empire and its rapid urbanization were helpful in concentrating the Jews in particular areas where it was easier for them to discover the legal position on the issues that concerned them, and so drew the community ever closer together under the authority of the Geonim. What happened was that people at a distance from the experts would write to them with their queries, and would eventually receive a reply, with the messages traveling on the increasingly good roads in the Islamic world which also, of course, increased trade. By the tenth century, the unity of the Islamic world came into question, and the subsequent conflicts of Muslims with each other led to a breakdown in communications and a very important development: far more autonomy on the legal front for local communities and how they interpreted the law. At various stages a central authority tried to impose some uniformity on what was being done, but to this day the local courts and institutions in the Jewish world are able to determine what is kosher, which conversions are genuine, when a divorce is valid and so on, without any prospect of appealing to a higher and final authority.

From what we know of the economy of the time, Jews were involved in a wide range of commercial and craft activities, often using their connections across the Islamic world, and beyond, to move goods around and import articles that were in short supply in the Middle East. They became progressively urbanized, and the large cities at that time were considerable cultural and commercial centers, on a global scale – and this was nowhere more the case than in Spain. When in the eighth century the Muslims invaded from North

Africa, they occupied a country with a varied population, and a Jewish community that had not been well treated by the Visigothic kings, who had sought to impose their religion on the Jews. As mentioned earlier, the Jews fought on both sides in the following centuries, and often achieved positions of high status in both Muslim and Christian Spain, but the former was more open to them than the latter. One thing that helped here was the fact that Spain was controlled by the remnants of the Umayyads from the east, who had been defeated in the heartland of the Islamic world by the Abbasids. The relative isolation of the Umayyads in the west of the Islamic world made them more dependent on what they found in Iberia, including the Jews. The stability of the unified state was broken up in the eleventh century, when Berbers from North Africa invaded and split the country into smaller units, which quickly began to compete with each other, and Jews were often employed as useful state subjects to help foster the ambitions of the local rulers and their courts. Of course, one of the effective recruiting motives for employing Jews was their lack of support in the local population, since there is much evidence that the idea of Muslim states being organized by Jews caused great offence among the Muslim population, and this made them all the more dependent on their employers.

But by the end of the eleventh century a new regime came into Spain from North Africa – the Almoravids – to fight the increasing Christian challenge to the Muslims, and they were far from happy at the idea of having a Jewish community under their control, even after their initial successes in repelling the Christians. An even more unfriendly regime – the Almohads – took over in the following century, and brought about the migration of Jews to the Christian territories in the north, who now became the patrons of the Jews. There was, however, a progressive decline in attitudes toward the Jews as the Christians became increasingly dominant on the peninsula, and eventually total Christian domination meant the expulsion of the Jews and the ending of the Jewish community. One wonders whether a similar success by the Muslims might have resulted in a similar conclusion.

As the Islamic world came under strain from the twelfth century onwards, its ability to feel comfortable about its minorities also declined. The Iberian peninsula was gradually lost, the Crusaders established a non-Muslim state for some time at the heart of the

Islamic world and, most significantly of all, the Abbasids in Baghdad were destroyed by the Mongols in 1258. This all led to a good deal of heart-searching as to what was happening to the land of Islam, a debate that did not alter when the Ottomans took over the region, for while they were indeed Muslims, they certainly were not Arabs. The occupation by the Ottomans was rather fortunate, since this foreign empire needed both commercial agents in various parts of the diverse empire as well as individuals who would owe their allegiance to Istanbul, not to the local population, and the Jews were in a good position to fulfill this role. When the Jews were expelled from Iberia, the Ottomans invited them to live in their empire, though not just anywhere, but largely where the Ottomans thought it would be best to have them. Not only Jews were used in this way, of course, and the other minorities also played a political role, sometimes leading to a good deal of rivalry and ill-feeling toward the minorities.

The Jews in the Ottoman Empire specialized in certain areas of work, with textiles and leatherwork being important, and all kinds of work with precious stones. Their links with their co-religionists elsewhere helped them act as go-betweens in both commerce and diplomacy. Once the empire broke up into its constituents, the Jews, and other minorities, found themselves with a very problematic status, especially with the creation of the State of Israel and the victories of the State against its many Arab and other Muslim foes. We should not over-emphasize the importance of Israel in this process, since other minorities such as the Christians throughout the Arab world, the Yezidis in Iraq, and the Baha'i in Iran, have all had difficulties in surviving in the region among a Muslim majority. There is a limit to what can be blamed on Israel, though one often admires the ways in which that limit can be stretched. Most of the Jews in the Islamic world moved either to Israel, the USA or Europe, and the very long-established Jewish communities in the Middle East, some going back 25 centuries, have now been entirely extinguished. It is worth contrasting the experience of the Jews in the Islamic world with those in the Christian world. While for long periods the former was a superior home for Jews over the latter, and there has been no Holocaust in the Islamic world (yet), Jews have not continued to survive in most of the Islamic world at all. There were plenty of anti-Jewish riots, murders and expulsions in the Islamic world, and, quoting the Qur'anic phrases 'There is no compulsion in religion' (2.256) or

'Not all of them are alike' (3.113), does not tell us anything at all about Islamic attitudes to Jews, since there are plenty of harsher passages also in the Qur'an, and in any case there is a tendency to interpret or adapt theological passages in any way that fits in with an individual's wishes. The refrain in the Arab world that the Arabs cannot be anti-Semitic, since they are themselves Semites, would be more persuasive were there fewer translations of the anti-Semitic classics in Arabic, and were they to be less widely disseminated in the Arab world. From there, they have moved on to the Islamic world as a whole.

On the other hand, there is always something rather ill-fitting about the incorporation of European racist works into the Islamic world. In most Islamic cultures there is not much of an idea that blood determines who you are, in the same way that there is in much of Europe, for example. When the Prophet married a Jewish woman he insisted she became a Muslim, we are told, but once that was accomplished, no distinction seems to have been made between her and anyone else. Over time, many Jews have converted to Islam, and while sometimes they are treated with suspicion, as is often the case with converts into any religion, on the whole Islam is successful at gaining converts and making them feel at home in their new faith. The large number of Jewish converts in the early years of Islam led to a whole series of sayings called the Isra'iliyat, based as they were on Jewish folklore and custom, and one of the main tasks of some of the scholars who deal with the *hadith* literature – the sayings of the Prophet and his Companions – is to segregate this material from much more genuine, in their view, Islamic source ideas. The idea that one remains a Jew for generations even after converting to another religion is entirely foreign to Islamic law and culture, and that is why it should not be thought that the contemporary taste for anti-Semitic literature in the Islamic world is the same sort of enthusiasm with which it was received outside that world.

Chapter IV

What Jews Do

The Commandments

It is often said that Judaism is not so much an orthodoxy as an ortho-praxy, and by this is meant that it consists more of what it takes to follow right practices than right beliefs. This is, of course, wrong, but it does bring out something that is true; namely, the emphasis in traditional Judaism on laws, on practices and on a system of rules that encompasses the whole of life, from the prayer said after going to the bathroom in the morning to the prayer said before going to sleep, what is worn, what may be eaten and so on. Yet these rules all have some basis in belief, they are far from arbitrary, and extensive legal discussions have developed out of the (already quite extensive) account in the Hebrew Bible of what Jews are supposed to do.

The commandments, or *mitzvot*, traditionally consist of 613 individual rules (*taryag mitzvot*). Many of these have to do with Temple ritual, which was central to Jewish life and worship when the Torah was written. On the other hand, some sacrifices seem to be limited to a specific holy place (according to Deuteronomy), while in Leviticus the Temple and Jerusalem are not required places for sacrifice. Others only apply in a theocratic State of Israel. It has been estimated that only about 270 of them – less than 50 per cent – are still applicable. The important thing about the *mitzvot* is that we are supposed to obey them because God has asked us, indeed has commanded us, to act in this way. He does not need the *mitzvot* to be carried out, but we do. If we forsake them, the consequences can be serious.

According to the Talmud, every day, like a grieving lion, God roars: 'Woe to My children! On account of their sins I have destroyed my house, set fire to my sanctuary, and exiled them among the nations!' (*Berakhot* 3a). The house in question is the *Bayt Mikdash*, the Temple. Presumably, God wants his people to learn from their mistakes, and he destroyed the Temple, which perhaps is better understood as he allowed it to be destroyed, in order to teach them a lesson. All the *mitzvot* of the Torah help us to become like God, in that he does what is right, and in following what he tells us to do we presumably also do what is right. Of course, it is difficult for a finite actor to be like the infinite, but as far as we can, we ought to, we are told, and here the Temple was important, since it was such a magnificent building that it inspired the imagination of the ordinary Jew and helped him to do his duty. So it looks as though God has made this harder for us by allowing this source of our inspiration to be destroyed. The point is, however, that it will only be rebuilt when the Jews realize a level of spiritual growth that makes the Temple of value to them again, a level they have seriously descended from up to now. This brings out another feature of the *mitzvot* that is nicely captured by the notion of *tikkun olam*, repairing the world. The *mitzvot* play a role in improving our spiritual and indeed our practical lives, since they represent how God wants us to live, and once we put ourselves under his authority, we change as people and come to achieve a more elevated way of seeing things, including ourselves and the world as a whole. God does not need us to obey him, but we need to obey him, it is in our own interests, and it does not really matter what many of the rules are that we follow so long as we follow them.

This is a point well worth considering when we look at how appropriate ancient laws are in modern times. It is difficult to see why divine legislation should change over time, since the nature of humanity and God does not change, and the laws binding them together should also stay the same. On the other hand, we do change, and what works imaginatively at one time to bring us round to the right way of thinking may no longer work at a different time, since things are now different. This suggests that the *mitzvot* ought to vary over time, something that Maimonides for one certainly accepted when it came to the progress from sacrifices, to prayer and finally to what he calls silent meditation (Leaman, 2008). Yet once we accept that they may change, the link that they have with God is in peril. It is worth remembering that according to traditional Judaism, not only the Written Law but also the Oral Law was given to the Jews on Mount Sinai, so it is taken to be an unchanging source of legislation, valid for all time.

The number 613 was first given in the third century CE by Rabbi Simlai, who divided the 613 *mitzvot* into 248 positive commandments and 365 negative commandments. Since this figure was first announced, many have undertaken to organize the 613 commandments. Easily the one with the most lasting significance is the twelfth-century list by Maimonides in his *Book of the Commandments*. Many Jewish texts explore ways of dividing up the rules into various numbers, and it is entertaining to see how this is done and to consider its significance. Is it just to show how clever one is to be able to do it, or does it have some higher purpose?

The number 613 has symbolic significance in that it is the numeric value of the word *torah*, plus the two commandments that existed before the Torah: I am the Lord your God, and you shall have no other gods before me. The division into 248 positive and 365 negative commandments is also of numerological significance: there are 248 bones and organs in the male body and 365 days in the solar year. However, the number of bones can probably be counted differently, and there are also leap years with different days (and one wonders at the significance of a solar year, since Judaism has a calendar in terms of lunar years).

We are told by Rabbi Simlai (*Makkot* 23b–24a) that 613 was reduced to 11 by David, who in Psalm 15 says:

> Lord, who shall sojourn in your tent
> Who shall lie on your holy mountain
> He who walks uprightly and does the right
> And speaks the truth in his heart
> He who does not slander with his tongue
> Nor does evil to his friend
> Nor takes up a reproach against his neighbor
> He in whose eyes a reprobate is despised
> But who honors those who fear the Lord
> Who swears to his own hurt
> And does not change
> Who does not put out his money at interest
> And takes no bribe against the innocent
> He who does these things shall never be moved.

But as though this was not enough, he credits Isaiah with further reducing the number to six in *Isa* 33.15, and Micah to three (*Mic* 6.8).

Isaiah comes back and brings it down to two (*Isa* 56.1), only to be followed by Amos (5.4) and Habakkuk (2.4) who reduce it to one. The
explanation goes:

> Then came Isaiah and reduced them to six: 'He who walks right-
> eously and speaks uprightly, who despises the gain of oppression, who
> shakes his hands free from holding a bribe, stops his ears from hearing
> of bloodshed and shuts his eyes from looking upon evil.'

> Then came Micah and reduced them to three: 'He has told you, O
> man, what is good, and what does the Lord require of you, Only to
> do justice, and to love kindness and to walk humbly with your God.'

> Then Isaiah came again and reduced them to two: 'Keep judgment
> and do righteousness.'

> Finally Amos came and reduced them to one: 'Seek me and live.'

> So did Habakkuk, who said 'The righteous shall live by his faithful-
> ness.'

These passages might suggest that the *mitzvot* are not that important,
if they can be reduced to a smaller set of principles. After all, if in a
mathematical calculation one can achieve a result with a smaller
number of operations, one should do so; it is more elegant and dis-
plays a more perspicuous grasp of the discipline to do so. Yet it is
worth noting that this passage comes in the Babylonian Talmud, not
a text which is well known for dispensing with ritual. When, in a
similarly reductive mood, Hillel tells a convert that Judaism is just
'What is hateful to you, do not do to your neighbor' (the convert says
he needs an answer while standing on one foot, which in the idiom
of the day meant immediately!), this is reported in the Talmudic
book of *Shabbat* (31a), which reflects on the laws connected to the
Sabbath. Hillel continues his answer, no doubt swiftly while the
questioner was starting to topple over, by advising him to study the
commentaries on this issue. Here we have the nub of how rabbinic
Judaism sees the links between the *mitzvot* and more general ethical
principles. The latter represent the semantics of religion, while the
former are the syntax. Judaism is all about getting the ethical principles right, but the way to do this is to embody them in a certain kind
of practice, and that involves being very careful about how one
behaves. The very precise rules of behavior that are to be followed,

according to the Talmud, represent the ways in which those principles can be acted upon, how they may be used, and without any rules
of converting the meaning of action into action itself, then we do
not have religion at all, just a set of abstract principles.

Food

One of the most common notions of Jewish practice deals with food.
Kosher is the English word for *kasher*, to make food fit for eating by
Jews according to the Torah. These rules were derived from parts of
the Torah, especially Deuteronomy and Leviticus. They were then
interpreted and developed, and some were modified, to take into
account changing technologies and situations, but the intention
among those committed to traditional forms of Judaism is to remain
faithful to the original formulations of the Law in the Torah.

A lot of food that has the word kosher on the label is in fact not
kosher at all, but shares the style of kosher food. The first point to
make about *kashrut* before going into the rules is that few Jews keep
these rules, or even know what they are. But traditional Jews go to
huge lengths to eat only what is kosher, and they also strictly segregate
food that has milk in it from food that has meat in it, basing their
decisions on the passage in the Torah that tells them not to cook a kid
in its mother's milk. Jews are allowed to eat ritually slaughtered beef,
sheep, goats and deer that display no flaws or diseases, and if the animals are killed in the right sort of way, by an approved *shochet* or
slaughterer, who says the right words before cutting their throats, and
who then drains as much blood as possible from the carcasses. No
pork, camel, rabbit, rodent, reptile or any animal that died of natural
causes or that was killed by a hunter can be kosher. Chicken, turkey,
quail and goose can be kosher, while eagle, hawk and vulture are not.
Salmon, tuna, carp, herring and cod are acceptable, but crab, lobster,
octopus, clam, swordfish and sturgeon are not. Wine and grape juice
has to be made under supervision, otherwise is not acceptable. Cheese
can be eaten provided the rennet that is used to make it is kosher. All
fruits, vegetables and grains are permissible (*Gen.* 1.29), with the
exception of grape products. Because of laws against eating or drinking anything offered to idols, and the fact that wine was often made
for pagan offerings and celebrations, all wine and grape juice that is
not made under Jewish supervision, as noted above, is prohibited.

Only animals that chew their cud and have cloven hooves are kosher (*Lev* 11.3; *Deut* 14.6). Thus beef, sheep, lamb, goat and deer may be eaten, while pork, camel and rabbit may not. These restrictions include the flesh, organs, milk and any by-products. So gelatin, if it is not made from a kosher animal like an appropriately slaughtered cow, is *treyf*, as are most hard cheeses, which are processed using rennet, an enzyme from the stomach lining of non-kosher animals. As noted above, these animals must have no disease or flaws (*Num* 11.22). Ritual slaughterhouses may well perform post-mortem examinations of the lungs, looking for adhesions. Animals free of these adhesions are designated *glatt* (smooth) kosher. This has come to mean that a more strenuous level of *kashrut* has been followed.

Animals must be ritually slaughtered in order to remain kosher (*Deut* 12.21). The primary goal of ritual slaughter is to rid the animal of as much blood as possible, since consuming blood is forbidden by the Torah, which makes many comments about blood throughout the text. Ritual slaughter involves cutting the animal's throat with an extremely sharp knife with no nicks. In the past, this could well have been the most humane form of slaughter, though this is not mentioned as the reason for the rule. The meat must then be kashered, or made kosher, by hanging the carcass up to drain it of as much blood as possible. The meat must then be washed, salted and cooked well-done, so there is no evidence of blood left on it. Some parts of kosher animals are non-kosher. The sciatic nerve in the hindquarters, and the fat surrounding the animal's organs, are not acceptable. Only domesticated birds such as chicken, turkey, quail and goose may be eaten. Birds of prey and scavenger birds, such as eagles, hawks and vultures, are prohibited (*Lev* 11.13–19; *Deut* 14.11–18). Only seafood with fins and scales is kosher. Fish do not need to be ritually slaughtered (*Num* 11.22). Today, insects are not eaten (*Lev* 11.12). The Torah allows for certain exceptions, but since it is difficult to know what insects are allowed, there is a blanket ban on all of them.

Meat and dairy products should not be combined or eaten at the same meal. This rule stems from a passage in the Torah merely prohibiting boiling a goat in its mother's milk (*Ex* 23.19; *Ex* 34.26; *Deut* 14.21), yet this is interpreted as forbidding meat and dairy products to be eaten together. Fish with dairy or eggs with dairy are permitted. It is not an issue of quantities, as even the smallest amounts of meat or dairy affect the status of food. *Pareve* (neutral) designates foods that contain neither meat nor dairy and can therefore be eaten with either one. What constitutes a 'separate meal'? Opinions differ somewhat as to the details, but most traditional Jews wait between three and six hours after a meat meal before consuming dairy products. This is because remnants of meat or fat tend to remain in the mouth for several hours after eating. By contrast, one need only rinse one's mouth and eat a pareve food after consuming dairy products to be able to eat meat. The rules of *kashrut* also extend to non-food products. Utensils like pots, pans, sinks, dishwashers, potholders and plates take on the status (*fleishig, milchig, treyf* or *pareve* – meat, milk, unfit or neutral) of the food they touch in the presence of heat. For example, a pan used to fry a sausage or a pot used to make chicken soup become *fleishig*. If the *fleishig* pot or pan is then used to boil milk, *kashrut* has been violated. Similarly, a bowl previously used for a meat product cannot be used subsequently for ice cream.

To give an example of the sort of complexity this law creates, let us look at a legal response to an example of it. A person sent to someone else a pot of meat into which some milk had spilt, and the sender asked whether it could be eaten. The answer from a rabbi, and the person who was supposed to receive the food, was that it could not. So it was thrown away. But it was later determined that this judgment was wrong. Who, then, in such circumstances, if anyone, has to pay compensation for the wasted food, the rabbi or the person who threw it away? R. Yaacov Reischer suggests it was not the fault of the rabbi, since despite his initial judgment being wrong, his intention was to do right. It appears that the man who threw away the food was at fault, but in fact he just did what he was told on good authority, so he is also not guilty. So no compensation is applicable in this case (*Responsa*, 106).

To try to avoid these sorts of difficulties, many kosher households have at least two sets of dishes and cutlery, one for meat and one for dairy. Cleaning is also important – separate dishpans, sponges, dish racks and dishwasher loads must be used for *fleishig* and *milchig* items. To *kasher* a utensil, or make it usable for any purpose, it must either be heated to a very high temperature (450°) or soaked in water for several days. Regular laundering of *kasher* items such as towels is necessary, but the rules of how to change the status of anything that has been used for one of the food groups according to the laws of *kashrut* are complex, which will not surprise anyone with any awareness of the rules that apply here. Since the presence of heat is required for the transfer of status from food to utensil and vice versa, cold food may be eaten on a clean plate regardless of its status, and the same knife may be used to cut meat and cheese, so long as it is cleaned in between. But in a sense it is simpler to have different kitchens or at least different sets of plates and cutlery, since then these issues never arise. When eating away from the home, unless in a kosher institution, it is often the case that disposable flatware and utensils are used, along with cups and drinking vessels, so that no issues of whether it has come into contact with the wrong food group arise. The items are used for the first time during the meal, and then discarded.

Most Conservative Jews are satisfied to read product ingredient labels to make sure their food is kosher, though it is not necessarily labeled as such, while Orthodox Jews tend to insist that foods are certified as kosher by a trained rabbi, called a *mashgiach*. The 'seal of approval' that indicates a *mashgiach* has observed and approved the product's preparation is called a *hechsher*. After all, even if all the ingredients are kosher, one does not know if the person handling the food items himself or herself has allowed the food to come into contact with forbidden foods.

Several symbols indicate kosher status. The most common are K inside a circle, which stands for 'kosher', and a U inside a circle, the certification symbol of the Union of Orthodox Jewish Congregations. Different religious authorities may be cited as the inspecting and validating agency. Other Jewish-oriented symbols include a P inside a circle, which denotes a food fit for Passover (when fermented foods are not permitted), the letter M to indicate a meat product, the letter D to indicate a dairy product, and the word '*pareve*' or '*parev*,' indicating a *pareve* or neutral food. Many foods are called kosher when in fact they are not. Sometimes kosher merely refers to a type of ethnic food, rather than to the fact that a *mashgiach* or inspector has supervised its production!

The Purpose of kashrut

The Torah offers no explanation for the dietary laws other than the implications that the Jews are God's chosen people and they are thus different from everyone else: 'You are to be holy to me because I, the Lord, am holy, and I have set you apart from the nations to be my own' (*Lev* 20.26). Why food *is* important is an interesting question, but then food is important and if one regards what one eats as being ordered by God, it does stimulate an appreciation of how the divine enters to a degree into all things. Why eating some things and avoiding others makes you holy is for many people a bit of a mystery, and the majority of Jews today totally ignore the dietary laws, and know very little about what they are. The Reform movement, which started in Germany in the nineteenth century, was openly contemptuous of these rules and set out to disobey them at every turn, regarding them merely as cultural rules appropriate to the past, but not to the present. On the other hand, the less traditionally observant members of the Jewish community have recently acquired a somewhat greater respect for the dietary laws, seeking perhaps not to create too strong a division between the different kinds of Jewish observance that exist.

It is worth saying, though, that many organizations have members' rules that have to be followed, and these are generally entirely arbitrary, and deal with what is to be worn, eaten, drunk and so on. In fact, it is often the case that the more meaningless the rules are in themselves, the more enthusiastic are the members about them. What following such rules says is that we belong, and that different people can fit in with each other through an agreement on practices and judgments. A very good example of this is grammar, which of course could have gone in any direction it wanted and often changes over time, so it is rather silly to regret such changes, since whatever the rule is in language one just has to follow it. If being understood means following the rules, then it is surely sensible to do so. These rules are arbitrary, but once they are accepted they become far from arbitrary if one wants to be recognized as a member of a community. This was King David's guiding principle: 'I have placed God before me at all times' (*Ps* 16.8); and it applies just as well to the laws related to everyday life, such as what we do and do not eat.

Some have argued that the Jewish dietary laws are there to preserve health. This is not satisfactory as a general explanation, though, since some of the animals on the forbidden list are perfectly healthy, and in fact the great Jewish thinker and doctor Maimonides expounds at some length on the healthy properties of eating pigs, though of course he did not advocate it for Jews. For him, one of the purposes of the dietary laws was to help us to control ourselves when

it comes to eating and drinking, and to not just eat or drink anything
as though our appetites must come first and be satisfied wherever
they might extend. But if we want some indication of the importance of food and drink, a good place to look is Exodus 24.9–11.
Moses and Aaron, Aaron's sons and 70 of the elders climbed up
Mount Sinai after Moses read the covenant out to the people, and
there they all saw God, something that is repeated in the text in
verses 10 and 11, a very rare honor indeed in the Torah. And what
did they do after they saw God? It says in the text that they ate and
drank. Now, many commentators argue this should not be taken literally, and by eating and drinking is meant spiritual nourishment,
since they were so moved in all their senses by the experience of
contact with the deity that they ate and drank in that heady
encounter. I prefer to read it literally, though, and when it says they
ate and drank it brings out the importance of our everyday activities
even during a meeting of such significance. We are physical creatures,
and eating and drinking is important to us, so it is quite reasonable
for a religion to seek to regulate these activities in some way.

There is controversy now over the stunning of animals before
killing them, which there is much evidence to suggest is less painful
than slitting their throats, however sharp the knife. According to the
laws of *kashrut*, however, this makes the animals *treyf*, since they are
damaged, and damaged animals cannot be considered kosher no matter how they are killed. Defenders of *kashrut* argue, despite the evidence, that stunning is not preferable from an animal welfare point of
view. In recent times there has been a move to extend the notion
of *kashrut* to include animal welfare, and the idea of animal slaughter
to feed people might in itself be regarded as suggesting that we should
not eat animals. This is a conclusion that Abraham Kook drew, suggesting that we were allowed to eat animals during a certain period of
our history, but that once we purified ourselves of our more animal-
like instincts, we could and indeed should transcend this sort of
behavior. This suggests that the references to blood and its equivalence to life are designed to make us think about the practice of
killing and eating animals when there are perfectly good alternatives.
Initially, perhaps, human beings were forced to eat other animals,
since there was a shortage of food and this struck them as highly
appropriate at the time. As we develop our moral consciousness,
however, we come to realize that this is an objectionable activity, and

the rules in the Torah that make eating animals complicated are designed to make us aware of this. A good analogy can be found in the rules on smoking on many American university campuses. It is legal to smoke in the USA, but it is also legal for a campus to discourage people from smoking by banning them from smoking on their property. As I was writing this in the winter of 2009/10, small groups of smokers could be seen on the borders of the University of Kentucky property braving the biting winds and snow to indulge their habit, a good example of how making an activity difficult is perhaps designed to make those who involve themselves in it think about whether they should really be doing it at all!

Prayer and Different Ways of being Jewish

Recitation of prayers is a significant part of Jewish worship. These prayers, often with instructions and commentary, are found in the *siddur* – the traditional Jewish prayer book. Observant Jews are expected to recite three prayers daily and more on the Sabbath and Jewish holidays. While solitary prayer is valid, attending synagogue to pray with a *minyan* (quorum of ten adult males for traditional Jews, ten adults for others) is considered ideal and is vital for some prayers to be said. In recent times a more ad hoc attitude to prayer has often been taken among Jews, most of whom today would not recognize a prayer if it hit them on the head. So we should not overemphasize the significance of prayer for the Jewish world as a whole. On the other hand, for many Jews, prayer is a significant part of their day, and it is important to know how this operates and what sorts of prayers occur regularly as part of various services.

An influential reform movement in Judaism arose in Eastern Europe, called Hasidism, from the Hebrew term *chasid*, or pious. This advocated a more ecstatic approach to prayer, and indeed to the laws, and its founder was called the Baal Shem Tov, or master of the good name. The movement based itself on charismatic leaders, the *tzaddikim*, from the Hebrew word *tzaddik* or righteous, who led a court which his followers attended, and very much laid down what they regarded as legal and what was not to be done. On the other hand, we should not emphasize their antinomian tendency, since they had a normal understanding of the Law; it is just that to a degree they accepted in certain situations that the Law could be suspended. For example, they were fond of stories to illustrate their points, and often the story would be about someone with great sincerity who for some reason could not act like an ordinary observant Jew, and the moral is generally that his behavior was superior to that of the latter. They very much set themselves up in opposition to the Mitnagdim, with their prime authority being the Vilna Gaon, who tended to emphasize a strict adherence to the letter of the law (*JT* ch. 9). Ironically, today these two groups are much closer to each other, and the Hasidim vie with other traditional Jews in faithfulness to the Law. The only difference is that they still have some unique features of belief depending on the group they belong to. They are often named after the town in Eastern Europe where they originated, so the Lubavitch Hasidim came from the town of Lubavitch in what is today Ukraine, and the Satmar Hasidim from Satmar in Hungary. The Lubavitchers are the most outgoing group; they set up what they call Habad houses all over the world in order to inspire Jews, and only Jews, to return to what they regard as the authentic tradition of how to practice the religion. Many of them venerate their late leader, R. Menachem Schneerson, so much that they think he is the Messiah, having the same sorts of problems that others have who think that the Messiah has already arrived, in explaining why nothing else seems to have changed for the better. The Satmarer are very hostile to the State of Israel, and all the different Hasidic groups have differences in dress, often quite slight, as well as appearance. Some feel that men should have beards, earlocks (*payot*) and wear their fringes (*tzitzit*) outside of their ordinary clothes, while others are clean-shaven and wear their *tzitzit* under their clothes.

There are very large differences in how prayers are performed depending on the type of synagogue one is attending, or the kind of Jewish affiliation the individual worshipper possesses. First, there is a difference in the rituals and prayers, as between Ashkenazi and Sefardi Jews. The former originate in Europe (*Ashkenaz* means Germany in Hebrew), while the latter come from Spain (*Sefarad* meaning Spain in Hebrew), and then moved to other parts of the world, largely the Middle East. There are also different rites for Jews from specific parts of the world, in Greece and Italy, for example, and, of course, local customs that prevail even when people move from one part of the world to another.

Then there are differences based on the denomination of the place of worship. The traditional communities tend to have long services, they meet frequently and the services are well attended by most of the members of the community. Men and women are segregated, and women play no part in the public part of the service, just staying in their part of the building and praying there. A *mechitzah*, or barrier, separates the men from the women. Worshippers may all pray, but they may also do other things in the synagogue, and the men in particular take an active part in the service, not necessarily at the same time as everyone else.

The closest to traditional Judaism is the Conservative movement in the USA, known as Masorti in the rest of the world. Here the liturgy is largely traditional, but there is rarely segregation of men and women, the services are more orderly and disciplined, and they are led by the rabbi. In traditional synagogues the rabbi may lead the service, but anyone can do so, and often the rabbi does not play much of a part in the service. His role is more a leader of the community and legal authority. However, in some synagogues the rabbi is more like a minister, and his or her role is to lead the service. Women are now ordained as rabbis in all synagogues apart from the traditional ones, and at the time of writing (2010) the first ordination of a woman as an orthodox rabbi in the USA has taken place, albeit not in a very central traditional rabbinic institution so far. There is also far more acceptance of gay people as rabbis, and gays as members of synagogues from all apart from traditional synagogues.

Reform and Reconstructionist synagogues have much shorter services than traditional and Conservative synagogues, and much more of the liturgy is in the local language rather than Hebrew. There is also much more development of new prayers, new worship rituals and so on, and the Reconstructionist *siddur* (prayer book) is quite entertaining in that the notes to the service tend to critique what they are commenting on! Men and women are not segregated and there are many women rabbis, services are orderly and the congregation is led by the rabbi, in what often resembles many church services. Services also tend to be relatively short, and the level of attendance is often low, with many only coming on special occasions such as the most important festivals of New Year and the Day of Atonement, and for events such as bar and bat mitzvahs. The festivals that last for two days in the traditional Jewish calendar, in the diaspora only last for one day for the Reform, and many festivals are totally ignored. One should not assume from this that Reform Jews take their Judaism less seriously than do traditional Jews, but comparatively speaking they certainly do not on the whole spend as much time on their religion or even know very much about it.

It will be interesting to see how the different denominations develop. In the USA the Conservative and the Reform movements are the largest but are rapidly shrinking, while the traditional groups tend to maintain their numbers and are in fact growing. There are, of course, a number of defections from orthodoxy, but families tend to be large and on the whole the scope for communities to be successful and grow, combining a deep religiosity with the ability to exist economically, is apparent in the USA. By contrast, the more modern approaches to Judaism are declining, largely because of the rapid rate of intermarriage, and the very small families of those who marry other Jews. Statistics suggest that, in intermarriage, only in a minority are the children likely to be brought up as Jews, and perhaps not that well either, and the relatively small number of children in any case means that the scope for growth is limited. Judaism is not a religion that encourages converts, though the Reform movement is slightly more enthusiastic about conversion than are the other denominations, and so at the start of the twenty-first century we have a situation where the Jewish population of Europe and the USA is relatively old, shrinking and increasingly living as singles.

The situation in Israel is different; there, the Jewish population is much younger than in the diaspora (though still older than the Arab population), and the traditional communities reproduce at a high rate, compensating for the low number of children among secular Jews. The issue of assimilation in Israel is very different from in the diaspora, of course. In the Middle East, religion defines the individual ethnically, and people will hold on to their religious label even if they do not have any particular religious beliefs, since that label is the name of the group to which they belong. Israeli Jews cannot disappear into the general population except by emigrating, which of course many of them do. In Israel most synagogues are traditional, but apart from the very religious groups, few Jews go to synagogue, and the non-traditional synagogues find it difficult to get a foothold, though there is no doubt that they represent far better the views of Judaism of most of the population. The State, in its continuation of

Ottoman policies on religion, identified traditional Judaism as the norm, though very few of the Zionist leaders, then as now, were themselves religious, and that practice has remained the case, with the orthodox hierarchy in charge of issues such as divorce, marriage, conversion and so on. The results have predictably been to alienate a large number of Jews or people who think they are Jews from the rest of the Jewish community in Israel, since barriers have been put up to make life difficult for them if they or their descendents do not conform to the strict rules of Jewish family law.

The general lack of enthusiasm for prayer in Israel apart from among traditional Jews may have something to do with the fact that prayer is not as an important a source of identity there as it is outside. Jewish children will be taken to the synagogue or temple in the diaspora by parents who want them to understand that they are not the same as everyone else, and are part of a long tradition that does things in a specific way. Jews learn (a bit of) Hebrew and go to different places to worship and on different days from everyone else. But in Israel all Jews know Hebrew, the festivals and Sabbath are holidays, and the distinctions between the different groups are well established and well understood. So, when the weather is fine there are far more people on the beach in Tel Aviv on the Sabbath than in synagogue, and when the weather is not fine there are still more people not in synagogue than otherwise.

Minyan

For many significant prayers, a quorum or *minyan* is required, and this is sometimes defined as ten men, and sometimes for less traditional Jews as ten adults, both men and women. In recent years in the USA an independent *minyan* movement has arisen, with *minyan*s being constructed in apartments and workplaces quite informally, rather than taking place in synagogues. This reflects the looser links today between American Jews and institutions such as synagogues and rabbis. For prayer, no rabbi is required in any case, as the role of the rabbi has very little to do with prayer in traditional Jewish practice. In the Reform movement, he or she has a role which is much more similar to that of a minister in a church: he or she leads the service and is often very much the focus of what takes place ritually in the temple.

An interesting theoretical issue arose about how to define a *minyan*, and in fact the question of what counts as a *minyan* often arises,

since it is so crucial for so many prayers. There are reports in the kabbalistic literature, in particular the *Sefer Yetzirah*, the Book of
Creation, of how it is possible to create a man. Could such a man be
counted among those in the *minyan*, since he might be regarded as
the child of his creator, and so a Jew? The Chatam Zvi suggests that
such a being cannot really be regarded as a man. In the story about
the creation of a man by Rava, in *Sanhedrin* 65b, he is sent to R.
Zeira, who promptly destroys him after getting no conversation out
of him. The principle here is presumably that, if he cannot speak,
then he is not really human. Did he then murder the man? Not
according to the Chatam Zvi, since he did not shed blood (*Gen* 9.8),
as there was no blood to shed. Had the being had a useful purpose,
such as making up a *minyan*, he would not have been destroyed. So
such a person may not be included in a *minyan* (*Responsa*, 104).

Music and Singing
As with most religious services, the length and content of the synagogue service depends on the sect and customs of the particular
community. In general, one can expect to hear the most Hebrew
used in an Orthodox service and the least in Reform services; and
services in Reform temples also tend to be shorter than those held in
Orthodox and Conservative synagogues. In recent years there has
been a trend for Reform to come closer to traditional Judaism, but it
is still the case that it uses far less Hebrew in its services. Some larger
synagogues have a *hazzan* (cantor), a professional or lay-professional
singer employed for the purpose of leading the congregation in
prayer. Reform synagogues often use organs to provide music in
their services, while traditional Jews disapprove of them, and in particular of mixed (male and female) choirs. Listening to women sing is
thoroughly disapproved of in the traditional Jewish world, stemming
from the Talmudic phrase *kol isha ervah* (*Berakhot* 24a). This labels a
woman's voice licentious and so to be avoided.

Kavanah
There is a notion of concentration (*kavanah*) for prayer, and in some
of the stories of the Baal Shem Tov, the creator of the Hasidic movement, concentration is taken to be even more significant than the
prayers themselves. The Master of the Good Name, as his title means
in English, was concerned at the dry character that traditional Jewish

worship and ritual as a whole had developed, and advocated a livelier and more emotional approach to the nature of prayer and everything that goes with it. Clearly, the point of prayer is to orient the mind toward God, and the rituals associated with prayer are all similarly designed. There is another problem with prayer, in that, as the prayers become familiar, it is possible to recite them without really thinking about them, especially when one has to recite them quickly, because there are so many of them, or they are in an unfamiliar language. Here, *kavanah* can become lost. As Halevi puts it, though: 'Actions without intentions and intentions without action are vain' (Halevi, 1947, 128.)

Dress and Artefacts
In most synagogues or temples, men wear a head covering, usually a dress hat or yarmulke (*kippah*), but most Reform (or Progressive) temples do not require people to cover their heads (neither Jew nor Gentile). Nevertheless, many Reform Jews now choose to wear a *kippah*. Parts of the services are recited standing, and the name of one prayer, the *amidah*, actually means 'standing'. Bowing is done at certain points in the service. A *tallit* (prayer shawl) is worn during the morning, and all day on Yom Kippur. Appropriate dress for a house of worship is expected in traditional synagogues: both men and women are expected to adhere to *tzniut* (rules of modesty) – long sleeves, long skirts and covering of the hair (married Jewish women only) for women, and men would be expected to wear trousers and cover their arms. In less traditional synagogues, a variety of styles of dress is acceptable. In wealthy communities, synagogues and temples are often criticized for being fashion parades.

Tallit
A *tallit* is a prayer shawl with fringes on all four corners. The *tallit*, or *tallet* (for Sefardim) *gadol*, is the large shawl that is worn for prayer, and the *tallit katan* a small one that is worn at all times in obedience to *Num* 15.37–40 and *Deut* 22.12 to wear fringes. It is traditionally worn only by men, but increasingly women are wearing it in egalitarian communities, and only in the morning, except on the Day of Atonement, when it is worn for all the parts of the service, and on Tisha B'Av, when it is worn in the afternoon rather than the morning. The person leading the service may well wear it in a synagogue

at any time of the day. It tends to be worn after bar and bat mitzvahs, though in some congregations unmarried men do not wear it. Men are sometimes buried in their *tallit*, with the *tzitzit* (fringe) removed, as there are supposed to be no knots in a coffin.

The Torah states, in Numbers 15.38, 'Speak to the children of Israel, and say to them, that they shall make themselves fringes on the corners of their garments throughout their generations, and they shall put on the corner fringe a blue (*tekhelet*) thread'; and in Deuteronomy 22.12, 'You shall make yourself twisted threads, on the four corners of your garment with which you cover yourself.' *Tzitzyot* are attached today only to Jewish religious garments, such as a *tallit gadol* (large prayer shawl). This is because today's clothes do not have four corners, and thus the fringes are not necessary. Traditional Jewish men wear a *tallit katan* (small prayer shawl) constantly, in order to fulfill this commandment at their own volition, and some consider it a transgression to miss a commandment that one has the ability to fulfill. The *tallit katan* is also commonly referred to as *tzitzit*, though this name technically refers to each of the fringes only. It is the *tzitzit* that are significant rather than the shawl part of the outfit, so the designation is quite appropriate.

The reason for the commandment is 'So that you will remember to do the commandments' (the whole passage *Num* 15.37–41 is relevant here). It is a reminder of the Exodus from Egypt (*Num* 15.40). Maimonides, in his commentary on the *Pirkei Avot* (2.1), includes it as a major commandment (*mitzvah*), along with *brit milah* (circumcision) and the *korban pesach* (the Paschal lamb). The *tzitzit* on each corner is made of four strands, each of which in turn is made of eight fine threads (known as *kaful shemoneh*). The four strands are passed through one or perhaps two holes, 25–50 mm away from the corner of the cloth. There are various ways of tying the knot, and quite a bit of discussion about the most appropriate method. The *Shulchan Arukh*, as so often, gives pretty precise instructions: The four strands of the *tzitzit* are passed through holes near the four corners of the garment that are farthest apart (10.1). Four *tzitzyot* are passed through each hole (11.12–13), and the two groups of four ends are double-knotted to each other at the edge of the garment near the hole (11.14–15). One of the *tzitzit* is made longer than the others (11.4); the long end of that one is wound around the other seven ends and double-knotted; this is done repeatedly so as to make a total of five double knots separated by four sections of winding, with a total length of at least four inches, leaving free-hanging ends that are twice that length (11.14). There are differences in Ashkenazi and Sefardi ways of doing this, as is so often the case.

Rashi uses gematria, and points out that the numerical equivalence of the word *tzitzit* (in its Mishnaic spelling) has the value 600. Each tassel has eight threads (when doubled over) and five sets of knots, totaling 13. The sum of all numbers is 613, traditionally the number of *mitzvot* (commandments) in the Torah. This reflects the concept that donning a garment with *tzitzyot* reminds its wearer of all the Torah commandments. Nachmanides disagrees with Rashi, pointing out that the biblical spelling of the word *tzitzit* has only one letter *yod* rather than two, thus adding up to the total number of 603 rather than 613. Some suggest that the blue color of the *tekhelet* is like the ocean, which in turn resembles the sky, and that helps us to think of God's abode. All this reminds us to consider the divine mission on which the Jews are supposed to be involved in fulfilling the divine commandments.

A set of *tzitzit* with blue *tekhelet* thread was the color that the Hebrew Bible commanded the Jews to use for some of the eight half-strings hanging down. The source of the blue dye was lost, however, and since then, Jews have worn plain white, undyed *tzitzyot*. *Tekhelet*, which appears 48 times in the Bible, is a specific blue dye produced from a creature referred to as a chilazon, all other blue dyes being unacceptable. Some explain the black stripes found on many traditional prayer shawls as representing the loss of this dye. Where *tekhelet* is used, only one thread in each fringe is dyed with it, the rest being left white generally. The dyed thread is traditionally made of wool, regardless of the material of the garment or the other threads. The other threads in the *tzitzit* (all the threads, where *tekhelet* is not used) are described as 'white'. The threads may be made either of wool or of the same fabric as the garment, but the whole garment is often woolen.

Karaites wear *tzitzyot* with blue threads in them. In contrast to Rabbinic Judaism, they believe that the *tekhelet* does not refer to a specific dye but just to the color blue. The traditions of Rabbinic Judaism used in the knotting of the *tzitzit* are not followed, so the appearance of Karaite *tzitzit* can be quite different from that of Rabbanite *tzitzit*. Contrary to some claims, Karaites do not hang *tzitzit* on their walls.

Kittel

The *kittel* is a simple white linen robe in which one is buried, and it is worn on a variety of ceremonial occasions, generally those that are very solemn, but some Jews also wear it at Passover.

Tefillin

Tefillin are phylacteries, small leather boxes worn on the forehead and on the arm, to fulfill the commandment to wear a sign on your arm and frontlets between your eyes. They are connected to the body by leather straps, and are worn during the morning service on week-days. The texts from Exodus 13.1–10, 13.11–16, and Deuteronomy 6.4–9, 11.13–21, are found in the boxes, handwritten in Hebrew by a *sofer* (a scribe). There is a reference in the Talmud to God wearing *tefillin*, one for the arm and one for the head (*Berakhot* 6a).

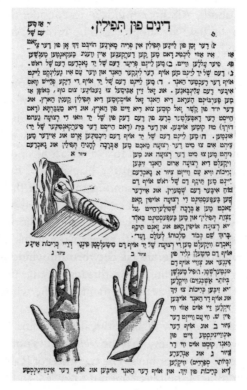

Tefillin *hand: Yiddish instructions on how to wrap the* tefillin *around the arm and hand, from a prayer book*

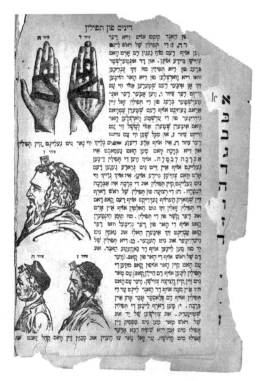

Tefillin *hand and head: Yiddish instructions on how to wrap the* tefillin *around the hand and head, from a prayer book*

Kippah (yarmulke)

Wearing of a head covering (*yarmulke*, skullcaps or *kippah*) for men came into effect, though on what scale we cannot tell, around the second century CE. Tractate *Shabbat* (156b) links a head covering with respect for God. The High Priest wore a hat (*mitznefet*) to remind him something was always between him and God. It seems that wearing a head covering all the time was once considered an optional *midat chasidut* (pious act), but today, full-time head covering is the normal practice for traditional Jews, more for the Ashkenazim than for the Sefardim. In Israel, the type of *kippah* that is worn often indicates the political affiliation of the wearer, and there are significant differences between different sorts of head covering, while wearing a *kippah* indicates your adherence to traditional Judaism, compared with the majority of Jewish citizens who are quite secular in their attitudes and behavior.

Mezuzah

The *mezuzah* (literally, doorpost) is in fact a box with the letter *shin* on it (representing *Shaddai* or the Almighty), which contains a handwritten parchment on which are the first two paragraphs of the *Shema*. These are quite literally the commandments that 'You shall write them on the doorposts of your house and upon your gates' (*Deut* 6.9, 11.20), and are on the right-hand side as one enters. Jews may kiss them or touch them and then kiss their fingers, the idea being to show respect for the Law as one enters and leaves the house. Sometimes when a family has been particularly unfortunate, Jews will change the *mezuzot* in order to improve the situation, or at least they will inspect the writing, the feeling being perhaps that there might be a mistake in how the letters were written and this has brought about the problems.

The Siddur *(prayer book)*

The prayers follow a pattern, and *siddur* means order. The prayer book for festivals is called a *machzor*. The Ashkenazi traditional prayers will be described briefly here, since the other forms of Judaism tend to follow the same sort of structure, albeit often with fewer prayers and less frequent meetings. The prayer book, unlike the Torah, is not considered to have come from God, even for traditional Jews, and so has been affected by a great deal of change and adaptation, yet the age of some of the prayers and the fact that they are linked with the Torah, since they often come from it, has done a great deal to increase their status. It is fascinating to see the changes that occur in prayer books. The Reform movement changes its prayer book quite radically at frequent intervals, while traditional Jews do not. Some traditional congregations do not even acknowledge the existence of the State of Israel and have no prayers for the State and its soldiers. Some rabbinical authority will have established the structure and the content of the prayers, and that is all that is required for them to have a resonance within the appropriate community.

The prayers are arranged to take place roughly at the same time as the Temple services, in the morning and in the afternoon/evening, for traditional Jews.

Shacharit

The morning prayers are called *shacharit*, from the word for dawn, *shachar*. Observant Jews say prayers when they get up and perform their morning ablutions, and upon putting on the *tzitsit* or fringes, *tallit* or prayer shawl and *tefillin*, boxes that go on the head and the arm. They then say the morning blessings, which are followed by blessings for the Torah and readings from biblical and rabbinic writings. The most common form of Jewish prayer is a blessing, or *berakhah*, and all blessings start with the same six words in Hebrew: 'Blessed are you, O Lord our God, king of the universe'. They start in the second person, addressing God as you, and continue in the third person, describing his actions. This perhaps represents a balance between the views of Rav and Samuel in the Talmud as to how God should be addressed. According to the former, he should be addressed familiarly when we pray, while according to the latter we should only refer to his actions and attributes, since to think that we could actually address him is to diminish him (JT *Berakhot* 12.4). A daily psalm is recited, based on a Temple ceremony. Next comes the first part only of the *shema yisrael*. In traditional services this is followed by a series of readings from biblical and rabbinic writings recalling the offerings made in the Temple in Jerusalem. The section concludes with the *kaddish*.

The *amidah*, which is made up of 19 blessings or *berakhot*, appears in both the morning and evening, and is sometimes called the *shemonah esreh* (eighteen) referring to the 18 blessings that are involved, though now there are 19, with the extra one being a curse rather than a blessing and applying to heretics. This prayer is said standing, not surprisingly, given that is what it means, and in the direction of Jerusalem. In Jerusalem, one prays in the direction of the Western Wall. The *amidah* is first said silently and then the reader repeats it aloud afterwards. There are slight variations to some of the blessings in the *amidah*, depending on the occasion, though the first and last three blessings remain the same. It begins by mentioning God's link with Abraham, Isaac and Jacob; God helped them and we ask him to help us now. God is called holy and asked to provide us with wisdom, forgive us for our misdeeds, help us when we are in trouble, save us from illness and free us from poverty. There is a request for the gathering together of the Jews from wherever they live, for good leaders, for protection from enemies, for the restoration of Israel and the arrival of the Messiah. It ends with a prayer for peace. There are changes to the structure of the *amidah* between festivals, weekdays and Sabbaths, and it is recited silently first and then afterwards with the congregation.

The next section of morning prayers is called *pesukei d'zimrah*,
verses of praise, containing many psalms (100 and 145–50), and
prayers made from a variety of biblical verses, followed by the Song at
the Sea (*Ex* chs 14, 15). This is followed by *barkhu*, the formal public
call to prayer which is recited when there is a congregation, and an
expanded series of prayers relating to the main recitation of *shema yisrael*. This is followed by the core of the prayer service, the *amidah*.
The next part of the service is *Tachanun*, supplications.

The Shema

The *shema* starts with the verse 'Hear O Israel the Lord our God, the
Lord is one' (*Deut* 6.4). It is followed by a non-biblical verse, 'Praised
be his name whose glorious kingdom lasts through all time', after
which the Deuteronomy passage continues, up to 6.9. This is followed by *Deut* 11.13–21 and *Num* 15.37–41. These recount divine
providence, the significance of the love of God and the importance
of the fulfillment of his commands, especially the use of the *tallit*,
tefillin and *mezuzah*, the first two of which would on a weekday have
been put on, and the last of which is always on the doorposts of the
house. The point of these artefacts is to encourage holiness, the study
of and instruction in the Torah, and the acknowledgement of the
spiritual goals of the escape from Egyptian slavery.

It begins like this:

> And you shall love the Lord your God with all your heart, with all
> your soul and with all your might. And these words which I com-
> mand you this day shall be upon your heart, and you will teach them
> carefully to your children, and you shall talk of them when you sit in
> your house, when you walk by the way, and when you lie down, and
> when you rise up. And you shall bind them as a sign upon your hand,
> and they should be like frontlets between your eyes, and you will
> write them on the doorposts of your house, and upon your gates.

In the rest of the prayer there is an emphasis on the unity of God and
his role in bringing the Israelites out of Egypt. He is the supreme
God and will rule for ever, the prayer concludes.

On Mondays and Thursdays, a short Torah-reading service is
inserted. Longer readings take place on the morning of the Sabbath
and during festivals. Some members of the congregation are honored
by being called up to the Torah, but generally someone else reads

from the scroll itself. The person called up will recite a blessing before and after the reading. Concluding prayers then follow and the prayers are finished, though those who do not have to go elsewhere may stay and recite psalms for a little longer. The service concludes with *aleynu*, a prayer for the general acknowledgement of God and his authority, and for the unification of humanity. Finally, the *kaddish* is recited. This prayer is a way of ending the service with hope. It exists in a variety of versions, and because of one of the version's association with mourning, it has a particular resonance when it is recited. It can only be recited in a *minyan*, a quorum, however that is defined. The *kaddish* is a very popular prayer, its popularity evidenced by it being in Aramaic, the ordinary language of most Jews in the past when they were living in Israel. It exists in a variety of forms, and basically looks forward to a time of general peace in a world controlled by God. Mourners recite it and it often serves to bring a part of the service to a conclusion before another part begins.

The Kaddish

This is the *kaddish* in its mourning form:

> Raise high and glorify the name of God throughout the world he created through his will
>
> May he build his kingdom in your lifetime
>
> During your days and during the life of the house of Israel
>
> Soon, and at a near time
>
> So let us say Amen
>
> Let the name of the holy one, blessed be he
>
> Be praised and glorified, exalted, raised up and honored, magnified and spread out
>
> We know he is beyond all praises and all songs of praise, and above all blessings, and all the soft words spoken in our world, and yet we say, Amen
>
> Let peace fall from the heavens with life for us and for all Israel, and let us say, Amen.
>
> Creator of peace in his high places, may he create peace for us and for all Israel, and let us say, Amen.

Mincha *and* Ma'ariv

The *mincha*, or afternoon prayers, and *ma'ariv* (or *arvit*), evening prayers, are generally linked. In many congregations, the afternoon and evening prayers are recited back-to-back on a working day, to save people having to attend synagogue twice. The Vilna Gaon, not surprisingly, given his unreservedly strict interpretation of everything to do with ritual, disapproved of this practice, and recommended waiting until after nightfall to recite *ma'ariv*. Of course, the possibility of going to a synagogue, or even a *minyan*, for prayers three times or even twice a day presupposes that one lives close enough to do this, and it has become progressively more difficult. The days when Jews all lived together in close-knit communities are long gone, except for the ultra-orthodox communities who do often still all live close to each other and even work not far from their co-religionists, so meeting during the day and afternoon for prayer is not difficult. Of course, if it is felt that communal prayer is an important part of life, then one takes care to live in close proximity to others within the same prayer group.

The afternoon service begins with *ashrey*, an acrostic poem praising God and his goodness, and is followed by the half *kaddish*, the *amidah*, a longer *kaddish* (*kaddish shalem*), *aleynu* and then the mourner's *kaddish*, should anyone be mourning. It tends to run straight on to the evening service, which starts with the *barkhu* and then the full *shema*, the half *kaddish*, the *amidah*, *kaddish shalem* and the *aleynu*, and again a mourner's *kaddish* when appropriate.

Friday night Services
Shabbat services begin on Friday evening with the weekday *mincha*, followed in some communities by the Song of Songs, and then in most communities by the *Kabbalat Shabbat*, the mystical prelude to Shabbat services composed by seventeenth-century Kabbalists. This Hebrew term literally means 'Receiving the Sabbath'. The Ashkenazi service is composed of six psalms – 95 to 99, and 29 – representing the six weekdays. Next comes the poem *Lekha Dodi*. Composed by Solomon ha-Levi Alkabetz in the mid-1500s, it is based on the words of the Talmudic sage Hanina: 'Come, let us go out to meet the Queen Sabbath' (*Shabbat* 119a). Many add a study section here, concluding with the *kaddish de-rabbanan*, the *kaddish* recited after a period of study. *Kabbalat Shabbat* concludes with Psalm 92 (the recital of

which constitutes men's acceptance of the current Shabbat with all its obligations) and Psalm 93, and is then followed by the *ma'ariv* (evening) service. The father may bless his children when he comes home from the synagogue, and recite a portion of the Proverbs to his wife, the part about a woman of valor. The meal starts with *kiddush*, praising God for having instituted the Sabbath and giving it to the Jews, and wine and bread are consumed. There are special songs, the *zemirot*, that are sung after the meal and a longer grace is also recited. Most Sefardi and many Ashkenazi synagogues end with the singing of *yigdal*, a poetic adaptation of Maimonides' 13 principles of Jewish faith (described in Chapter VI of this book). Other Ashkenazi synagogues end with *adon olam* (eternal Lord) instead.

Saturday morning Services

Shabbat morning prayers begin in the same way as the regular morning services. Of the hymns, Psalm 100 is omitted, its place being taken in the Ashkenazi tradition by Psalms 19, 34, 90, 91, 135, 136, 33, 92 and 93. Sephardic Jews maintain a different order, add several psalms and two religious poems. The *nishmat* prayer is recited at the end of the *pesukei d'zimrah*, the verses of song which are a selection from the Psalms. This has the theme that everything with breath praises God, 'who neither slumbers nor sleeps', and supports and directs the whole of Creation. The blessings before *shema* are expanded, and include the hymn *el adon*, which is often sung communally. The Torah scroll is taken out of the Ark, and the weekly portion is read, followed by the *haftorah*, a passage from the Prophets or Writings which changes each week. The custom of reading the Five Books of Moses in one year follows the Babylonian practice; in the Land of Israel the practice was over a three-year cycle. As so often, the Babylonian ways of doing things prevailed in the Jewish world which, after all, was to be a community that, like the Babylonians, lived outside the Land of Israel.

Seven people are called up to read from the Torah, and one person reads the portion from the Prophets – the *haftorah*. Generally, this selection has some link with the Torah reading. In the afternoon, three people are called up for the first part of the following week's portion of the Torah reading. After the Torah reading, prayers for the community are recited. Prayers are then recited (in most communities) for the government of the country and for the State of Israel.

Musaf

The *musaf*, or additional service, on Saturday morning starts with the silent recitation of the *amidah*. This is followed by a second public recitation that includes an additional reading known as the *kedushah*. Then follows a reading on the holiness of Shabbat, and a reading from the biblical Book of Numbers about the sacrifices that used to be performed in the Temple in Jerusalem. Next comes *yismechu*, 'They shall rejoice in Your sovereignty'; *Eloheynu*, 'Our God and God of our Ancestors, may you be pleased with our rest'; and *retzey*, 'Be favorable, our God, toward your people Israel and their prayer, and restore services to your Temple.'

After the *amidah* comes the full *kaddish*, followed by *ayn ke'eloheynu*. In traditional Judaism this is followed by a reading from the Talmud on the sacrifices that used to be performed in the Temple in Jerusalem. These readings are not normally carried out by Conservative Jews, and are invariably omitted by Reform Jews. The *musaf* service culminates with the Rabbi's *kaddish*, the *aleynu*, and then the Mourner's *kaddish*. Some synagogues conclude with the reading of *an'im zemirot*, 'The Hymn of Glory'. Reform Jews omit the entire *musaf* service.

Shabbat Mincha

The Sabbath *mincha* (afternoon service) commences with Psalm 145. The first section of the next weekly portion is read from the Torah scroll. The *amidah* follows the same pattern as the other *Shabbat amidah* prayer. After *mincha*, during winter Sabbaths (from Sukkot to Passover), *barekhi nafshi* (*Psalms* 104, 120–134) is recited. During summer Sabbaths (from Passover to Rosh Hashanah) chapters from the *Pirkei Avot,* one every Sabbath in consecutive order, are recited instead of *barekhi nafshi*.

Havdalah

A ceremony takes place at the conclusion of the Sabbath to mark the division, *havdalah*, between the day and the rest of the week. Some wine overflows a container, to symbolize the hope that the joy of the Sabbath will to a degree flow into the week, there is a lighted taper which reminds us of the fact that lights cannot be lit over the day of rest, and there is a spice box that can be taken to mark the special flavor of the day that has passed. It can also represent the need to revive one's spirits on the ending of the special day.

The Rules of the Sabbath

The Sabbath owes its status to a passage in the Bible, when, at *Gen* 2.1–3, God finished the Creation and rested on the seventh day, and he blessed the day as a result. It has a rather nice human feeling to it, the idea that when your labors are at an end you rest, and then you celebrate that rest, and may continue to celebrate it from then on, thinking back to the work that led up to it. It is first mentioned as a day of rest to be observed in a particular way during the journey in the desert when the Jews were collecting manna, and they were told to collect two lots of manna on the sixth day so that they would not have to exert themselves doing it on the seventh (*Ex* 16.23). The idea seemed to be that the people were not supposed to leave their places on the seventh day (*Ex* 16.28–9), and in the Ten Commandments, as they are popularly known, a more detailed set of rules appears about the Sabbath in which a ban on work figures largely, not only for the individual but for everyone connected to him (*Ex* 20.8–11). Sometimes it is connected to the exodus from Egypt (*Deut* 5.12–15) and sometimes to a covenant with God (*Ex* 31.12,16). The ban on work came to be much discussed by the commentators and a list of 39 types of activity that counted as work were enumerated and have been expanded constantly since then, so that for traditional Jews the Sabbath is really distinct from the rest of the week. Despite this plethora of rules, there are things one is allowed to do, such as defend oneself, save a life and avoid being harmed by a dangerous animal.

The source of the restrictions on what can be done on the Sabbath are in Tractate *Shabbat* 7.2 of the Talmud, where a wide range of different categories of what are called work are listed and classified as desecrating the Sabbath. These 39 categories have been expanded to include an even wider group of forbidden activities, but they do not include anything that can save a life (*pikuach nefesh*). For example, if a building collapses on someone on the Sabbath, it is permissible to dig him out to save his life. On the other hand, if he is dead, his body should be left there until after the Sabbath (*Yoma* 85a). Saving a life comes before almost all the laws, except for those banning idolatry, incest and committing bloodshed. So helping someone seriously ill on the Sabbath is allowed, even encouraged, even though it involves desecrating the day (*Yoma* 84b).

The seriousness of the Sabbath and its observance is obvious, since its violation is a capital offence (*Ex* 31.13–16). The Sabbath represents a covenant for all time, and goes very much along with circumcision, another sign of the covenant. The laws of what counts as work not to be done on the Sabbath are complex and have expanded vastly over time, and a good example of this can be seen in a response by R. Shlomo Luria to the issue of whether, in a very hot country, it would be acceptable to put an egg on the roof, where it would be cooked by the sun. Generally, the answer is that this would be permitted, provided there was no sand on the roof. If you bury it in the sand, that is work and so is wrong, and it is even wrong if you do it before the Sabbath, or just to keep it warm (*Responsa* 72).

The prophet Micah produces a comment that is often taken to be critical of formal prayer, when he wonders sarcastically whether God would be pleased with 'thousands of rams or ten thousands of rivers of oil', referring here to the sacrifices, which is often taken to refer to complicated rituals we perform on behalf of God. He goes on to say that God has shown us what is good, and here he refers to humanity, not just the Jews, and that is to act justly, to love *chesed* (righteousness) and to walk humbly with your God (*Mic* 6.7–8). It is this balance that is important, and so easy to upset as we often observe in our lives, in the three things we are told the world rests on: Torah, or study of the holy texts; *avodah*, or worship; and *gemilut chasadim*, righteous deeds (*Pirkei Avot* 1.2). Torah comes first in the list, since it is taken to lead to the others, although clearly it does not have to. One could spend all one's time devoted to studying the Torah, and some people do, and the suggestion here is that this is not right. Even Torah study and prayer is not enough, but needs to be combined with good deeds, and how can one perform good deeds without being part and parcel of the everyday world which enables one to earn money and provide for a family? We should remember that the rabbis themselves who wrote the *Pirkei Avot* all had occupations by which they actually earned their living, unlike the often sleek and heavily subsidized rabbis of today.

Chapter V

Festivals and Rites of Passage

The Calendar

The Jewish calendar is lunar, and each month consists of 29 or 30 days. A 13th month, Adar sheni (Second Adar), is added occasionally in order to resolve the gap between the lunar and solar years.

A day begins at sunset and ends at nightfall the next day on the solar calendar. Nightfall is taken to be when three stars in the sky can be seen.

The months of the year are listed below, with important days noted:

Nisan
14   Fast of the firstborn
15–22   Passover
16   Start of Counting of the Omer
17–20   Chol Hamoed

Iyyar
5   Yom ha-Atzmaut (Israel Independence Day)
14   Second Passover
18   Lag B'Omer (33rd day of the Omer)

Sivan
6–7   Shavuot

Tammuz
17   Fast

Av
9   Tisha B'Av

Elul
The *shofar* is blown on weekdays during the month, with *Selichot* or penitential prayers recited in the last week.

Tishri

1 & 2	Rosh Hoshanah
3	Fast of Gedaliah
10	Yom Kippur
15–21	Sukkot
21	Hoshanah Rabbah
22 & 23	Shemini Atzeret
23	Simchat Torah

Mar Cheshvan

Kislev

25–2 or 3 Tevet	Chanukah

Tevet

10	Fast

Shevat

15	Tu beshvat (New Year for Trees)

Adar

13	Fast of Esther
14	Purim
15	Shushan Purim

Festivals

The Pilgrim Festivals
There are three festivals when male Jews are told to go to a designated place, and as it were appear before God. These are the Passover, Shavuot and Sukkot (*Deut* 16.16).

Passover
Passover, or Pesach, is celebrated over eight days in the diaspora, seven days in Israel, and runs from 15 to 22 Nisan. The name itself

comes from the tenth plague, when the Jews' houses were passed over by God, who was intent on punishing the Egyptians through killing their first-born sons. This is the festival when Jews are commanded not to eat any leavened bread, now broadened to include a range of other products, and all leavening and the utensils and dishes used with it are removed from the house by the evening of 14 Nisan, and the bread is ceremonially burnt the next morning, while the utensils are sold to a Gentile, for the week. The first night, and outside of Israel the second also, there is a service which now takes place in the home, the Seder, which is the carrying out of the commandment of relating the story of the exodus to children, strictly speaking sons, and what God did to make this possible (*Ex* 13.8). Even in fairly unobservant families, Passover is often celebrated, the emphasis on children and food making it doubly attractive, and the ritual involves a great deal of preparation and display that participants often enjoy. On the table are a variety of objects designed to represent important themes of the event. Three *matzot* are put on the table, two representing the double gift of manna in the desert and the third the bread of affliction. There are four glasses of wine, and a fifth for Elijah, who is supposed to prefigure the Messiah, bitter herbs that represent the bitterness of slavery, parsley for spring, *charoset* (a paste combining nuts, wine and apples) that remind the attendees of the mortar used by the Jews in their labors in Egypt, a roast lamb bone which represents the lamb sacrificed in the days of the Temple, salt water that refers to the tears of the Jews and the sacrificial salt, plus a roasted egg that also indicates the Temple sacrifices.

The haggadah may owe its origins to the late Tannaic period (c. 170 CE–200 CE or 220 CE, and the first mention of a *seder* service is in the Mishnah, *Pesachim* 10.5) by Rabbi Gamaliel the Elder (or Rabbi Gamaliel I) of the first century CE, who was President of the Jewish legislative body in Jerusalem (known as the Sanhedrin), who declared: 'One who has not said [perhaps better interpreted as not understood the spiritual implications of] these three words, *pesach*, *matzah*, and *maror* has not done his duty' (or 'Whoever has not discussed these three things at Pesach has not fulfilled his obligation: the Pesach, Matzah, and Maror'). Between the eighth and ninth centuries CE, the Geonim (the leaders of the Jewish academies of learning in Sura and Pumbedita, Babylonia – now Iraq) compiled the version of the haggadah as it is known today. It used to be contained in the prayer book and was shorter than the modern version. Originally in Spain, the seder was recited in the synagogue by the congregation, but in time it developed into a ceremony to be carried out largely in the home. By the fourteenth century the service was available as a separate book, and for those who could afford it, as a very fancy illuminated manuscript. Over the following centuries the text changed slightly to include a few songs that were popular, and in recent years quite radical changes have been made by Jews seeking new ways of celebrating the Passover, but it is remarkable how faithful to the very old format the haggadah has remained over the last seven centuries or so. The festival is very popular even in an increasingly secular Jewish world, and yet much of the text is uncompromising with its rather dry, commentatorial structure, with discussions by rabbis on the meaning of some of the key phrases and items in the seder service, hardly very riveting material by any standard for a general audience, especially one with many children present. The songs toward the end of the seder are lively, but they are only reached after reciting the stately but ponderous Hallel, verses praising God that are sometimes thought of as repetitive and are certainly not very exciting. The book has for some centuries concluded with the *chad gadya*, an Aramaic song that is very funny and difficult to recite, given its plethora of consonants, the perfect way to end the evening on a high, but with the consoling thought that God is in charge of everything.

When one looks closely at the haggadah, it is difficult to conclude that it is very suitable for the purpose it sets itself. Much of it is obscure and consists of rabbinic commentary, asking questions that are not very interesting or central about the precise meaning of some of the words used to describe the events linked to the Passover. Apart from the fact that the order of service is traditional, and so reminds observers of how it has been performed continually for centuries (although there have in fact been changes), it is certainly not the most perspicuous way to design a series of prayers dealing with the events of the Passover, despite what many of the commentaries say. Much of the text is convoluted and takes the shape of rabbinic commentary, which is never very exciting, and here takes its time to work out some of the principles behind the Passover rituals, and what needs to be done during the festival. One surprising part of the festival is that, despite the concentration on the exodus from Egypt,

Moses is never mentioned. It is as though he never existed, and all the credit for the rescue of the Jews is given to God. This is not only surprising, though it goes along with the rather critical attitude that Judaism often takes to heroes, but also interferes with the drama of the account in the haggadah. Incidentally, in the illustrated *haggadot* (*haggadahs*) that were produced from the Middle Ages onward, Moses and Aaron often figure visually as central characters, since God cannot appear directly in any case. The illustrations often seem to make good the omissions in the text itself.

We could ask in a similar way why, in the afternoon service on the Day of Atonement, is the traditional reading from the Torah the passages about forbidden sexual relationships? This part of the Law is not even supposed to be discussed as part of study, merely recited in a service. The Talmud suggests that this is because, on that date in the past, a great deal of dalliance would take place between young men and women, and dancing would result in marriage proposals and so on. The idea is that the afternoon of the Day of Atonement would signal the end of the solemn part of the service, since it was assumed that God had by then forgiven everyone. The rather grim laws on sexual relationships were designed to calm people down and restrain their behavior (*Ta'anit* 4.8). This is a possible explanation for the selection of this particular passage, though it has to be said that unless one had been eyeing a fellow congregant lasciviously it really does not seem that relevant to ordinary life. Yet it brings in the way that religions try to regulate human behavior by creating a degree of balance in our relationships with each other and within ourselves. Often, balance can be achieved not by anything that is directly appropriate, but by something that is familiar. When a loved person dies and is remembered affectionately by those who were close to him or her, it is often the little things that he or she said or did that are remembered, but in themselves they are of no significance at all, or even rather ridiculous. This may make them even more impressive, since they became part of the character of the person we are remembering. Yet they do not really tell us anything about the person and have no significance in themselves. It may be the way he laid down his spectacles in the evening, or what she hummed as she made a cup of tea. These charmless actions become charming when they are remembered as part of the aura of the departed person, and religious ritual often acts in the same way. We should not expect them to reveal why they are significant, we just know they are because of how they are connected to what is in itself significant, in this case God. The laws the Jews are supposed to follow have no rationale on the whole except that which reposes in their source, and many of the prayers we enjoy reciting are exactly the same – in themselves rather unimpressive and even repetitive, yet they become part of a ritual that in the end is familiar and comforting.

Shavuot (Pentecost)

Shavuot is celebrated on 6 Sivan, and outside Israel among the non-Reform community, also on 7 Sivan, and the word literally means 'weeks' (*Ex* 34.22; *Lev* 23.15–16; *Deut* 16.16), since it is seven weeks after the second day of Passover, the first day when the *omer* sacrifice was brought to the Temple. The dating of this festival proved to be very controversial and played a large part in the separation of the Jews, on the one hand, and the Karaites and Samaritans on the other, since the latter two took the Torah literally and disagreed about the precise understanding of when Shavuot ought to begin. They took the reference to the Sabbath from when the counting should start literally to mean the Sabbath, and not the week, and so for them the festival always starts on a Sunday. The festival is based on Exodus, chapters 19–20, and deals with the giving of the Law on Mount Sinai. Since it occurs in summer it is often accompanied by flowers, and dairy food is eaten. It may well have originally been something of a harvest festival (*Ex* 23.16), since there is a reference to an offering of the first fruits of the wheat harvest (*Num* 28.26; *Ex* 34.22) and the Book of Ruth is read, with its harvest themes. The rural theme is often used in synagogue decoration during this period, with plants and agricultural products on display in the building. The link with the giving of the Law is made with the reading of the Ten Commandments, more accurately called the Ten Sayings in the Hebrew Bible.

Sukkot (Tabernacles)

Sukkot takes place on 15 Tishri, lasts for seven days (*Lev* 23.42–3) and commemorates the period when the Jews were living in the desert in temporary houses or booths; hence the name Sukkot, from the Hebrew *sukkah* meaning 'booth'. Observant Jews live for at least part of the day in a booth, with a roof covered in plants and branches.

A variety of species of plants are eaten and even used in the synagogue, where a *lulav*, or palm branch, and *etrog*, or citron, and myrtle and willow are brought into the service and seven perambulations are made around the Torah. It is mentioned at *Deut* 16.13–15, *Ex* 23.16 and *Lev* 23.39. At the end of the festival, Shemini Atzeret and Simchat Torah are celebrated – in Israel on the same day – the end coming on Simchat Torah with the finishing of the cycle of reading of the Torah, while all the sifrei Torah, the scrolls of the Law, are taken out of the ark in which they are kept and paraded around the synagogue. After the last reading from the Torah, a start is made from its beginning.

New Year and the Day of Atonement

Most of the festivals in the Jewish calendar commemorate historical events, but the New Year and Day of Atonement do not. The whole period is extended by a long build-up through the month of Elul. The *shofar*, or ram's horn, is blown at the end of the weekday morning services in Elul, and only ceases one day before New Year. Additional prayers are said, in particular the *Selichot*, before the morning service – for Sefardim, for the whole month, but for Ashkenazim for a more limited period.

Rosh Hoshanah, or the Jewish New Year, is celebrated over two days, even in Israel, on 1 and 2 Tishri, and begins the ten days of penitence that culminate in the Day of Atonement. The Reform stick to one day, which, after all, follows the Bible. The theme is judgment, and many of the prayers during this period refer to the significance of repentance and the power of prayer and good works. The synagogue is often transformed in appearance by the use of white material to cover the ark and the *sifrei torah*, plus the clothes of the celebrants. The *shofar* is blown throughout the services, perhaps to symbolize the sacrifice of Isaac and his replacement by a lamb (the Torah reading for the second day is *Gen* 22.1–24), and to wake up the participants to the need for repentance and a change in their way of life. The *shofar* is not blown on Shabbat. Jews sometimes go to a place of flowing water after *mincha* on the first day of Rosh Hoshanah to cast off their sins symbolically (this is called *tashlikh*), but again not on Shabbat, and a sweet new year is represented by having honey instead of salt with bread, and some fresh fruit. These pleasant customs precede a rather grim week of extended prayers, including the *Selihot*, that call on us to repent and lead up to the Day of Atonement, a day of fasting from sunset to nightfall, evening to evening (*Lev* 23.27, 32). No food or drink is to be taken by those considered of a suitable age, though if there is a relevant medical condition the fast should be moderated. Before it starts, many Jews try to ensure that any conflicts with other human beings are resolved, since God can only be called on to forgive our sins against him, not against others. The evening service is often called Kol Nidrei, after the starting prayer, which is a recitation of the significance of vows, and became highly controversial since it was taken by some Gentiles, wrongly, to imply that once a year Jews could get rid of their obligations to keep to agreements. Throughout the evening and the following day the prayers frequently have a confessional flavor, the dead are recalled and many Jews stay in the synagogue through the whole day. There is not much point in going home, since the fast continues until the evening. The afternoon service has the book of Jonah as the *haftorah*, appropriately, given its theme of repentance and the power to avert the evil decree. In the evening after the festival it is traditional to make a start on the building of the *sukkah* for Sukkot, which follows a few days later. The blowing of the *shofar* brings the synagogue service and the fast to an end.

Chanukah

Chanukah is in fact a minor festival, though the most familiar in the USA because of its proximity to Christmas. The Seleucid Empire under Antiochus IV intervened in a civil war in Judea when a former high priest, Jason, attempted to re-establish himself in that role, and marched on Jerusalem with a group of armed supporters. In 167 BCE, Antiochus interpreted this as a revolt against his rule and decided to end once and for all this notion of a separate religion of Judaism. He was basically siding with those Jews who favored a more Hellenistic lifestyle against those who were perhaps less sophisticated and wished to maintain their old traditions. The revolt was led by a priest, Mattathias and his sons, including Judah, known as Judah Maccabee, from the Hebrew for hammer, *makabi*.

They won after two years of conflict and re-established Jewish worship in the Temple, and we are told that when they lit once again the menorah or candelabrum in the Temple they found only enough

Hebrew heroes: Judah Maccabee inspires his troops

oil for one day, yet it served for eight days, the miracle that the festival celebrates with the lighting of what, strictly speaking, should be called a *chanukiyah*. The strange thing about the festival is that the rabbis have in the past been rather critical of it, while ordinary Jews have been very enthusiastic. This is hardly surprising, since the holiday is a very relaxed one as far as one's religious duties are concerned, and there is money to be given to children, doughnuts and latkes (pancakes) to be eaten (the theme of the holidays is, after all, oil), and it is the celebration of a victory. The rabbis are rather suspicious of anything that emphasizes human power, and the book of Maccabees is not in the Jewish Bible, only in the Apocrypha, perhaps for that reason. Jewish tradition often interprets the festival as a religious reaction to Hellenism, but in fact it seems to have been more against Jews who were enthusiastic about Hellenism. Even the victorious Maccabees had no problems in maintaining links with outside civilizations. In fact, they made contacts within the Roman Empire that led to the ultimate downfall of the independence of the country when Pompey intervened in the civil war between Aristobulos and Hyrcanus a century later, and, of course, ultimately the destruction of the Second Temple.

The festival is minor, there are no prohibitions on work, and all that is involved is the lighting of a menorah or *chanukiyah*, a set of eight candles plus an extra one called a *shammash*. Each day one extra candle is lit to symbolize the miraculous nature of the oil that was found in the re-dedicated Temple. It is customary in many communities to give children presents, sometimes one each day, perhaps as a sort of consolation for not celebrating Christmas. Games are played with a top, a *dreidel*, and fried food is eaten to follow up the general theme of oil. A vigorous hymn is sung on each night, the *maoz tzur*, which recites four instances of divine redemption, the exodus from Egypt, the return from Babylon, the escape from Haman, and finally the victory of the Maccabees. It ends with a rather bloodthirsty reference to the restoration of the Temple and the spilling of the enemies' blood that will ensue, which led to it being banned or reformulated by some Reform communities, but it has remained popular throughout the Jewish world. Most Jews in the diaspora who recite the Hebrew probably have no idea what it means anyway.

Purim

Another minor festival is Purim, on 14 Adar, which celebrates the escape of the Jews in Persia from their enemies, particularly the evil Haman, and the word *pur* in Hebrew means 'lots'. Haman cast lots to decide on which day the Jews were to be killed. On the evening of the festival, the scroll of Esther is read, often in a humorous way, and people dress up in fancy costume, this being a big carnival event in Israel and a huge excuse for a riotous party in the diaspora.

When the name of Haman is mentioned in the reading, children boo and stamp their feet, and rattles are used to make more noise.

Purimspiel

Though Jews do not have much of a reputation for excessive drinking, on this day one is allowed (even encouraged) to drink to such an extent that it becomes impossible to distinguish between Haman, the villain of the story, and Mordechai, the hero.

Fasts

There are various fasts in Judaism, and potentially there are many occasions for fasting, but these are generally not observed or are avoided by some study taking place, which obviates the need to starve for less serious fasts. Among these less serious fasts are the Fast of the Firstborn, which commemorates the delivery of the Israelite firstborn from the fate of their Egyptian peers before the departure from Egypt. There is also the Fast of Esther before Purim, in commemoration of her fast before she approached the king to try to save the Jews in Persia. There are four other fasts through the year to remember events connected with the fall of Jerusalem.

1. The Fast of Gedalia is on the day after Rosh Hashanah (3 Tishri); the Bible calls it the fast of the seventh month (*Zech* 7.5, 8, 19).

Gedalia was the governor of Judea, working for the Assyrians, and he was assassinated by Ishmael b. Netanya. This led to the final exile from the area. Had Gedalia not perished, the situation of the Jews would have been much better, and they could have stayed in the Land.

2. On 10 Tevet, Nebuchadnezzar laid siege to Jerusalem (2 *Kings* 25.1); the consequent famine and suffering were the beginning of the end (*Ezek* 24.1–2). The Chief Rabbinate of Israel has named it as the general Kaddish Memorial Day, for those whose date of death is unknown. It is often linked with the Holocaust and the six million who were murdered then.

3. On 17 Tammuz, according to the Mishnah, the tablets from Sinai were broken, the daily offering ceased in the First Temple, the walls of the Second Temple in Jerusalem were breached, and Apostomos burnt the Torah and set up an idol in the sanctuary. These three fast days are from daybreak until night.

4. On 9 Av, it was decreed that the Exodus generation would not enter Israel; that day both Temples were destroyed though, according to Jeremiah, the First Temple was burnt on 10 Av (52.12ff.); 2 *Kings* claims that Nebuchadnezzar came to Jerusalem on 7 Av and burnt the Temple (25.8ff.). We are also told that on this day the independent Jewish metropolis, Betar, was captured, with its leader, Bar Kokhba, and Turnus Rufus leveled and ploughed the area of the sanctuary in the defeat of the revolt against the Romans.

Maimonides suggests that in the time of the Messiah these would no longer be fasts, but actually celebrations (Hilkhot *Ta'anit* 5.15, referring to Zechariah 8.19). Presumably this is because Jerusalem would have been re-established in all its former glory and so it could be then regarded more cheerfully.

Jews fast from before sunset until the following evening, as noted above for Yom Kippur.

The Fast Day Torah readings
On all rabbinic fast days, the readings are Exodus 32.11–14 and 34.1–10, in the morning and afternoon, except on Tisha B'Av morning. In *Ex* 32, Moses tries to restrain God's anger against the people who are supposed to be following him, after the incident

of the Golden Calf; he reminds God how much he invested in them in the exodus, and of the dire consequences to the divine name should the Egyptians hear of their destruction. The Patriarchs, and the divine promise through the covenant to give Israel to their descendants, are recalled. God is assuaged and the principle is established that he will not totally despair of the Israelites whatever they do. In *Ex* 34, Moses ascends again to Sinai, at dawn and alone, and hews two new tablets. God descends in a cloud, standing with Moses, and reveals some of his attributes: 'God, God, the Lord, merciful and gracious, slow to anger, with much love and truth, granting love to the thousandth generation, forgiving sin, rebellion, and error' (*Ex* 34.6–7). Moses quickly worshipped, and again asked God to forgive Israel, and to accompany them on their mission. God promises a covenant that will be manifested in front of the people through miracles. The fast day *haftorah* in *mincha* is *Isa* 55.6–56.8, which calls on us to seek God when he may be found, and his willingness to respond appropriately.

The Tisha B'Av reading in the morning is *Deut* 4.25–40. Prosperity in the land of Israel will lead to corruption and idolatry, which brings about divine retribution. Moses warns that exile and destruction will be the inevitable result. Jews will survive as small minorities in the far-flung diaspora. There they will worship dead gods of wood and stone, fashioned by human hands. After the Jewish people have undergone the long painful exile, they will, at some point, return to God, their Lord, and finally grasp the meaning of what has happened to them. He never forgets the covenant with their fathers. The Jewish miraculous experience of the exodus from Egypt, as well as God's appearance at Sinai, are unique testimony to divine revelation and providence.

The *haftorah* is *Jeremiah* 8.13–9.23, and explains that God sees destruction and exile as the only way to redeem Israel, which has become thoroughly corrupt. Jerusalem will be desolate, and the Jews forced to improve their behavior in the diaspora. Eventually, after a long period of mourning, the Jews will understand the source of their exile, and return to God and the Torah. The Book of Lamentations is read. The first word of chapters 1, 2, and 4 of the book are the name of the book – '*aychah?*' – 'How could it happen?' The same word is also used by Moses to describe his despair, unable to handle the awkward Israelites (*Deut* 1.12). This lack of a relationship with Moses may have led to the Jews' rebellion, following the incident when spies brought back a discouraging report from the land of Canaan. This, in turn, led to Moses and his generation not being able to enter Israel; had they, rather than their descendants, been the conquerors, it could have been done without bloodshed, and the destruction of the Temple and exile need not have occurred, according to some commentators. Jerusalem has now sunk into the depths of despair. The Jews' false faith in apparent allies and friends having evaporated, they once more return to their only true helper – God. Once they return to him, their former glory will return in full force. In the Midrash, both occurrences of 'aychah' are said to recall an even earlier use of the word. In Genesis, when Adam and Eve violate the single commandment they were given, God calls to them in the Garden of Eden: 'ayekah?' – 'Where are you?' In Hebrew, the consonants are the same; only the vowels are different. The connection between 'ayekah' and 'aychah' hints at a connection between the two questions. When there is dispute and dissension, when things go wrong, God is saying, 'Where are you? What has happened to you?'

Asceticism in Judaism

The conclusion of the Sabbath is marked by the *havdalah* ceremony, which emphasizes the distinctions that exist between things; obviously here referring to the distinctions between the holy and the profane, the Sabbath and the rest of the week. Spices are involved, and wine, and some have suggested that the point of the ceremony is to prepare the individual Jew for another week of ordinary life before the next Sabbath can be enjoyed. On the other hand, there is also criticism of those who make too much fuss of the Sabbath by comparison with the rest of the week, and some Jews given to asceticism actually fast from Sabbath to Sabbath, or undertake other physically difficult tasks on ordinary days in order to emphasize the significance of the Sabbath. This is nicely captured by a Hasidic story reported by Buber, where a Jew restricts his intake of water leading up to the Sabbath in order to increase his pleasure in the day, and where, just before a particular Sabbath, he feels a tremendous pride in managing to control himself on this and other occasions. Once he realizes that he now has incurred the sin of pride, he breaks his fast and the comment his rabbi makes, and the name of the story, is 'Patchwork' (Buber, 1991). The idea is that when one takes on ascetic tasks there is the danger of one's life ceasing to be a unitary process, in which one combines the natural with the spiritual, but rather one sees one's spiritual life as a struggle to dominate the natural. That sort of struggle makes life a patchwork, and basically unsatisfactory. It is this sort of behavior that is criticized in *Nedarim* 41b, where we are told that 'someone who imposes vows of abstinence on himself is as though he put an iron collar round his neck, he is like someone who builds a prohibited altar, he is like someone who takes a sword and plunges it into his heart. What the Torah forbids is enough, do not try to take on further restrictions.'

Yet some groups did go much further than the law prescribed. In the Second Temple period, a group called the Essenes turned their backs on the Temple and Jerusalem and set up their own community in the desert, where they seem to have followed ascetic rules and practiced celibacy. They had their own writings, which were certainly connected with those of ordinary Judaism, to whom they were linked in that they regarded themselves as a righteous remnant of those who had returned from Babylon. In his book *On Dreams*, Philo refers to a similar group in Egypt who disregarded money, pleasure, society and nourishment, except in so far as they needed to stay alive. They spent hardly any money on themselves, slept on the ground and disregarded the elements in their determination to live simply (I, 124–5). He says they were called Therapeutae and lived south of Alexandria, spent their days in prayer and the study of religious texts, and clearly he is very impressed with them. They ate only at night, since they thought that philosophy should be pursued in the light, and the needs of the body in the dark. They did not eat meat or drink wine and had the very simplest of diets (*On the Contemplative Life* III, 22–37, 64–90). On the Sabbath and festivals they came together – which is unusual, since they spent the rest of the week in seclusion – and prayed and studied together, both men and women (though they remained physically quite separate in so far as this was possible), and in this way presumably the distinction between the Sabbath and the rest of the week was emphasized and noted.

Yehuda Halevi wrote a book called *Kuzari*, which deals with a discussion between the ruler of the Khazar nation, who many believe was to convert to Judaism, and a number of other people, including a rabbi and a philosopher, and each participant gives his point of view on the issues that were bothering the Khazar. Halevi defends Judaism in the book, the rabbi definitely has the best lines, and the full title of the book is *Kuzari: The book of proof and argument in defense of the despised religion.* The rabbi suggests that the problem with asceticism is that it overrides the principle of balance that is so important a part of Judaism. Someone who earns a lot of money and spends it on things that are appropriate to him and his family, and acceptable to his religion, is perfectly aligned with what he ought to do, and the idea that we should be poor and deny ourselves what we would otherwise wish to enjoy does not accord with the Law. It is because we do not ourselves know how to establish this sort of balance that the Law tells us what to do and helps us to act appropriately. What the observance of the Sabbath does, the rabbi suggests, is to help us acknowledge the omnipotence of God, since the Sabbath is a celebration of the creation of the world by God, and his miraculous deeds on behalf of the people whom he chose, and the places he chose for them. So it is the actions that are legally prescribed for the Sabbath that provide the proper ways to approach God, rather than through extreme ascetic practices (Halevi, 1947, 77–9).

Problems with Prayer

Is the modern prayer book in Judaism a problem? By 'modern' is meant both the traditional prayer book and the various reformed versions, since if there is anything we know about modern Judaism, it is that most Jews have a marked disinclination to pray. This is despite, or perhaps because of, a development of many different prayer books, which is perhaps not such a new development after all, since we do know of the existence in the past of specific books of prayers for women, who make up, after all, half the Jewish popula-tion. There is today an Open Siddur project, which is putting on line every single prayer that has ever been performed by Jews within Judaism and inviting viewers to compile their own prayer book, mix-ing and matching whatever they fancy, or to put it more seriously, the prayers they find meaningful.

One of the features about this personal selection of prayer that is remarkable is precisely that it is personal, whereas normally Jewish prayers are communal. The idea of a prayer book is that a group of people all do the same thing, roughly at the same time, together, and in this way presumably everyone supports everyone else and brings into the activity some of the pleasant (and also, of course, less pleasant) aspects of sociability. There is certainly a difference in how the notion of community is regarded today: with the ubiquity of the computer and the internet, many people feel closer to individuals with whom they are in contact electronically yet have never met than they are with those who are physically closer to them. On the other hand, it does have to be acknowledged that even in the traditional synagogue not all the prayers are recited all the time, there is scope for some alteration of what is said and done, and the prayers are often not all said together at the same time, since people may come and go at different times and so will often be at different stages of the service. And, of course, what congregants are actually thinking about may be very different from what they are reciting, and what they subsequently do may also be very different. This is hardly news; we all know that people who pray may be thinking about something else, and that they may recite prayers valuing certain things and activities that in real life they show no inclination to favor. All this provides an argument for the traditional prayer book, in that the prayer book need not be something that encapsulates every aspect of each individual's personal theology, but it should contain material that one can think about and wonder how to reconcile with one's own beliefs, and so provokes an encounter that is potentially satisfying and worthwhile. On the other hand, if the worshipper finds the *siddur* obscure or worse, incomprehensible and thoroughly out of date, then it might be harder for him or her to use it in this way. Yet this might be more of a reflection of his/her personal failings of imagination than anything else. It could be said, however, that despite there also being much in the Bible and the Law that is obscure, incomprehensible and out of date, most Jews would find in these works something worth responding to, at the very least. This brings out the notion of Judaism as the first postmodern religion, where many of its perhaps less than willing adherents struggle to find meaning in its core practices, and so discover new ways of developing that meaning, often without any essential link to those practices themselves.

Death

Death is often referred to in the Bible, but the notion of an afterlife is quite vague, except in the book of Daniel, and cadavers are quite quickly dealt with in modern Jewish custom. There is some debate about how to define death, whether it is just the end of the breathing process or brain death, or some combination of the two, given that in modern times it is possible to keep people alive with technology in ways not feasible in the past when the classical legal texts were written. It is generally not allowed to speed up death, but there is no need either to prevent it from coming about through natural methods once the ordinary means of averting it have failed. The general idea is that God is the true judge, the phrase much used in a prayer of resignation said on hearing bad news about the death of someone, and the dying person should be treated well, not left alone, and when he or she has died, should not be left alone either. The dead person is cleaned and washed, often by a special society, the *Chevra Kadisha*, who are of the same sex as the deceased, and treat the body with great respect, so it is covered at all times. It is dressed in very simple clothes, including often a *kittel*, a shroud, and, in the case of men, with the *tallit* minus its *tzitzit*. Prayers are said before going to the cemetery, and again at the cemetery, finishing with the *kaddish*. The dead person is placed in a simple coffin, which remains closed and is buried very quickly, usually within 24 hours of death unless a Sabbath or festival intervenes, or there is some other major problem in bringing together the mourners. The chief mourners shovel some earth on to the coffin in the cemetery. The grave is marked with a small wooden post with the person's name, and later a headstone replaces the wooden post. The funeral service is brief and the mourner's *kaddish* is recited. Everyone washes their hands before leaving the cemetery, acknowledging the pollution associated with death.

From the time of death up to the burial, those closely linked with the dead person are not obliged to perform their normal religious tasks, a tear is made in an item of the mourner's clothing, and on returning after the funeral they sit *shivah* (seven), for seven days from the funeral, on low chairs and are visited by others who seek to comfort them. There is a break during Shabbat, when mourning is not allowed, and a festival will bring the *shivah* to an end. The end of the shivah sees the start of the *sheloshim* (thirty) when, for the next 30 days, one can return to work but must not cut one's hair or shave. *Kaddish* is said every day, and for parents, every day for a year. Children continue to mourn for a year, at the end of which it is customary for them to light a candle on the anniversary of the death, recite *kaddish* in synagogue and perhaps read the *haftorah* also. Reform congregations do not observe many of these rituals, but some of them are to a degree part of their mourning and death rituals.

Family Life

Children are much emphasized in Judaism, though today outside the world of the traditional Jews, families are generally small. After all, the first commandment to humanity is to be fruitful and multiply (*Gen* 1.28). After a child is born the mother is considered ritually impure for a set time. A boy is named at his circumcision, a girl in the synagogue the first time the Torah is read after her birth. Children get a Hebrew name, with the name being extended for boys with *ben*, son of, and for girls, *bat,* daughter of. There is a cere-mony for first-born boys whose fathers are not Levites or Kohanim, called *pidyon ha-ben*, which involves a small payment to avoid them being consecrated to the Temple (*Ex* 13.2), which of course no longer exists. Boys should be circumcised (*Gen* 17.9–11), and this is performed by a *mohel* if the child is healthy enough on the eighth day after the birth. At 13, a boy is able to take on the commandments or *mitzvot* fully and becomes *bar mitzvah*, and in egalitarian communities a similar status (*bat mitzvah*) is bestowed on girls at around the age of 12. Today, this has become a huge event, but originally it was far less significant as a public celebration, although no doubt just as, or per-haps more, significant for the individual concerned. The boy or girl typically read a portion of the Torah, perhaps also the *haftorah*, and they may give a speech displaying some mastery of Jewish texts and the Law. Initially, the Reform movement disapproved of this cere-mony and replaced it with a general confirmation event, but it has become so popular in recent years that they have reverted to the more traditional formula. The advantage of confirmation is that it tended to be at a more advanced and appropriate age, in the late teens, by which stage children have perhaps reached a more mature stage in their relationship with their religion. On the other hand, in the USA, the idea of a party for young teenagers has become so

popular that even non-Jews sometimes ask their parents to organize
something similar for them.

The laws of betrothal or marriage are very complicated, and there
are a large number of people who are not allowed to marry each
other because of their family connections or their status in Jewish
society. The wedding itself may be quite elaborate, and traditionally
the bride and groom will stand under a *chuppah*, or canopy, and the
marriage document, or *ketubah*, will be read out and signed by them.
It has details of the date of the marriage, the participants, the
obligations the husband has to his wife, and what the husband will
pay if there is a divorce. In egalitarian weddings these obligations are
written up as being mutual. Traditionally, seven blessings are recited,
a ring or rings are exchanged and a glass is broken. This is often
interpreted as being a reference to the destruction of the Temple in
Jerusalem, but may also be superstitious to avert the evil eye, or to
remind the participants during a time of happiness that things may
turn out badly. Weddings can, of course, be elaborate or simple, and
do not have to take place in synagogues.

Similarly with a divorce, the document of divorce, the *get*, will be
read out to the participants so that it is clear that they accept it
willingly and understand its implications. Divorce is mentioned in
the Torah (*Deut* 24.1), but over time the rules concerning divorce
have become complex. In the traditional community only a man can
divorce his wife, not the other way around, and 90 days later the
woman is free to remarry. The delay is to ensure that she is not
pregnant. If a husband refuses to divorce his wife, she can suffer the
status of being an *agunah* or chained woman, since she is unable to
move on and remarry within the orthodox community as a result of
his refusal. Reform Jews merely treat divorce as a civil matter and do
not involve themselves in Jewish laws on this issue.

The Synagogue

The word 'synagogue' in English comes from the Greek translation
of *bayt ha-knesset*, or house of assembly, since synagogue means
assembly. In America, the Reform community often uses the term
temple for synagogue. But it must be emphasized that there is nothing consecrated or sacred about the synagogue, and prayer can take
place virtually anywhere.

It used to be thought that the synagogue was created after the destruction of the Second Temple in 70 CE, but we now know that they existed all over Palestine and the diaspora, even while there was a Temple. They even existed in Babylonia during the exile in the sixth century BCE, and no doubt played a significant role in maintaining the notion of Jewishness in an alien land. It would have looked improbable for a faith so centered on the Temple to survive once that link was broken, but it seemed not to have happened like this at all; the distance from the destroyed or even the renovated Temple may have enhanced rather than diminished Jewish identity.

There are differences between traditional and less traditional synagogues, and between Ashkenazi and Sefardi synagogues. Traditional synagogues tend to have a separation between men and women, and the others do not. This can be a *mechitzah*, a curtain, or even just an aisle between the sexes, or there can be a separate balcony for the women. There is an *aron kodesh*, a holy Ark in which the scrolls of the Law are kept, and a *ner tamid*, an eternal flame, that is a reminder of the menorah that was always lit in the Temple. Synagogues in the West tend to have their seats pointing east, toward Jerusalem, and those in the east point west, toward the same place. The *sefer Torah*, the scroll of the Law, is carried around the synagogue and then placed on the *bimah*, a raised dais in many buildings, and read to the congregation. Some synagogues are enormous and very grand, while others are tiny and modest; and some have substantial additional facilities, while others are very basic.

In Eastern Europe in the past, when there were large Jewish communities, the synagogue was often the hub of the village, perhaps the only place that was warm most of the time, a place where travelers rested and where education was centered. The rabbi was often the head of the community, and everyone would go regularly to the synagogue, or to one of the synagogues in a town, and the whole of the community's social life was built around it. In modern Western society, synagogues are much more like churches. In the USA they often contain the facilities that churches have, such as gymnasia, health facilities, libraries and educational facilities, and Reform temples also resemble churches in that they often contain organs to provide music during services, and the rabbi very much leads the service. In traditional synagogues this is less the case, with the rabbi being more the expert on legal and ritual issues, someone who is respected as a leading scholar in the community, while others often lead the service, or parts of the service. In the Reform temple, the rabbi is often the reader from the *sefer Torah*, while in traditional synagogues this is often a member of the congregation.

Synagogue buildings vary greatly in style and generally follow the local culture, though in the past they had also to take into account local regulations on how high they could be and what sort of presence they were allowed to project. In Europe and the USA in the nineteenth century, synagogues often took on a Moorish design to distinguish them from churches, while in the Middle East they were often very similar to mosques, though they took care never to be bigger. The synagogue in Groningen, in the Netherlands, pictured here, is a good example of a building somewhere between a church and an exotic Eastern building. Like so many European synagogues, it is no longer used as a synagogue, and in a distinctly Dutch way is in the red light district. Most of the Jews in the city were killed by the Nazis. In Greek and Roman times, synagogues incorporated aspects of classical design, while in Byzantine areas they resembled the local style of architecture, though they tended to have less representative material compared to churches, at least of anything that resembled a

Synagogue, Groningen, Netherlands, front view (left) and side view (right)

human being. Animals often figure in synagogue art, and communities that were wealthy were keen to display what they possessed through the embellishment of their local house of prayer.

Conversion to Judaism

Conversion (*giyyur*) to Judaism is when a non-Jewish person wants to become a full member of the Jewish community. One of the differences between Judaism and the two religions that emerged from it, Christianity and Islam, is that Judaism has for a long time been totally uninterested in converting others to the faith. There were in the past obviously periods of conversion, and when alien communities were overcome in war they may well have become absorbed into the Jewish community. In the first few centuries of the Common Era the literature suggests that conversion was quite prevalent, and it only came to an end when a more aggressive Christianity forbade it. Non-traditional Jews follow much more relaxed conversion principles, and so traditional Jews do not generally accept the converts. There is also the problem that the Reform regards the child of a Jewish father and a Gentile mother as being Jewish, while for the traditional community it is the reverse. The disagreements about conversion and about who is legally Jewish has led to a great deal of argument and confusion, with some rabbinates converting people whom other rabbinates reject as not being Jews. In 2009, for example, many conversions carried out in Israel by the orthodox rabbinate were not accepted by the orthodox rabbinate in Europe.

A male convert is a *ger* (female, *giyoret*), which in English is often translated as proselyte from the Septuagint translation into Greek. *Ger* means a stranger, but also someone who travels or lives with someone else, and the meaning here originally in the Bible is to refer to those non-Jews who accompanied the Israelites out of the land of Egypt on their sojourn through the desert and eventually to the Land of Israel. They were a symbol in a sense of how assimilated the Israelites had become in that others naturally felt they ought to accompany them, and were in effect members of the same community. After all, the word *ger* comes from the Hebrew root word *gar*, meaning 'to dwell' or 'to sojourn [with]'. These people were both living with the Israelites and traveling with them. *Lev* 19.34 states: 'As a citizen among you shall be the *ger* (the stranger) who lives among you, and

you shall love him as yourself, for you were *gerim* in the land of Egypt
– I am the Lord your God.' In the Bible it is clear that there was no
formal conversion as there is today, though there is a reference to a
gerut, or conversion process, as the circumcision undergone by the
male stranger (*ger*) before eating the Passover offering (*Ex* 12.48),
which seems a rather demanding requirement before having a meal,
or even participating in a significant ritual.

In the Talmud, *ger* is used in two senses: *ger tzedek refers* to a
'righteous convert', a proselyte to Judaism; and *ger toshav*, a non-
Jewish inhabitant of the Land of Israel who observes the Seven Laws
of Noah and has repudiated all links with idolatry. Today, *ger* refers to
a Jew by choice, and all the varieties of Judaism, with the exception
of Syrian Jews, accept converts, though the conversion procedures
are all quite distinct. Even the Karaites have ended their ban on
conversion in modern times.

For Rabbinic Judaism, the laws of *gerut* are based on codes of law
and texts, including discussions in the Talmud, through the *Shulkhan
Arukh* and subsequent interpretations. Jewish Law is generally
interpreted as discouraging proselytizing, and religious *gerut* is also
discouraged. Rabbis are technically required to reject potential
converts three times, and if the would-be converts remain adamant,
only then setting up the process by which they can be converted. This
is because the laws that Jews are supposed to follow are more stringent
than they consider are required by other religions; a person who
would be considered derelict of religious duties under Jewish Law
could easily be, without a change in his or her actions, an entirely
righteous Gentile. For example, Noah is called 'good in his time', the
implication being that, by the general standards applying to Gentiles,
he behaved well. By the standards of the Torah, his behavior might
not have been appropriate for Jews, however, but this is no criticism
of him. Why, then, should a Gentile be expected to wish to convert,
when he or she could live a perfectly honorable life as a Gentile? Jews
have suffered regular and often severe persecution throughout the
ages, culminating perhaps in the Holocaust, when an estimated third
of the Jewish population was murdered, so a proselyte is exposing
himself or herself to potentially mortal danger. Why should someone
wish to be exposed to these problems if there is nothing wrong
according to Judaism with living the life of a Gentile, and if an
individual need not convert to Judaism in order to be a good person

and live virtuously? He or she can do that quite easily as a non-Jew. However, if the individual has a deep and committed wish to become a Jew, then the conversion process is designed to make it possible.

A rabbi convinced of the prospective *ger's* sincerity may allow him or her to follow the process of *gerut*. For traditional Jews, this involves appearing before a Jewish religious court known as a *beth din*, consisting generally of three judges to be tested and formally accepted. A person who converts formally to Judaism under the auspices of a halakhically constituted and recognized court receives at the culmination of the process a certificate of conversion. One of the unusual aspects of the Reform movement is to actually welcome converts, and in the Pittsburgh Program, the founding principles of the movement, this is stated quite clearly but then, of course, the movement was setting out to distinguish itself from other forms of Judaism. The requirements of Reform Judaism for conversion are generally lighter than with the other denominations, and vary according to the local rabbi and community. Circumcision and immersion in a *mikveh* are not generally required, but there will be a course of study and induction into Jewish practices and worship, which over a period will qualify an individual for conversion.

The Amoraim who produced the Talmud set out three requirements for a *gerut* to Judaism (*Keritot* 8b), which must be witnessed and affirmed by a *beth din*. These include circumcision (*brit milah* or *hatafat dam brit*) for men, immersion (*tevilah*) in a ritual bath (*mikveh*) for both men and women, and offering a sacrifice (*korban*) in the Temple (the *Bayt Hamikdash*) – this requirement is deferred while the Temple does not exist, until such time as it may be rebuilt. The consensus of halakhic authorities also requires a convert to understand and accept the duties of the *halakhah*, classical Jewish religious law. This is sometimes assessed by a test or an interview. The result, of course, is that the convert generally knows a lot more about Judaism than those who are born Jews. Yet it is worth pointing out also that the standard response to potential converts is not to ask them what beliefs they are going to affirm, but rather why they want to join the Jewish people, given the harsh way in which Jews are often treated by others. This brings out nicely the fact that Judaism is just as much, or even more, an ethnic identity as a religion. After confirming that all these requirements have been met, the *beth din* issues a certificate of *gerut* certifying that the person is now a Jew.

There was a lot of discussion about conversion in the Roman Empire before the Mishnah began to formulate rules, and from accounts that exist, there was quite a strong interest in converting to Judaism. The debate, as always, was between those who sought to make it difficult and those who were in favor of a more lenient approach. A big issue, and one that Christianity did well out of, was physical circumcision, which must have put off many men, and there is some evidence that it was mainly women who converted during this period. R. Joshua argued that, beside accepting Jewish beliefs and laws, a prospective Jew must undergo immersion in a *mikveh*. In contrast, R. Eliezer makes circumcision a condition for the *gerut*. A similar controversy between the School of Shammai and that of Hillel is given (*Shabbat* 137a) regarding a proselyte born without a foreskin: the former demanding the spilling of a drop of blood of the covenant; the latter declaring it to be unnecessary. The rigorous view is echoed in the Midrash: 'If your sons accept my divinity I shall be their God and bring them into the land; but if they do not observe my covenant in regard either to circumcision or to the Sabbath, they shall not enter the promised land' (*Genesis Rabbah* xlvi). There is the even more unfriendly 'The Sabbath-keepers who are not circumcised are intruders, and deserve punishment' (*Midrash Deut Rabbah* 1.21).

In the USA, Reform Judaism rejects the concept that any rules or rituals should be considered necessary for *gerut*. But there has been a tendency for Reform to come closer to traditional Judaism in modern times, and so more stringent requirements for conversion are often applied nowadays. American Reform Judaism does not require ritual immersion in a *mikveh*, circumcision or acceptance of *mitzvot* as normative, since these are not rituals they regard as important in any case. Appearance before a *beth din* is recommended, but is not considered necessary. Converts are asked to commit to religious standards set by the local Reform community. Various forms of Liberal Judaism in Israel, the UK and other countries reject this approach. Many Liberal rabbis in these countries hold that it is necessary for a man to have a *brit milah* or *brit dam*, that both men and women require immersion in a *mikveh*, and that the *gerut* must only be allowed at the end of a formal course of study, before a *beth din*. This is a common view among many Reform rabbis in Canada and the UK, as well as a small but growing number in the USA.

Halakhah forbids the mistreatment of the convert, including reminding a convert that he or she was once not a Jew, and hence little distinction is made in Judaism between those who are born Jewish and those who are Jewish as a result of *gerut*. However, despite *halakhah* protecting the rights of *gerim*, some Jewish communities have been accused of treating converts as second-class Jews. According to Orthodox interpretations of *halakhah*, converts face a limited number of restrictions. A marriage between a female *ger* and a *kohen* (members of the priestly class) is prohibited, and any children of the union do not inherit their father's *kohen* status. While a Jew by birth may not marry a *mamzer* (someone who is the product of the union of people who are not officially married according to Judaism), a convert can marry a *mamzer*. King David is descended from Ruth, a convert. (*Ruth* 4.13–22). In Orthodox and Conservative communities that maintain tribal distinctions, converts become *Yisraelim*, ordinary Jews with no tribal or inter-Jewish distinctions.

Talmudic opinions on *gerim* are numerous; some positive, some negative. A famous quote from the Talmud labels the convert 'Hard on Israel as a blight' (*Yevamot* 47b). Many interpretations explain this quote as meaning that converts can be unobservant and lead Jews to be the same, or converts can be so observant that born Jews feel ashamed. The latter appears more likely, given the enthusiasm of converts for their new religion. Today, the term 'Jew by choice' is often the label that converts give themselves. But a real problem exists in the different rules and regulations that exist within the Jewish world, and this has implications for who counts as a Jew, who can be buried in a Jewish cemetery, who can marry another Jew and so on, and in particular has even more serious implications under Israeli law. Even within the orthodox community there are many disagreements about which apparently orthodox conversions are acceptable, and so there is no possibility that amity across the denominations will ever exist.

Conversion from Judaism

During the onslaught on the Jewish community in Christian Europe, two charges were often repeated by the Christian side of the debate: that one should not dignify the debate as a debate in the sense that it was hardly a free exchange of views – the result was always going to be the overwhelming of the Jews by the Christians; and there was no real willingness on either side to be persuaded by the other. But the Christian charges are serious and deserve to be considered seriously, and they were. The first is that Judaism takes too literal an approach to the Bible and thus misses out on the real meaning of what is contained within it. The second is that Judaism is too material a religion, a defect that is rectified by Christianity. In fact, in the view of many Muslim commentators on the two earlier versions of the truth, as they see it, this approach is very much accepted, with Christianity being seen as too spiritual, and Judaism as too material. Islam is the religion in the middle, as it were, balancing the two extremes and getting it right. This identification of Judaism with materialism is a protracted theme in anti-Jewish polemics, and survives to the present day. It is worth looking at the implications of this accusation, especially as it was developed in the period of Iberian history when Christianity was recovering its power and no longer felt the need to put up with religious minorities within its realms.

The two charges are, of course, linked. If one takes a literal attitude to something, then one regards the material account to be relevant in explaining what is meant by the text, and this is not easily distinguished from being what might be called materialistic. As we know, though, a good deal of Jewish commentary on texts is far from literal, in the sense that Abraham ibn Ezra and Moses Maimonides, two great Iberian exegetes, produced quite fanciful interpretations of the Bible, by any stretch of the imagination. It has to be said that there is no general Jewish interpretation of the way that interpretation ought to take place, and some Jewish thinkers, like Maimonides, had a rather critical view of the matter and all that was involved with it, and a distinct penchant for asceticism, something that was only emphasized later by his son and grandson. After Christianity proved to be so effective a counter-force to Judaism, the latter even developed some doctrines that copied the new religion, like a sudden interest in the afterlife and the immortality of some element, whether body or soul or both. It is a bit strange that the Christians were particularly exercised by the Talmud, since this is a work that takes on occasion a very non-literal view of scripture. The facts are clear. Both Jews and Christians interpreted what they each regarded as their basic religious texts, and the debate was really about what sorts of interpretation ought to be accepted and what should be avoided. The Jews were often left to answer a ragbag of minor complaints about what the Talmud says about Jesus, and about how Gentiles are to be treated, what they think God is unable to do, and a whole variety of accusations based on Jewish texts often taken out of context or misrepresented entirely. The fact that some of the Christians attempting to convert the Jews had originally been Jewish did not generally raise the tone of the 'debate', though some of their objections are well chosen and must have been quite effective in the debate. Abner of Burgos is a particularly thoughtful interlocutor, but on the whole they were challenged quite effectively by many of the Jewish representatives, who did not, of course, have much difficulty in refuting the more outrageous charges against them. It is always difficult to know what to say when different religious claims are put up against each other as though they were arguing, when what they really need to be doing is more along the lines of defining what their main principles are, and then offering them up in competition as more or less accurate descriptions of the truth.

One of the effects of this defense of interpretation is the search for the basic principles or roots of religion. This was a continuing project in Judaism, only eschewed by a few thinkers such as Isaac Abravanel. It is not obvious how this is linked with the charge of literalism, but when one reads what thinkers such as Maimonides and Joseph Albo say about what they are doing, it is clear that they at least declare what they see as the significance of what they are doing in such straightened conditions. When one's religion is under attack, and skilled debaters seek to undermine it, one needs a clear and confident account of the faith, even perhaps a summary of it, to help maintain one's adherence to the faith. After all, Islam and Christianity both have creeds, and one of the reasons why Judaism has survived so long despite the constant pressure on it from competing religions is its ability to adapt by incorporating to a degree what it finds desirable in its competitors. While attempts at constructing creeds were designed to bring the religion down to its basic parts that then could be defended, presumably the idea initially was to give co-religionists a perspicuous grasp of what they should seek to defend and what their religion is really all about. It is a matter of seeing the wood for the trees, and without that sort of knowledge one can easily get lost and perhaps stray into an inappropriate environment completely.

This has nothing to do with the so-called literalism of Judaism, but, on the contrary, with defending a particular interpretation of the Bible and the Law that develops out of it. There is no reason why the tools of the enemy should not be employed in this regard, to develop a view of Judaism that meshes both with what is seen as tradition and avoids the charges drawn up against it. What we tend to concentrate on when looking at debate between religions is the ways in which they emphasize the differences between them; so, for example, Judaism tends to be rather scornful of doctrines such as that of the Trinity and the notion of Jesus as the Messiah. What is more interesting, though, is the emphasis on what unites them; in particular, the basic adherence to monotheism, and the elevated position of the Jewish Bible and its putative role in pointing toward the following revelations, if they were, by Jesus and later through the Prophet Muhammad. From a Christian point of view, the Jews and the Christians all start on the same journey, but the Jews stop too soon; while for Muslims, both Jews and Christians stop too soon, and in doing so they also damage the integrity of the revelations they received. The Jews stopped a long way behind the Christians, and do not even adhere to the Law they were given by God according to Islam, for which he punishes them, but they pretend to find it difficult to understand how to observe that Law. The second sura of the Qur'an, The Cow, goes into this at some length, so the literalism of the Jews is only apparent. They do not really want to observe the strict letter of the Law; they want to give the impression that the Law is so complicated that they have no idea what they are supposed to do, and so avoid blame for not doing it! A result of this is that God punishes them by making them wander in the desert for so long, and subsequently, according to much Muslim exegesis.

The search for roots and basic principles is part of responding to these claims, and they are not, it has to be said, ridiculous claims at all. Whatever one thinks of the claims of Christianity, it does seem rather arbitrary for Jews to deny that any prophet could arise after the last of the biblical prophets, and a whole range of different people have been widely recognized to be the Messiah. Some of these beliefs persist in the face of the most obvious failure of their mission, something that could be said of Jesus also. The point of laying out the axioms of a particular religion is to suggest that the practices of that faith are linked not just to tradition and the familiar ways of doing things but more significantly to a set of ideas and principles that the practice actually embodies in some way. The important idea is that these principles of Judaism are not much different from those of Christianity and Islam, something Jews are said not to appreciate and so they go about doing things in the wrong sort of way.

This might seem to be wrong, since the Christians at the time argued that the Jews failed to make the right connection with the teaching of Jesus, sent after all initially to the Jews, his community, and so the Jews are left with the wrong set of principles. But on the whole there was general acceptance among its enemies that Judaism as a religion had just stopped developing when it should have gone in a Christian direction, and by implication the principles from which it started were acceptable. So how is it a helpful strategy in trying to resist Christianity to emphasize such a point that the Christians themselves were propounding? It is useful because it suggests that whatever else can be said in favor of Christianity, it is not something that fundamentally affects the basis of Judaism. The Christians believe in one God (sort of), in the divine origin of the Torah and in a system of reward and punishment, and so do the Jews, according to Albo in the fifteenth century. His discussion of the afterlife has attracted a lot of criticism in the commentaries on it, since he appears to waver between those thinkers who believe in a purely spiritual afterlife and those who insist the body is also involved. But his point is not to come down on one side or the other, it is just to show that there is such a general notion in Judaism and a lot stems from it. So it is wrong for the Christians to assert that Judaism does not have a powerful notion of an afterlife; when it became necessary, Judaism quickly developed one, and so the charge of materialism cannot make much headway, at least when talking about the afterlife. Similarly, the charge that Jews do not recognize the lack of necessity of pursuing all the laws in the Torah does seem like a small detail, given the very general agreement between the religions on many significant fundamental principles, or so Albo would have us believe. As a rhetorical device, this could go in two ways, one of which would be to suggest that, if Judaism and Christianity are in agreement on many fundamental issues, then why not convert if it is advantageous to do so? The other way it could be taken would be to suggest that unless one happened to accept as true the additional beliefs that Christians needed to recognize, why bother to convert?

Fighting Conversion with Pictures

It is remarkable, given the huge pressure for conversion, that more Jews did not convert, though many of course did. It is interesting to compare the fate of the Dönmeh in Turkey and the Frankists in Poland. Jacob Frank (1726–91) was a follower of Shabetai Zvi, who left Turkey around 1755 or so for Poland, in an attempt to gain followers for the messianic cause. There he was strenuously opposed by the rabbis, and the fact that the group were totally rejected by the Jews made them join the Roman Catholic Church in large numbers. By contrast with the Dönmeh, the Frankists are regarded as having disappeared into the general population, even in a country so unsympathetic to Jews as Poland, but even after conversion the former Jews had very different experiences, based on the religion and Turkish culture they had joined, or thought they had.

One might think that resistance to conversion in Iberia was because many Jews had a strong sense of separateness because of their position in the peninsula, and did not want to jeopardize that for the new religion, but when we look at the lifestyle of Jews in the Iberian peninsula it seems to resemble very closely that of their Christian and Muslim peers. They spoke and wrote in the local languages, wore locally popular styles of clothing, and as far as material culture was concerned, adopted the Spanish style of art and architecture. As far as we can tell, the synagogues of the period closely resembled the religious buildings of the majority communities, and the illustration of religious books, in particular the *haggadot* for Passover, are remarkably close to contemporary Christian religious illustrated works. Given the critique of Judaism as materialistic, it is difficult not to see them as defiant celebrations of ordinary life at the time, displaying as they do scenes of eating, drinking, preparing food, wearing fine clothes and following the normal occupations of people in town, preparing for and enjoying the festival. One assumes that the illustrators were often, if not exclusively, Christian, since they follow exactly the style of the Christian books of this kind; and no doubt their Jewish patrons had told them the sorts of themes they wanted produced, and expected them to produce these in the style of the time – that is, in the Christian style. There is, for example, in the products of Iberian culture no hesitancy about the human body or face, even within a Jewish community that in other places was a bit more reticent in this regard. These books bring out how integrated culturally the Jews thought themselves to be, while at the same time holding on to their distinctive religious and ethnic identity, in so far as they were allowed to. As we know, when cultures feel themselves to be under pressure there is a tendency for individuals to feel a pull toward tradition and the old certainties, and there was certainly a move away from philosophy toward kabbalah and a narrower religiosity at the time. However, these books represent a retreat, perhaps, into the enjoyment of religious events and what is associated with them, as a way of revalidating these before the community and its members. In the same way that the upper echelons of Christian society could pay for the production of fine illustrated volumes celebrating the major themes of their faith and its rituals, so the Jews could copy them and in so doing brought out the religious meaning, for them, of the everyday material activities of ordinary life. It was this, of course, that represented the precise target of many of the Christian polemics against the Jews.

This is not to deny that the Christian iconography of the time did not equally celebrate the everyday events of the lives of the Christians, and, of course, their lives and those of their Jewish peers were very similar. For the Christians as well as for the Jews, many of the characters illustrated are wearing the clothes of the period and carrying out the customary activities of ordinary people – cooking, cleaning, building and so on. The themes are, of course, often different, but sometimes in ways that seem obviously to contrast, with the *matzah*, for example, often serving as a counterpoint, in Jewish books, to the Eucharist in Christian ones. Both books often bear some official regal or municipal seal to indicate the official connections of their owners and commissioners. It is sometimes argued that the preponderance of children in the Jewish books are designed to contrast with the Virgin Mary and her one child, and with the ideal of virginity, very much not an ideal in Jewish thought. There are plenty of family scenes in the Jewish books, often linked with the Bible and its main characters, yet it seems to be rather far-fetched to represent this as specifically designed to contrast with Christianity. In the Christian books there are also plenty of families when their presence is called for by the topic, and surely the ordinary lives of the readers of these books were just as involved with children and domestic affairs as those of their Jewish peers. One should always be cautious in ascribing meaning to images at a point in time so distant from us today, and where there is so little corroborative evidence, but it is certainly plausible to think that more was going on here than merely the copying of the hegemonic culture's style of illustration. We need to think about how any culture seeks to survive within the context of another that has a leading role in the state, and is still able to preserve some aspects of its distinctiveness – we can clearly see this in the illustrations of the Spanish *haggadot*. They use the symbolism of the general Christian culture, but obviously use it to validate the Jewish way of looking at the world, and in particular what we might here call materialism – the notion that the world is there to be enjoyed and was created by God in that way. They tend, like the haggadah itself, not to be directed at the next world, though there is nothing in them to deny the existence of such a world, yet by contrast with a lot of Christian themes that involve heaven and hell, they are firmly directed at Jewish history and the events described in the haggadah itself, plus the production of many of the Passover items that are to be consumed during the festival itself. We do need to bear in mind that the modern custom of having a family meal on the first two nights of the Passover is of quite recent origin, and that the festival and the haggadah were apparently used in the synagogue for a long time, with the meal following a communal meeting there for prayer; and so the *seder* did not necessarily have the sort of meaning that it does for modern Jews. This actually makes the point even more strongly that, in their emphasis on materialism, the Jews of the time were setting out to celebrate an aspect of their lives as participants in a religious tradition, not just a familiar social event that emphasizes to a degree food and drink. Food and drink are represented since they are part of the religious ritual, and in the *haggadot* they are portrayed joyfully and intimately, perhaps as a way of defying the overwhelming forces that surrounded them and wished to destroy them and their practices, both physically and intellectually.

We might raise the question of how we know that these representations of ordinary material life are about vindicating ordinary material Jewish life, by contrast with the alternatives? And of course we do not know, and we shall only be able to argue that this is a plausible interpretation of what is going on here. Many interpreters of the iconography of these images are very sure of what they represent, and what each item in them stands for, and one can only admire their certainty in such an interpretative process. This is

far from the approach adopted here, and yet we should take on board
the idea that a culture that is not generally illustrated visually will
take a particular pleasure in it. This is especially the case if it can
copy, or at least use, the paradigms of the dominant, hostile culture.
Whatever the rights and wrongs of the different iconographic
approaches, the general idea that we like to see what we do displayed
in pictures, especially when what we do is criticized by the state, is
surely a sound notion. Making a culture visible validates it, in the
view (a term not chosen lightly here) of many of its practitioners.

One of the features of medieval Christian society is that, as time
went on, the books and their patrons became more widely available
down the social scale, so that whereas they began with the aristocracy
and even the royal family, they eventually became the valued
possessions of the wealthy bourgeoisie. The Jews also wanted to
participate in the activity of illustrating books, or at least owning
them and displaying them, and in Spain many of the books that
survived have some royal or city seal, boasting of the high
connections of the owner and giving them some sort of official
imprimatur, a sort of secular *hechsher* that this was something
appropriate and important. A book is ultimately a possession, one of
the things that the Jews were criticized for valuing, and the *haggadot*
displayed the possessions of Jewish history and culture, how they
overcame their enemies and were rescued by God when in great
danger of disaster in the past. The pictures in the *haggadot* often
portray relevant biblical scenes, but just as often do not, containing a
litany of Jewish biblical history that celebrate the notion of Jewish
continuity and existence over time, precisely what was being attacked
so fiercely in many periods of Jewish life in the Christian world. Sed-
Rajna notes, quite rightly, that the sequence of illustrations in many
haggadot have nothing to do with the Passover story, and seem to
come from elsewhere and to be prepared for a different sort of book
(1992, 144). It would be better to say that they are not there precisely
to illustrate the Passover story, but to validate the whole institution on
which the story is based, and we should not take modern ideas about
what should be in a haggadah as definitive for all time, pictorially
speaking. While the text may be fixed, the art certainly is not. The
pictures are there to celebrate Jewish life and the way that Jews see the
Bible and the stories in the Midrash attached to it. They represent a
form of resistance to the Christian hegemony of the time even more

The Israelites crossing the sea, and Miriam's song

powerfully than the counter-arguments of the Jews at the disputations. So we see the Pharaoh not drowning in the crossing of the sea of reeds, very much a facet of the Midrash, and the willowy Israelite women dancing in celebration under Miriam's direction.

There is a tendency to concentrate on the arguments between the different religions when conversion was at issue, as well as the issue of force that was often applied to the weaker religion in order to induce its members to convert. It is quite right that we should spend time on these topics, since they are very important, but what is also important are the decisions of the individuals concerned to devise ways of fighting off the pressure to convert that were probably based not on intellectual arguments nor on an objective consideration of the advantages and disadvantages of changing religious allegiance, but rather on a stubborn disinclination to abandon tradition and well-established ways of doing things for something different coming from an oppressive force. What is helpful in this attempt at holding on to the past is some way of representing it, either visually or in some other, perhaps literary way, and that will not necessarily involve a different sort of representation, just a different topic from the norm. In fact, it is very important that the form of representation is the same as that of the leading culture of the time, since that means that the deviant story can be displayed so as to appear quite normal. This suggests to those in the subservient culture that while the story is indeed different, it cannot be so dissimilar, and is deserving of respect, at least in their own eyes. This validates their resistance, and cocks a snook at the symbols of oppression and authority, while at the same time appearing to accede to its hegemony. There is nothing specifically Jewish about this – minorities who are oppressed, or regard themselves as oppressed, have often followed this strategy and continue to do so today. We may note the parody that characterizes the performance, but we may also observe that ordinary people trying to live their lives in conditions of difficulty do what they can to achieve a state of normalcy despite the hostile pressures, and this means trying to find a modus vivendi with those pressures. The most frequent way of doing this in Jewish history was to try to remain Jewish, while finding something in the local culture that could be used to facilitate this.

It is difficult to over-emphasize the significance of what we see. Moses was called a remarkable prophet, since he was apparently the only person who has seen God face to face, and Job came to understand the divine message when he said that he saw God, compared to just hearing about him. The important feature of sight is that it makes something stand out in front of us in a way that makes it difficult to doubt. It calls not only on our intellect but also on our emotions, not that our other senses cannot do this, of course; yet seeing something is surely the most direct form of experience familiar to human beings. When Jews first saw their ordinary activities portrayed in books in non-hostile ways, it must have had an impact on them. When they saw themselves represented much as the Christians represented themselves and their history, it must have had an even deeper impact. For a culture that was about to have to leave, or to go into hiding or convert, this would all become a source of nostalgia, but must have played a role in sustaining the morale of those vulnerable to the powerful forces that were to engulf them.

Chapter VI

Issues

The Jews have Always Longed to Return to Israel

We are often told that the Jews have always longed to return to Israel, but there is no evidence to support this idea. It is mentioned a great deal in the traditional prayer service, but largely as part of the messianic age and the rebuilding of the Temple. The Reform movement tended to be disapproving of such aspirations, seeing the original countries of Jews today as their appropriate homes, though in recent times there has been a move toward a more enthusiastic approach to Zionism. Some traditional Jews are also critical of the idea of returning to Israel without the leadership of the Messiah, seeing devotion to a piece of land as standing in the way of devotion to religion. The most significant factor to mention here, though, is the simple fact that since the State of Israel was formed, Jews can return to Israel, yet most do not even when no obstacles exist for such a move. It is difficult, then, to suggest that there is this universal aspiration, since an aspiration that can be realized quite easily, and is not, hardly deserves the name of an aspiration. Even 25 centuries ago, when Ezra and other Jews from Babylon returned to the Land of Israel, few others accompanied them, though they could quite easily have done so. One even wonders whether all the Israelites in Egypt left with Moses, or whether many stayed, and the unenthusiastic comments of the Israelites on their journey through the desert suggests that not all were committed to the task on which they were engaged – to move to the land that God had promised to them.

There was a cynical description of Zionism before the State of Israel came about, as a process through which one Jew gave money to another Jew so that a third Jew could move to Palestine. The connection between Jews in the diaspora and Jews in Israel is complex. Most Jews in the diaspora are concerned with Israel in the sense that they hope it flourishes, and they will support it when it is in trouble. On the other hand, they show little enthusiasm for going there to live. Some Jews, a small minority but significant nevertheless, are staunch opponents of Israel and Zionism as a whole. They are perhaps linked to the original Jewish movements that were opposed to Zionism. These were sometimes religious and based on the idea that Israel should only be re-established through the intervention of the Messiah, when God decides the time is right: anything else is heretical. Or they were secular and socialist, and argued that the Jews should throw in their lot with the local progressive movement, and not seek to distinguish themselves by opting for a move to a distant country. Today, both groups are far smaller than they were. Until the Nazi period, the prospect of a national home for Jews in Palestine seemed very remote indeed to most Jews, and perhaps also not that desirable, since in many cases they were well established in their own countries. The way in which Europe suddenly seemed to turn its back on the Jews, and the rest of the world with it, during the Nazi onslaught was a shock that provoked a reaction in terms of a new enthusiasm for the idea of a country that would be specifically Jewish. There was a popular saying among German Jews who went to Israel in the 1930s that they were not there because of Zionism, but because of Hitler. They would have preferred in most cases to continue with their established lives and careers in Germany, but given that they could not, Israel was a reasonable alternative, and they often did what they could to create in Israel a version of the Germany they had left.

After the dire facts of the Holocaust became known, the Jewish population in the diaspora revolted against the idea that the Jews who had survived the massacres in Europe were now being prevented from going to Palestine by the British holders of the mandate. They put so much pressure on the President of the USA that he reacted with rather typical anti-Semitic remarks on how he was being treated by those selfish Jews! The near disaster of the War of Independence in 1947–8 – which Israel should really have lost and the Jews there would then have had a very uncertain future, if any – further engaged diaspora Jewry. The successes and reverses of the next few decades meant that it was difficult not to identify with this small, vulnerable country (in the eyes of most Jews), surrounded as it was by large and powerful enemies. The situation of Israel in the Middle East closely represented, it seemed, the situation of the Jewish minority in the diaspora in former times: threatened, wildly outnumbered and the target of prolonged hostility.

Prayer and the Synagogue became More Significant after the Temples were Destroyed

For a time, what we now call Judaism had its roots in a ritual based on the Temples in Jerusalem. These roots are remembered in the rituals of the prayer book and on particular festivals such as Yom Kippur, at least in traditional communities. Yet it is worth remembering that the Temple period was quite short, in relative terms, in that most Jewish or Israelite history took place either before the Temples were built and rebuilt, or after they were both destroyed.

The institution of the Temples put a certain group of people in charge of the religion, and there must have been opposition to this level of authority, especially since it had financial advantages. The centralization of the religion on the Temple and Jerusalem must also have annoyed some, as well as the noise and bustle of the Temple events themselves. The rabbis in the Talmud spend a lot of time talking about the magnificence of the Temple, yet it is possible that, for many, life around them would have palled, or seemed far less significant than more restrained activities such as small groups of people praying and carrying out rituals in their own environment. Maimonides certainly implies that the Temple and its ceremonies represented an important period in the development of Judaism, but one that was well past by his time, and the idea of resurrecting those ceremonies and going back to the sacrifices would no doubt have seemed strange. The point of religion is to move people's thinking along a continuum from an earlier period, when it is cruder, to a more perfect level, a move for Maimonides from doing things in huge groups to reducing the size of the groups, until finally people are by themselves and contemplate silently what is higher than them.

To a certain extent, quite the opposite occurred when the Temple was destroyed, in that the Sadducees were quite rapidly overtaken by the Pharisees, and this created a more complex form of Judaism, since in many ways the Oral Law came to represent the Temple and its ceremonies. The Sadducees were more reliant on the Written

Law, and priests were closely linked with the ways in which the rules of that Law were to be carried out in the Temple, but once there were no Temples they became rather superfluous and their beliefs too abstract in the public's mind to replace the Temples and their ceremonies. They were contemptuous of the often imaginative aggadic nature of much of the Oral Law, and perceived clearly how many of the Pharisaic doctrines on the afterlife had no connection to the written text of the Jewish Bible. Yet, without the Temple, were the Pharisees not correct in thinking that something needed to be installed in the public imagination to maintain the link with religion once the institution and building of the Temple was no more? Even magic could seem a tempting option when the central institutions of the religion are no longer functioning.

Magic pot: Demon surrounded by magical Hebrew incantations, Nippur 1000 CE

In a moving poem from the eleventh century, Gershom Meor ha-Golah has this verse:

> The holy city and its environs
> Are exposed to derision and plunder
> All its treasures are buried and hidden
> And nothing remains except this Torah

By Torah, he certainly meant the oral as well as the written Torah, since he was an important figure in both the French and German Talmudic colleges, and the Oral Law can be seen as an important displacement activity for Jerusalem and its Temple rites. Here we need to take seriously the ways in which religions set out to change the pattern of thinking of their followers. In Exodus 11.2, God asks the Hebrews to borrow from their neighbors gold and silver articles, and in the picture from the haggadah in Chapter I of this book we clearly see them carrying away gold and silver objects. These seem strange things to want when leaving a country quickly, especially if the Hebrews are going to spend a lot of time in a desert, as God surely knew he had this in mind for them. Yanai in the Talmud suggests this was to keep a promise made to Abraham, that when his descendants left Egypt, they would be wealthy (*Berakhot* 9a–b), referring to *Gen* 15.14. Perhaps it was to put the period of slavery behind them, and by taking these valuable items as symbolic payment for their past work, the Hebrews could start thinking of themselves in a new way, as free people. The midrash on Exodus suggests that this was a difficult task for the Hebrews, to go to their former masters and get them to pay for what in the past they had done for nothing. This put them on the path to reversing their lack of enthusiasm with which they had greeted Moses and his mission in the beginning (*Ex* 6.9). When they went through the desert, the Hebrews often had periods of being depressed and regretting having left Egypt, thinking back nostalgically to how relatively comfortable life had been in a country where at least they were fed and were able to drink. According to Maimonides, they spent 40 years in the desert in order to change their thinking processes from those of slaves to those of free people, since such a change is a gradual process. What is really important here is imagination, developing new ways of thinking about oneself, and a way of starting the process is by taking things from your oppressors. This begins to make you think you can be in control. The gold and silver were symbols of the new people who were leaving the country to go elsewhere. In reality, the great treasure they were going to receive on leaving the country is often taken by the commentators to be the Law they are going to receive. The gold and silver is a material indication of something even more valuable, but less material, that is in prospect.

Once the Temple was destroyed, the Jews needed a new symbol to represent who they were and how they should relate to God. It is

really the Oral Law, not the synagogue, that stepped into this important role. The Oral Law is full of *aggadah*, of stories designed to flesh
out the character of the Bible and the Mishnah, and these provide the
reader with the imaginative basis of exploring their relationship with
God. These stories are supplemented by other stories, stories from the
Kabbalah, the Jewish mystical literature, and from later thinkers, all of
whom sought to affect readers in their attempts to understand what
they should do and how they should pray now that the prayer HQ, as
it were, was gone. Often, though, when the headquarters are
destroyed, the campaign that was led from it continues, and with
redoubled vigor. This certainly happened with Judaism, and in one of
those ironies that history seems to delight in presenting, it is happening today in exactly the same way with the Palestinians. The Israeli
army scores one crushing victory after another against the Palestinians
in their various political and military permutations, and yet they are
not only not destroyed, but seem to be ever more powerful and determined. And the Israelis are increasingly puzzled. Should the
Palestinians not by now have given up the struggle, they wonder? The
fact is that, just as the Jews for thousands of years had in their minds an
imaginative narrative of their links with the Land of Israel and their
eventual return to that territory, so do the Arabs, and what fortified
the Jews in what they now perceive as being their long and ultimately
successful struggle is just as likely to fortify the Arabs.

Though Maimonides severely criticizes imagination (Leaman,
1988) and its role in coming to know things worth knowing, it is
vital in religion. There is an interesting rabbinic response by Rabbi
Shlomo Duran, the son of the distinguished thinker Shimon Duran,
to the question of whether worshippers should remove their shoes in
the synagogue, as Muslims do in the mosque. The questioner refers
to Maimonides' saying that this was not necessary. The reply is that
one should go by the rule of the area in which the synagogue is situated. In the Christian world, keeping your shoes on does not mark a
lack of respect for the building in which one goes, but in the Muslim
world it does. What is important here are the local conditions that
prevail and what implications they have for what counts as respect
(*Responsa* 38). Why are the local conditions relevant? They are relevant since they reflect how people think.

In the past, the idea of returning to Israel played a part in binding
the community together, and it was mentioned (and still is) in many

prayers and practices. Today, when it is an easy process for Jews to return to Israel, many prefer not to, so they need something else to value as an aim, and for many this is support for Israel and its struggle against its many enemies. Often they have in mind not a real country with the usual range of problems that countries have, but an idealized place where the desert was made to flower and the people nobly defend the land against a ferocious foe. Imagination works with ideal conceptions and constructs them to organize and orient our thinking. Yet we should beware of assuming that, just because some idea is often mentioned in the liturgy and otherwise, it is really an important motivating notion. It may be, but it is unlikely to work in that way as it is simply presented, and once one qualifies the idea and sees exactly how it is understood by different constituencies in the community, it loses its clear and direct role in unifying those in the group.

A final point worth making is that Jews have often, both in the past and the present, been rather proud of where they are living, or where they have come from, rather than particularly eager to return to Israel. For example, Maimonides often used al-Qurtubi as part of his name, the Cordoban (referring directly to his father). Hermann Cohen (1842–1918), in his opposition to Zionism, suggested that Germany was the promised land for the Jews, not the Land of Israel. There is a certain pride in Babylon in this Talmudic verse: 'When the Torah was forgotten in Israel, Ezra came from Babylon to restore it, when it was forgotten again Hillel the Babylonian came to restore it, and when it was forgotten once more, Rabbi Hiyya and his sons came from there and organized it once more' (*Sukkah* 20a). Yet Babylon was a place the Jews were taken to as prisoners and the first Temple was also destroyed by the Babylonians, so it is interesting that the place should be held in such high esteem. Even when there was another Temple in existence, most Jews seemed to have stayed quite happily in Babylon, and so it seems that synagogues and prayer could coexist quite easily with the existence of the Temple of the time. Hence it is probably not true to say that they only flourished in the absence of the Temple.

Judaism is a Religion based on Common Beliefs and Principles

There is a protracted controversy in Judaism as to whether the religion is based on a creed. Some influential thinkers believe it is and others that it is not, and in fact what we have here is a general issue about religions. Do religions base themselves on certain principles that cannot be altered and which define them, or are they far looser bodies of practice and belief? Religious authorities tend to argue for the former, since it is the basis of their status. They can then interpret and explain the basic axioms of the religion. It also very much accords with our intuitions about religion, but here, as so often, our intuitions let us down.

According to Maimonides, there are 13 principles of Judaism (see his commentary on the Mishnah, tractate *Sanhedrin*, chapter 10). These are:

- Belief in the existence of an independent creator
- The unity of the creator
- God has no body, so any anthropomorphic language used to describe him is merely to help us get an idea of what, from our perspective, he is like. It is not to be taken literally
- He existed before everything and will exist when everything comes to an end
- Only God should be worshipped, not anything he creates
- The prophets are perfect and have tremendous intelligence
- Moses is by far the greatest of the prophets
- The Torah comes from heaven
- It is complete and should not be added to nor anything taken away from it
- God knows whatever we do
- God rewards those who obey his commandments and punishes those who do not
- The Messiah will come
- The dead will be resurrected.

The trouble with any such list is that it is difficult to know how to interpret it, and as Maimonides produces these tenets of the religion he is obliged himself to explain briefly what he means by these principles, and to indicate that if he were to explain them properly it would take a long time. So it is not at all clear what it means to say that every Jew must accept such principles, since it is not clear what they are committing themselves to believing in and accepting that they are true.

When talking about a number of different languages, the Jerusalem Talmud comments, 'Aramaic for lamentation and Hebrew for speech' (*Megillah* 1.9). This brings out a feature of Hebrew – at least as it appears in much of the Bible – that it is on the whole a clear and fairly down-to-earth language. It is very good for describing things, especially things that were important to people at that time and place – the weather, the landscape, the livestock, how people reacted to events and so on. There is a great confidence in the ability of language to get things done and to communicate, throughout the Bible and in later commentaries on it. Mystics tend to argue that language is not enough, that we also need forms of special experience and more direct contact with the supernatural, and that language has to be analyzed with special interpretive mechanisms that can show us the secrets that lie within it. As so often, though, this is not the standard view of the use of language in the Bible. It should certainly be explored and plumbed, and is by the commentators, and connections are drawn between terms in unusual and indirect ways, sometimes even by transposing letters or juggling with the numerical value of different terms; and a distinction is often drawn between four accounts of meaning.

A term may have four forms of analysis: *peshat, remez, derash* and *sod*. The first is the plain literal meaning; the second uses allusion; the third parable; and the last refers to a secret, and so is the most obscure meaning. The four initial letters of each word are used in the term *pardes* (significantly, perhaps, not originally a Hebrew word), or paradise, literally a garden but here referring to the garden of paradise. It is important to apply all these different ways of looking at meaning, since if only the first three are used, the initials make up the word *pered*, or mule, and *Psalms* 32.9 is quite clear on the intellectual limitations of that animal! This suggests that, if you stick to the ordinary level of interpretation, you really do not get very far, and Maimonides, for example, is quite critical of the ordinary believer and his/her limited grasp of what s/he does, and why. But he is not appealing here to a deeper mystical knowledge that should be more generally available – quite the contrary; he is advocating that religious people should embrace, as part of their religion, being self-aware. In the same way as moral individuals should ask themselves why they do what they do, since this is part of morality, not just the blind following of rules, so followers of a religion have a duty, according to Maimonides, not only to read their holy book, but should also discuss it and try to work out its implications.

Hebrew is the language of speech, we are told in the Jerusalem
Talmud. This means it is a way of understanding how people communicate with each other, and provides users themselves with a
channel of communication. Hardly surprisingly, there is among the
commentators a great pride in the Hebrew language, the unique
possession of the Jews, and something they wanted to defend no
doubt when their co-religionists were attracted to other languages
such as Greek and Aramaic. When we examine some of the very
complex and sophisticated approaches to the Hebrew language
among the commentators, we need to recall the basic premise from
which they began, which is that the language is clear and perspicuous, and a reader or listener can readily work out what is being said
and meant. Learning a language is often a matter of rote, learning
rules, memorizing spellings and so on, and learning Hebrew is
exactly like that, yet the emphasis on education in the early Jewish
community brings out nicely the way that the language is not only
supposed to be acquired but also mastered in such a way that it can be
used by the individual, with appropriate guidance, to enable him or
her to know what is going on in the language. What the commentators do is to supplement that knowledge with additional suggestions
and comments. However, as the commentary became more and
more complex and influential, it tended to get in the way of understanding the language itself, and the situation arose where it was
thought that all anyone needed to know to understand the Bible was
commentary, not the grammar of Hebrew, since all readers needed to
know was embodied in the commentary. Exploring grammar inde-
pendently, as it were, could be dangerous and subversive, and give
rise to interpretations that were unbalanced and inappropriate.

This is a dispute that often arises in religion, where an elite group
has the power to interpret texts and is reluctant to give up that
power to others. One of the features of the Enlightenment, or
Haskalah, in Judaism was to stress the significance of understanding
the Hebrew language once again as a medium of speech, as something perspicuous and accessible. The whole *Wissenschaft des
Judentums* movement in Germany not only directed its attention to
the language, but also to the social conditions within which the
important Jewish texts were produced, and the intention was to provide another way of understanding those texts, a way that took
power away from the traditional religious authorities and their layers

of commentary and tradition. In religion this move was quite revolutionary and religions do not often recover from such a change, as indeed Judaism as a unitary religion has never recovered. Once it is felt that no single group of thinkers has the power to determine the meaning of a religious text once and for all, since they no longer have a monopoly on understanding the language of those texts, then power is wrested away from them and given to someone else, not necessarily to anyone superior to the ancient regime, but at least someone different.

We are often told that, over time, the grip of the Temple priests and those close to them was weakened as the Temples were destroyed and the Jewish community spread throughout the world. We are also told that, also over time, the influence of the Babylonian academies became less significant as distances grew greater between Babylon and the rest of the Jewish world, and so more reliance came to be placed on local religious authorities. This is all true, but what it represents is not so much a particular historical development unique to the Jews but a normal religious feature, the democratization of religious knowledge over the years, the inability of great religious centers of authority to hold on to their power and to project it as successfully as they had in the past. One of the features of this is the desire to represent the religion in a simplified way that makes sense to people and can be used easily by them, without their feeling that the religion is inaccessible or mysterious in some way. Here, the idea of principles is useful, a creed that defines the religion and expresses clearly what distinguishes it from other religions. We can see quite clearly from where the enthusiasm for such axioms and principles comes, but this does not mean that we have to accept that it provides an accurate account of the religion.

If there is no creed, then does this not suggest that anything is acceptable? The answer is no, since the problem with a creed is not that it limits what can be brought under the rubric of the religion, but on the contrary makes the religion infinitely extendable. This is because the set of principles that is said to encapsulate the religion has itself to be interpreted, and so what purports to make the issue simpler is itself the source of further complexity. This is not an issue that just affects Judaism, but all religions, and we need to challenge the idea that religions are obviously equivalent to some list of ideas. This is not only false, but dangerous, since it is then not difficult to attack a religion by producing one of its statements and claiming that that statement encapsulates the religion itself. After all, the defenders of a particular religion often focus on such statements, which they then represent positively, so why should its enemies not do the same? Religions are far too sophisticated, and mixed up with practice as well as belief, to be readily definable in terms of any easy-to-grasp principles, and Judaism is no exception here.

Jews are Motivated by a Great Concern for Justice

Jews often see themselves as being particularly interested in justice, and there are certainly plenty of references in the Bible to justice and its significance. In the Reform community, prayer has largely been replaced by what is called *tikkun olam*, which is taken to mean repairing or improving the world, easily identifiable with improving justice. There is also the observation that many Jews have been involved in social movements, and today a large number of Jews are enthusiastic participants in even pro-Palestinian movements. In Israel, some Jews do a great deal to defend the rights of Palestinians, who may themselves show no sign of any interest in the welfare of their Jewish neighbors. Jews who set themselves up against the majority of the Jewish community often appeal to their upbringing as Jews in defense of their position, as though Judaism involves a special enthusiasm for justice that they have internalized and is the main driver of their actions.

But all the Abrahamic religions talk a great deal about justice, and it is difficult to argue (which is different from saying that it has never been suggested) that one is more oriented toward justice than the others. What Judaism does have in its legal system is a bias toward the toleration of disputes about what Judaism involves. As far as the Law is concerned, the consensus of how it should be interpreted does not have to involve everyone to be valid. The important thing is that there should be agreement on what the Law is, otherwise the ordinary Jew will be confused as to what he is supposed to do. Agreement does not mean that everyone agrees, but that most people do, and the dissenters are allowed to continue to put forward their views, albeit only as theoretical alternatives and not in a way that affects actual practice (*Sanhedrin* 11.2). The rabbis were so keen on emphasizing the legal process that even God was said to

work with a *beth din* (house of judgment), to which he teaches
something new on Law each day (*Genesis Rabbah* 64.4). We find in
the Jerusalem Talmud *Sanhedrin* 1.1, 18a a series of comments on R.
Ishmael b. R. Yose's suggestion in the *Pirkei Avot* 4.8: 'Do not judge
alone, for only one judges alone.' R. Judah b. Pazi is not satisfied with
this and extends it to suggest that even God does not judge alone. R.
Yohanan says that God never does anything without discussing it
with the heavenly court; and R. Eleazar that the use of the term 'the
Lord God' refers not just to God, but also to his court. This could be
typical rabbinic hyperbole, but it is worth noting that, if even God is
said to take advice, then it is even more important for human beings
to do so.

Does God need anyone's help in working out what to do, what is
just or what shape the Law ought to take? Surely not. But we do.
This requirement to take other peoples' views into account does
mean that we have to be open to other people and cannot rely on
ourselves to work everything out. In *Pirkei Avot* 4.1, Ben Zoma asks
'Who is wise?', and he answers, 'He who learns from everyone.' Ben
Azzai expands this idea in 4.3 to suggest, 'Treat no one and nothing
as a waste of time, for everyone and every comment has a value.' This
general theme of respecting humility is prevalent through the *Pirkei
Avot*, and probably reflected the difficulty of the Tannaim, the commentators from around 100 BCE–200 CE, both laying down rules of
how to behave and also not thinking of themselves as very special. It
is not easy to be an authority in any area, especially religion, and not
to think of oneself as a rather elevated sort of person. Indeed, the
style of the Mishnah is quite restrained, in that the Tannaim do not
issue orders, but describe behavior, obviously with the aim that it
proves a useful guide. When the Amoraim, the later commentators
who were working between 200 CE and 600 CE, discussed the
Mishnah and other Tannaic hermeneutic works such as the various
midrashim and *baraitot*, they often did not agree on their legal implications, but were content to go with the majority line on the issue. As
Hannah Arendt comments:

> Unanimity of opinion … destroys social and personal life, which is
> based on the fact that we are different by nature and by conviction. To
> hold different opinions and to be aware that other people think differ-
> ently on the same issue shields us from that god-like certainty which

stops all discussion and reduces social relationships to those of an ant-heap. A unanimous public opinion tends to eliminate bodily those who differ, for mass uniformity is not the result of agreement, but an expression of fanaticism and hysteria. (Arendt, 1978, 182)

There is, of course, the very famous passage about how to kasher (purify) an oven, on which a group of rabbis have one opinion and Rabbi Eliezer has an opinion that is supported, apparently, by God (*Bava Metzia* 59b). The rabbis tell God to mind his own business, albeit politely, using as support the biblical passage 'It is not in heaven' (*Deut* 30.12), to suggest that the solutions to legal disputes are not to be found in heaven, but in the collegial decisions of the rabbinate. Yet that biblical passage is actually stretched rather a long way to give that reading. It comes in a long speech by Moses, in which he emphasizes the significance of the Israelites doing what they are supposed to do, and the reference to 'it is not in heaven' is working out what their duty is. God says that it is not difficult to work out what they are supposed to do, since he has told them and has not hidden that information somewhere inaccessible – in heaven, for example. How one gets from this to the argument that it is for rabbis and not God to determine how we are to act is a bit of a mys-tery, but not untypical of much Talmudic reasoning. Perhaps this extension of the phrase is allowable as deriving an additional signifi-cance from it, but in any case it does bring out something that is true about law – that it is a matter of what is agreed at a particular time among qualified people.

So, at the heart of traditional Jewish ideas about how decisions should be made – even by God – is the idea of consensus, agreement and not disrespecting the minority opinion, all constituents in what we tend to call justice. This is a formal feature of justice, and does not have any particular political implications. Yet one of the features of Jews that has often been noted is their tendency to be attracted to the left in politics. Even in the USA, where Jews have generally pros-pered and have a higher income than the norm, they are heavily overrepresented in radical causes. Political scientists often say that Jews live like WASPS (White Anglo-Saxon Protestants) and vote like Puerto Ricans. So, for example, in the presidential election in the USA in 2008, the only group more heavily in favor of Barack Obama than Jews were African-Americans. In the fight for desegregation and voters' rights in the South in the 1960s, Jews often made up half the volunteers, and two out of the three men killed by the Ku Klux Klan in Philadelphia, Mississippi in 1964 were Jews. In radical groups such as the far left, and feminist and gay liberation movements, Jews figure strongly, and have done for a considerable time. Yet this is not what is predicted to happen. As minorities prosper and move out of their original neighborhoods, they are expected to identify more with conservative ideas and reflect this in their voting. Yet even when the whole country is voting Republican, Jews prefer the Democrats, and have done for the last 21 elections. That is not to say that there are not some notable right-wing Jewish thinkers and politicians, there certainly are, but the mainstream of the Jewish electorate has stuck to what they see as progressive candidates.

There have been many debates as to why this should be the case. Some have argued that justice serves as a displacement activity for traditional religion. With the arrival of the Enlightenment, religious ideas were pushed into the background and something else had to take their place as a unifying motif, and ultimately this was justice, which is, after all, an entirely desirable aim for anyone. But why should this arouse the enthusiasm of a community that was radically separated from the calls for justice in the Bible, since it no longer had much contact with or interest in the Bible's teachings? It is difficult also to argue that the determining factor here is memories of anti-Semitism and the support that doctrine received in the past on the right. Today anti-Semitism is just as likely, if not more likely, to be found on the left, and yet so are Jews. Perhaps, though, the long history of persecution makes Jews still think of themselves as potential victims, and makes them identify with other victims who at this time do have problems.

It is possible that this has an effect. The references to the stranger and the respect with which he or she ought to be treated often refers back to the phrase 'for you were strangers in Egypt'. The Passover service frequently invites the participants to think of themselves being back in Egypt, and events throughout the Jewish year often refer to past persecutions and sacrifices. Yet it is difficult to understand the mechanism by which this message reaches Jews, since most of them do not participate very much in festivals and synagogue activities, let alone study the Torah. Most American Jews will attend a seder, but how far they actually consider the nature of the words in the service is a moot point. The experience of actual anti-Semitism is so far away from most modern Jews that it is difficult to see it as a powerful motivating factor.

In any case, in countries outside the USA, Jews generally vote in line with their socio-economic status, and this orientation toward the left no longer exists. In Israel, for instance, the first three decades of independence saw governments of the left, but since 1977 they tend to be more on the right. Is that because the traditional Jewish commitment to justice only exists in the USA, or only takes a polit-ical direction to the left in the USA? Is there any evidence that, in their personal dealings with others, Jews are any more just than are other people? Surely not. How about traditional Jews, who will at least be aware of the emphasis on justice in significant Jewish texts? Non-traditional Jews will probably have no knowledge of the Bible, or at least only a superficial acquaintance with it, and so it is difficult to know how this enthusiasm for justice, if it exists, emerged. As with so many generalizations about Jews and Judaism, this apparent enthusiasm for justice needs to be treated with great suspicion.

Had Israel Existed, the Holocaust would Never Have Happened

The idea of Israel as a home for Jews is a potent one, especially in times of disaster such as the Holocaust. One of the cruel responses that the Nazis made to appeals for the welfare of their Jewish victims was to ask who wanted to take them, since the Nazis were happy to see them go elsewhere. In most cases, there was nowhere for them to go and so they were murdered in countries from which there was no possibility of escape. Had a Jewish national home existed at the time, they could have gone there.

This idea is rather simplistic, though. The Nazis did not just want the Jews to relocate but to be eliminated, and it is difficult to think of a world dominated by such people which would allow an Israel to survive. On the other hand, during the earlier period they did allow Jews to leave Germany, provided they left their assets behind, and there is some evidence that as the Final Solution began to be planned, it was a reaction to the fact that the Reich was in control of large numbers of Jews and other groups of people they did not want, and nor did anyone else. A country capable of issuing visas would have been able to take in Jewish refugees, though the idea that the Palestine of the 1930s and 1940s could have absorbed the whole of European Jewry is extraordinary. Would Germany in any case have wanted or tolerated a small and hostile state to emerge not that far from the borders of its growing empire, a state whose citizens were its most hated ethnic group?

There is an important fact about Israel: that it serves as a haven for Jews in a world in which other forces are also prepared to support them. Though a good deal of emphasis is placed, rightly, on the skill and determination of the Israelis to defend themselves, and there is no doubt of their ability to do so, we must acknowledge the wider context in which this takes place. Would Israel have achieved independence without the heavy importation of arms from Czechoslovakia during the armistice, itself brought about by the Soviet Union? Would Israel have survived the attrition in the 1973 war with Egypt and Syria without the heavy replenishment of military equipment from the USA? The fact that Israel is so firmly within the Western sphere of influence has surely given its enemies room for caution, however aggressive their language has often been.

This might seem a strange remark to make, since surely Israel would always have been considered as part of the Western sphere of influence? In its early decades, though, Israel was oriented politically very much to the left, and the State was enthusiastic about controlling the economy. It is only after the protracted hostility of the Soviet Union and its allies that the left in Israel finally gave up on warmer relations with the socialist bloc. Being allied to the West is by no means a guarantee of security, however. Many countries are part of the West, in much more integral ways than Israel, and have been allowed to fall by the wayside. Greece is a good example. Created in the nineteenth century out of the Ottoman Empire, and the source of the word meaning Europe, Greece was the object of a great deal of enthusiasm by those in Christian Europe. Yet when, in the twentieth century, first the Armenian and later the Greek population of Turkey was either massacred or expelled, this had very little impact on Europe as a whole. One can point also to the fate of Georgia in the twenty-first century, a country that was invaded briefly by Russia in 2008/9 and which has modeled itself on the West in an almost painful manner. In two of these cases, such severe reactions were brought about as a result of military adventures that went wrong, but it still suggests that a vague sort of sympathy for a country is not very cashable currency in the survival stakes. Hitler himself is supposed to have referred to the lack of continuing interest in the fate of the Armenians when contemplating a similar massacre of the Jews.

Perhaps the significance of Israel is not that it will prove to be a haven of safety for Jews, but that it represents the fact that the Jews will no longer be impotent when their enemies confront them. When one considers the nature of the Middle East and the growing power of those hostile to the Jewish State, and the fragile nature of the support it has received, it is difficult to be confident in Israel's ability to survive. The internal divisions are just as worrying, or even more so. A rapid growth of a potentially hostile Arab-Israeli population and a lukewarm traditional Jewish population means that the basis of the State is losing its foundations, in that fewer and fewer of the population are prepared to serve in the military. The growing antagonism of the world's 1.5 billion Muslims for the 14 million Jews is a trend that surely can have only one eventual conclusion. In parts of Europe, Jews have already been marginalized or driven out by constant aggression from local Muslim populations, who find it rather easier to attack individual Jews going about their business compared to confronting the Israeli army in the Middle East.

Before the Holocaust, the Jews were the largest non-Christian minority in Europe, but now they are vastly outnumbered by the new Muslim population of the continent. This is not necessarily a problem; it could be that this new minority will adapt to the mores of Europe and take on an increasingly secular lifestyle, which will enable them to coexist happily with the largely post-Christian culture that now characterizes Europe. On the other hand, it could also be that this will not happen, and it is difficult to believe that the increasingly hostile attitude of Europe toward Israel at the end of the twentieth century and beyond is not affected by the growing political influence of its Muslim citizens. The low birth rate of the general Jewish population in the diaspora, together with high rates of intermarriage, suggests that Jewish influence will decline progressively despite the existence of Israel. Finally, the concentration of Jews in relatively few places gives any determined enemy the opportunity to kill a large proportion of them very effectively. Even when he totally controlled Europe, Hitler had to gather Jews from many different places and take them to the concentration camps before he could kill them in large numbers. Today, the majority of Jewish children in the world live on the Mediterranean coast of Israel, in a few cities and smaller communities, a very tempting prospect for those who see the Jews as an enemy that must be annihilated. As some enemies of the Jews in the Middle East have suggested, the ingathering of the Jews will only make them easier to destroy when eventually the balance of power alters.

The point of this approach is not to suggest that Israel will not survive, nor that its neighbors will necessarily always seek to destroy the inhabitants of the State of Israel. There is, however, little evidence that Israel has made Jews safer, either in the State or elsewhere, than they would otherwise have been. The Jewish State has taken on the pariah status that Jews had (and still have in many parts of the world), and it is difficult to see how that will contribute to Jewish survival in the face of its many enemies.

Judaism is a Total Way of Life, Not (just) a System of Beliefs

All religions are a way of life, not (just) a system of beliefs. Supporters of a particular religion often try to stress its practical aspects, to show how serious the religion is, perhaps in contrast to others. It is certainly the case that someone who follows Jewish Law in his or her life has a great number of rules to follow, and anyone who studies the Talmud as a guide to practical life will base their activities very much on their interpretation of their religion. But this is just the same for Muslims and Christians; it is not as though all they have to do is accept a number of beliefs and then they can do whatever they want. Here again we need to distinguish between different Jewish attitudes to Judaism. For many Jews there is no difference at all between their lifestyle and that of their Gentile neighbors. They are Jews in the same way that most people acquire their nationality – through birth.

Yet there are some Jews for whom their religion is totally demanding as a lifestyle. It envelops them completely and they organize their life around it, obeying rigorously Judaism's laws and rituals, as specified by some form of traditional religion. It regulates how they live, who they live with, what they eat, wear and so on during every waking moment. It does not just affect a part of their life, but is all-encompassing. It is true that few religions have such a complex legal

structure which regulates even apparently minor aspects of life as
Judaism does. The *Pirkei Avot* (Ethics of the Fathers) in the Mishnah
suggests that Jews should be as careful about a minor commandment as
about a major one, and indeed the distinction is not always that easy to
make in any case. But is not the important distinction here between
people who take their religion seriously and those who do not? The
pious Muslim or Christian may have fewer dietary laws to consider
when thinking of his or her obligations, and yet there are plenty of
other things to think about that are important to individuals in following their religion. Monks and nuns are difficult to characterize as not
thinking about Christianity as all-encompassing, and many Muslims'
lives are built around prayer and study of religious texts to a degree that
really can be said to define them. Some Christian groups take the
Sabbath very seriously and have complex rules of behavior rather like
those of the Jews, and the Jains in India take extraordinary steps to follow their very strict laws on what they can eat and what involves
killing living things, something they take stringent measures to avoid.

We are often told that there is something very different about a
specific religion which makes it unlike all the others. Sometimes this
is positive, and often it is not. At the time of writing, there is a lively
discussion in Europe as to whether Islam is so different from the other
religions of the continent that it cannot fit into the accepted rules of
secular Western society. Islam is not just a system of beliefs, but a
whole lifestyle, we are told, and seeks to dominate any other religion
with which it comes into contact. This follows from the very nature
of the religion. However, this is far from the truth and the experience
of the very ordinary lives of European Muslims. Religions have survived so long because they are capable of adapting and changing to fit
in with different environments. When Jews report with some pride
that their religion is far more a way of life than any other religion,
they are wrong. Many religions are strict on how their followers are
to live, they all do it in different ways, and the prioritizing of one at
the expense of the others in this respect is very questionable.

Jews are a Race

Are the Jews a race? They are often referred to as such by their enemies, and even sometimes use that sort of language themselves. God
made two covenants with groups of people – the covenant with

Noah which covers everyone, and the covenant with Abraham and later with Moses and the Israelites, which is taken to apply to their successors, the Jews. In the Bible itself, the origin of many of the children of the patriarchs is quite mixed, in the sense that they had Israelite fathers and pagan mothers, which goes against the contemporary rules about who is Jewish among traditional communities. Here, the criterion of who is Jewish depends on the mother and of course the faith of the child himself or herself when adult. For the Reform movement, the Jewish parent can be either male or female for a child to be Jewish, which does, it has to be said, accord better with the biblical evidence. On the other hand, as traditional Jews quite rightly say, most biblical events pre-date the giving of the Torah, and it is then, they say, that the rules they apply were enunciated and came into force. The Israelites leaving Egypt were an *eruv rav* (*Ex* 12.38), which is often taken to mean a mixed multitude. Did they become a race some time later, perhaps when Moses (in *Ex* 24) organizes the sacrifice of bulls and pours half the blood on to the altar and half on to the people, referring to it as the blood of the covenant? This is the only time that blood is actually applied to the people (and the only time that Moses carries out priestly duties). It seems far-fetched, as since that time different people have become Jews, and certainly many Jews have left the community.

We cannot overemphasize the significance of blood in Jewish rituals. It plays a huge part even after the sacrifices, when of course it was even more important. There were blood rituals in other ancient religions, and while religions often criticize the rituals of others and set up their own, they pay attention to the alternatives and often shape what they do with reference to them. If blood is significant in religion, then each religion needs, or needed, to have some blood rituals in it, and Judaism, of course, held on to the circumcision ritual, with its essentially gory features, unlike Christianity which quite early in its history presented itself as being too refined for this to be necessary. Menstruating women produce blood in just the same way that males do when they are circumcised, it was argued, and this provides some sort of cosmic balance that the kabbalists discussed, while Christians do not avoid menstrual blood and hence that balance is essentially upset because of the subsequent pollution. Christians in the Middle Ages were unimpressed by the Jewish practice of circumcision, and there were claims that Jewish men were in fact women who menstruated. In Spain, after the expulsion of the Jews, much emphasis was placed on the purity of blood, so that the Old Christians could distinguish themselves from the New Christians, who were really, as it was implied, Jews in Christian clothing. This view was naturally opposed by the New Christians, but it did become part and parcel of a good deal of Sefardi practice, whereby there was much emphasis put on the precise nature of one's origins in the Sefardi community, and there was often an attitude of superiority to Jews from elsewhere. This is an excellent example of how a discriminatory practice and doctrine against a minority is taken up by that minority and recycled to discriminate against other minorities, or indeed is transformed into a discriminatory doctrine against the majority, or of course both. What is clear in all this confusing variety of ideas is that blood is often taken to be a simple way of distinguishing between people, and so a Jew will always be a Jew, a Sefardi Jew always a Sefardi Jew, and so on, whatever Jewish or any other religious law says about the matter. There is something so powerful and basic in the idea of blood that it transcends the sorts of subtle distinctions that are made which suggests it is not so important.

Of course, for centuries the blood libel linked the Jews with blood in the public imagination, and continues to work in modern varieties of the libel even today. It is hardly relevant to point out in response that Judaism specifically proscribes the use of blood in any form in food, since at the time blood was regarded as something to be consumed and having the ability to harm one's enemies. To personify an enemy as someone who wanted to consume one's blood makes a lot of sense, even if it is not literally true, and of course the Jews were well known as people who did take things as literally true much of the time, so the idea that they literally sought to take Christian blood, after having taken the life of Jesus, is quite plausible. One of the themes of a lot of Jewish poetry is that link between *dam* (blood), *adamah* (earth) and Adam, the first man. The Christians who accuse the Jews of designs against their blood are those who in reality have taken the blood of Jews for generations and built their civilization on it, and in modern Zionist verse this is reversed, where the Jews for the first time, or so they represent it, stand up and are prepared to fight and spill the blood of their enemies in order to defend themselves. In early Zionism, the idea of the land being redeemed through blood is a potent one, and often used. Yet the suggestion that Jews are actually different from non-Jews through their blood is not much used as an idea by Jews themselves, it seems to corroborate many of the traditional anti-Semitic stereotypes.

The evidence from genetics for the existence of a separate Jewish race is quite varied. The priestly class, the Kohanim, are indeed closely related to each other, and a tribe in South Africa, the Lemba, are also related to them, giving credence to the story of priests in Yemen moving to Africa and presumably mixing with the local people. Yet the same is not the case for the Levites, in that the Ashkenazi Levites are not linked with the Sefardi Levites, or even other Jews. They are, however, closely linked with non-Jewish Eastern Europeans. The conclusion is that there is a good deal of genetic uniformity in the Jewish population as a whole, but other people have at various stages entered this gene pool and linked it with non-Jewish people. Even far back in history, we know that the Assyrians and Babylonians removed many of the Hebrews from the Land of Israel and replaced them with other people. The Romans also, in their very effective repression of the Jewish revolts, killed many Jews and encouraged the importation of other people to dilute the Jewish nature of the country.

What is interesting about the genetic research is that it seems to be largely irrelevant. It is not difficult for some such as Koestler (1976) and Sand (2009) to continue to argue that the Jews today are largely descendants of people who had nothing to do genetically with those who received the covenant, and nor were they descended from the patriarchs. We know very well that many people who were not orig-inally part of the Hebrew community entered the Land of Israel and linked up with the people there. We know also that Jews who lived in different parts of the world clearly often intermarried with the local population, though how extensive this was is unclear. Those who see the Jews as essentially part of the people descended from the patriarchs and those linked with them can continue to argue in this way, since there is certainly some evidence of such continuity. The important thing, of course, is not what is actually the case, but what people think is true. This is sadly very much the case for anti-Semites who often condemn those who have even a remote connection with a Jewish ancestor. Yet it does raise the real question of how far the covenant can impinge on those who might not even be linked with the people who originally made it with God, or with those who confirmed it later with God. It is not as though they are converts who voluntarily took on the obligations of the covenant. On the contrary, the obligations they regard perhaps as theirs because of their history, and yet that history could be entirely different from what they assume it to be.

Here we need to acknowledge that it is much harder to distinguish between what some have called pseudo-history or even voodoo history, and the respectable variety. There are all these strange histories or fantasies about where the Ten Lost Tribes went to, and similar far-fetched accounts of how Jews arrived in strange parts of the world and what happened to them afterwards. They all seem to end in an account of some huge conspiracy, and imply that giving us information about the genetic background of people tells us a lot about them. But of course it does not. It matters not at all if a particular Jew is truly a descendent of the patriarchs. What matters is what he thinks he is and, even more, what others think he is, and what implications that has for how he is going to be treated. Some suggest that, if the Jews are not a race, then the idea of the Jewish people 'returning' to the Land of Israel is nothing more than a Zionist invention, and probably quite a late one (from the nineteenth century, according to Sand). It follows, then, that the State of Israel lacks legitimation, since its whole *raison d'être* is the return of the descendants of its original inhabitants. This is surely not accurate, though, since even if the majority of the Jews today are descendants of Alexandrian, Berber and Caucasian converts, if they are regarded by others as Jews, and regard themselves as such, then they do form a people, the *Am Yisrael*, the People of Israel – and so perhaps deserve a piece of territory to call their own.

Jews are Clever

How much of what is perceived as Jewish intellectual success is a matter of nature or nurture? In modern times, as well as in the past, Jews have been very much involved in a variety of intellectual pursuits, and in vastly greater numbers than is representative of their proportion of the population at large. While Jews constitute about two-tenths of 1 per cent of the world's population, they receive an extraordinary number of Nobel Prizes. By 2009, they had won 27 per cent of the Nobel Physics prizes, and 31 per cent of the medicine prizes. They are 54 per cent of the world's chess champions. In the USA, about 2 per cent of the population is Jewish, as are 21 per cent of the Ivy League students, 26 per cent of the Kennedy Center honorees, 37 per cent of Academy Award winning directors and 51 per cent of the Pulitzer Prize winners for nonfiction. Jews have been found to have an unusually high mean intelligence, as measured by IQ tests, ever since the first Jewish samples were tested. Jews are only about average on the subtests measuring visuo-spatial skills, but extremely high on subtests that measure verbal and reasoning skills. This accounts for the fact that Jews have often seen themselves as physically limited, but successful in more intellectual areas.

It is worth pointing out that exceptional intelligence is not enough to explain exceptional achievement. Qualities such as imagination, ambition, perseverance and curiosity distinguish between the bright and the innovative. It is difficult to argue that, through the difficult situations Jews have often experienced, only those who were the fittest intellectually survived, since often survival was a matter of chance, not intelligence. When Jews had the option to escape through conversion, many of them did, and some of the most intelligent apparently, given the level of discussion then produced by the converts trying to encourage their former co-religionists to join them. Some have argued that the great achievements are really limited to Ashkenazi Jews and to those who lived in parts of Europe, where occupations for Jews were limited to finance, trade and selling – all activities where intelligence is significant, unlike farming or similar activities. Of course, Sefardi Jews were also involved in these activities, but far less so, and the Sefardim were particularly concentrated in crafts, stimulating less intellectual ways of thinking, or so it is often said. In any case, it is perhaps true that the sorts of skills that crafts encourage are not as flexible as those of more abstract forms of thought. Against this thesis is the evidence that Jews in the Sefardi world were also outstanding in intellectual achievement and in a range of the sciences, as well as in more practical activities.

There are reasons also for thinking that nurture, not nature, played a significant role. After all, the Jews, alone in the world, had effectively established universal male literacy and numeracy. On the other hand, this could serve as an argument against the continuing existence of the brighter part of the population as Jews. One of the biggest declines in the Jewish population occurred between the first and sixth centuries CE, when the world's Jewish population went from about 4.5 million to 1.5 million or fewer. Many were killed in the Roman wars and the consequences these had for the Jewish populations of Judea and Egypt. Joshua ben Gamla's instructions on universal Jewish literacy occurred at about the same time as the destruction of the Second Temple – 64 CE and 70 CE, respectively. This was the period when Judaism began to transform itself from a religion centered on rites and sacrifices at the Temple in Jerusalem to a religion based on prayer and the study of the Torah at synagogues, or so we are often told. In fact, this was not such a break, since even with the Second Temple, synagogues existed and there was plenty of decentralization in Babylon and in the diaspora as a whole, but also in the Land of Israel. It is certainly true that rabbis, scholars and local communities came to the fore rather than being poor reflections of what was going on at the Temple. In any case, prayer and worship could not be left to the priests in Jerusalem but had to be practiced locally, and this meant everyone had to be able to undertake the task of being able to read the prayers and to a certain extent study the Torah. Later, even women were expected to pray, albeit often only at home, at least in a vernacular language.

It could be argued that to carry out the basic religious tasks then became an intellectual activity of some complexity. It involved not only knowing the prayers, but also the ability to participate in the interpretation of Jewish texts, and we should remember that Hebrew was not necessarily a language well known to any of the Jewish communities by this stage. Perhaps those Jews who found literacy difficult were more likely to abandon their religion than those who did not. Perhaps they were concentrated in agricultural occupations and did not find much value in literacy outside of religion, in the sense that they did not need it to farm. On the other hand, perhaps the only reason why Judaism had such a strong, and unusual, commitment to education is because the Jews were already genetically predisposed to make a success of such a commitment. They were the only people who made education so important because they were uniquely situated to benefit from it. That is why, perhaps, over 2,000 years ago, Shimon ben Shetach said that all children should go to school (JT *Ketuvot* 8.11).

Nurture cannot be dismissed so easily, though. The early enthusiasm for education did mean that Jews had many centuries of practice

Ruth.

Deutsches Gebet- und Erbauungsbuch

für

israelitische Mädchen

zur häuslichen Andacht und zum öffentlichen Gottesdienste

bearbeitet und herausgegeben von

J. Brandeis.

Mit Festbetrachtungen

von

Dr. D. Feuchtwang und **Dr. M. Güdemann.**

Als Titelbild eine Wiedergabe der „Ruth"
von Henry Ryland in Lichtdruck.

Breslau 1908.
Verlag von Jakob B. Brandeis.

Ruth: A book explaining the prayers in German to Jewish women for use in the home

and experience in literacy before everyone else, at least in so far as most of the community were concerned. The fact that they were urbanized so rapidly was both helped by this and encouraged it, presumably, since a range of occupations were available in the cities and towns that made education helpful. On the other hand, the idea that the less intelligent Jews moved on to a less demanding religion from an intellectual point of view is not convincing. We should not exaggerate the demands of a Jewish education. It could involve very detailed study and considerable skills, but does not have to mean this – a fairly basic grasp of what is going on might be enough. There are certainly plenty of stupid Jews today and no doubt there were in the past also, and in fact there is a whole category of stories about them based on the village of Chelm, in which the most stupid, and thoroughly Jewish, people live.

It is wrong to think that the emphasis in Judaism on study is going to nurture Jews into being brighter than other people. For one thing, today very few Jews are brought up with a sound Jewish education, and so the instruction to study and the various rules about studying are largely ignored or even unknown. Even for those Jews who do concentrate on Torah study, and of course the many commentaries, the wider applications of this work are difficult to observe. Often they are so narrow in their approach to the study that they do not perceive any connection with anything outside of the restricted world in which they live, and indeed seeking such a connection would be in itself unwelcome and forbidden. A great deal of emphasis is placed on memorization, rote learning and prayer, and none of these activities probably does much to foster intelligence. Finally, it has to be said that the leading principle of much of the traditional movement, especially all that is more traditional than what is called modern orthodox, is to restrict the questions that can be asked and the issues that may be raised. The study that then takes place can be restricted, and the parameters of discussion are accordingly severely limited. It is difficult to think that this sort of intellectual inquiry is really of much value in leading Jews to broader topics or to tackling a range of problems that are of interest to most people today. The secular knowledge of the modern haredi, or ultra-orthodox community, in Israel, for example, and their colleagues elsewhere, is slight, and this is hardly surprising since they wish to cut themselves off as far as possible from the horrors of the modern world.

We need to be very careful about linking the performance of Jews academically with their education in the traditional Jewish texts, since so few modern Jews have received such an education. As with the argument that Jews are particularly interested in justice because they spend so much time reading texts which discuss it, or the idea that they are enthusiastic about Jerusalem since it crops up so often in prayers, this comes up against the rude fact that most Jews for some time have not on the whole read those texts or know those prayers. Nor now do their parents, or perhaps even their grandparents, so the idea that they were influenced in some way through them is also difficult to accept. We are left with the vague idea that just because someone is a Jew then they are likely to be intelligent, and this certainly explains why many Jews try to live up to that image, but it fails to explain how the stereotype arose in the first place.

Christianity is based on Love, Judaism on Law

It is often argued nowadays that Paul did not really set out to establish a huge distinction between Judaism and the new religion of Christianity, though he is often credited with, or blamed for, this accomplishment. He seems to be arguing most of the time against Christians who insisted that in order for a Gentile to be a Christian, he or she would have to convert to Judaism first. This seemed to Paul to be an exaggerated demand, and he opposed it. Provided the Gentiles agreed to abide by the seven Noahide rules that all righteous people are supposed to follow, they can become Christians. This was, of course, a clever move for the new religion to make and greatly increased its attraction. The notion that Jewish Law is harsh and inflexible is sometimes suggested in the New Testament, but just as often Jesus speaks of the Law with respect and denies that he has come to overturn it. Many would say that the dichotomy between love and law is a false dichotomy in any case.

The thing about the Law is that it establishes rules that apply to everyone in the community, and establishes rules of how to live that make it possible for the individual to understand and follow a religion. In doing this, he or she acts in the way that God wishes people to act, as they see it, and there is nothing harsh and inflexible in itself about this. There are certainly rules that are difficult to follow, and the two legal schools of Hillel and Shammai often distinguished themselves in terms of how difficult they made life for those following them. The school of Hillel was invariably gentler than the school of Shammai, and saw this as a virtue. Whether we should see it as a virtue depends on whether one thinks that religion should present the individual with relatively easy or relatively difficult tasks to perform.

It is not difficult to find reasons to be compassionate in Judaism. First, we need to pay attention to the reason that human beings were created in Judaism. Adam was created by divine breath to look after the garden. Adam is made from the dust of the ground and his role is 'to till it and care for it' (*Gen* 2.15). He is assisted by the creation later of a woman to be his companion, but before the woman arrived he was with the animals, whose names he was taught. After the Flood, God says to Noah and his sons, 'I now make my covenant with you, and with your descendants after you, and with every living creature that is with you, all birds and cattle, all the wild animals with you on earth, all that have come out of the ark' (*Gen* 9.8–11). Some have argued that one can deduce the preference in Judaism for vegetarianism, given the very explicit rules for treating animals (relatively) well and the idea of general compassion for all living things that God evinces in the Torah. The ox and the ass are not to be yoked together, presumably because one is stronger than the other and this would be unfair, and on the Sabbath the animals are supposed to rest and can be looked after, even though this might constitute what would otherwise be forbidden work. There are many stories about how animals have important roles in the life of the world, and how our attitudes to them say a lot about us. Moses and David, for example, as shepherds, are supposed to have behaved in ways that would suggest strength in a leadership role, since a good shepherd has to pay attention to the weakest of his followers and those most prone to going astray. Levi was the brother who discovered Benjamin's money in his sack, it is also suggested, because he, unlike the others, attended to his animals' needs before his own, a meritorious disposition displaying care and compassion for weaker creatures. Not sacrificing parents and children together is another rule that perhaps allows parents to enjoy, at least for a time, the companionship of their offspring and vice versa.

The Jewish mode of animal slaughter, *shechitah*, is complex, but basically involves, after a short prayer, the quick cutting of the throat of the animal with a very sharp implement, and the rules are clearly designed to avoid causing the creature pain as far as possible. However, in modern times there are other methods of killing that seem to most observers to be more satisfactory. For example, if an animal is first stunned, then killed, surely the pain is even less? The problem from a Jewish point of view of this procedure is that if the animal is first stunned, it is not possible for it to be killed appropriately according to Jewish Law, since its status as being undamaged before being killed is in question. This has led to a debate about whether Jews should be allowed to kill their animals in ways that contravene ordinary standards of animal welfare, though of course talking about animal welfare when this involves killing millions of animals is perhaps a strange form of expression. In recent times, the debate has been widened to include broader issues of cruelty where factory farming is an issue, though the kosher nature of the slaughter is technically not in question. If the Torah emphasizes compassion for all creatures, and indeed care and concern for all life, then should Jews be allowed to treat the earth and the creatures on it as being available to them to be used and exploited, or should they rather see themselves as being in partnership with our environment and responsible for taking care of it?

Abraham Kook is an unusual thinker on the treatment of animals. He was a very traditional rabbi, indeed the first (Ashkenazi) chief rabbi of Palestine, yet regarded Judaism as advocating vegetarianism. He suggested that the very complex rules about eating animals were designed to make us think that it would be better to give up that practice! For example, Jews are supposed not to mix meat and milk, so rules developed about what constitutes meat and milk products, and what degree of separation should exist. Some go so far as to have two kitchens in which meat and milk products can be prepared, and two sets of cutlery and crockery for each type of food. Then dead animals that have been slaughtered appropriately might still raise an issue, such as, if a drop of blood found on the animal rendered it potentially unacceptable, a visit to the rabbi might be required. Keeping everything kosher is time-consuming and often difficult, and Kook suggests that perhaps the strict rules about meat and its consumption and production are designed to make us wonder whether we ought not to do without it altogether, which he saw as raising us to a higher level of moral consciousness. The Torah works with us rather than against us, and realizes that we tend to enjoy meat and may see the world as our possession to use as we wish, and seeks to wean us gradually from this notion by putting in front of us obstacles in the form of Jewish Law, which do not prevent us from doing what we want, but make it harder.

Kook is using here a very important idea in Jewish thought, an idea that Maimonides enunciated very clearly, and that is that God could just create in us a disposition to behave in whatever way he wants us to, but prefers to allow us to get to that disposition gradually through our own efforts, albeit aided by his law. After all, a disposition, a way of doing things and thinking about them, is acquired by us gradually on the whole, over time, and the point of a religion is to get us to think about what we are doing, and why, through the mechanisms of that religion. We go to pray and though the prayers may be familiar to us, we are supposed to think about the words we are using, and we reflect on them and on what they might mean in a particular situation. We perhaps give some money to charity, and then think about why we do it, and we eat a cracker that has a *hechsher* on it, a symbol that it is kosher, either dairy or pareve (neutral), and we think about the laws of *kashrut*.

According to Maimonides, unless we explore the reasons for the commandments we are really operating at a very superficial level in following them. It is better to follow them superficially than not to follow them at all, of course, but the whole point of the *mitzvot* and even the *hukkim*, the major commandments and the ceremonial ones, is to change us as people, to make us acquire the right frame of mind and the ability to understand why we act in the ways we do and have the feelings we possess. God has given us laws he wants us to follow, not for his sake, since he needs nothing from us, but for our sake, since these ways of acting are in our interests. They are in our interests as actions in particular because if we think about what we do, we start to change into the sort of people who take an intelligent and self-aware view of who we are. There is a nice story in the Talmud of a calf who escaped from the slaughterer and who went into the prayer house and hid under the cloak of the great Judah Hanasi, the compiler of the Mishnah, pleading with him to save him from the knife. Hanasi said, quite reasonably, that the calf should return to the fate that had been established for him, presumably with slaughter as its end. The passage ends with criticizing him, despite everything he says being technically correct, since it is rather heartless to reject such an appeal from a creature who manages to escape from the knife. Heaven was not pleased with his actions here, or rather absence of actions, and it is said that, for that reason – his lack of compassion – a lack of compassion was shown to him. He relieved the situation, though, later when his servant uncovered a group of kittens in his house and was about to destroy them, only to be prevented by Hanasi quoting the verse *Ps* 145.9: 'His mercy is upon all his work.' As a matter of custom we often do treat animals who escape in situations like that of the calf rather differently from the rest of the animals who eventually are simply killed. Why are we compassionate about this particular case, and apparently encouraged to be so by the Talmud

(*Bava Metzia* 85a), when in general we have no compunction, as a culture, in doing to death for our pleasure huge numbers of similar creatures? Why were the kittens spared, and their sparing approved by heaven, when presumably there is nothing wrong with destroying animals in our houses that we regard as objectionable?

This raises an intriguing question about compassion, which is: how can we justify limiting our compassion to particular objects? If it is right to be compassionate in all cases where a certain situation applies, which surely it is, unless compassion is to rest on nothing more than a whim, then should we not be compassionate in all such cases? This is the point of the commandments, according to Maimonides; they help us to move from the particular to the general by helping us think about why we do what we do. So, for example, we follow the very complex rules of *kashrut* and then come to wonder what the point of these rules are, except to obey the word of God. It must be more than that, and surely, as Kook says, it might be to question the whole activity of killing and eating animals, the source of the complexity of *kashrut*. But it is not the complexity per se that should make us think about the rationale for what we are doing, Kook would argue, but the fact that so much care is taken to ensure that the killing and eating of animals is done in the right sort of way. That should get us to think about the whole process, and in his terms, to raise the issue of how we reconcile that with the compassion we should feel for other forms of life on the earth.

Despite his argument and also that of Maimonides, that the Law makes us think about what the deeper purpose of what we are doing involves, there is an argument that the Law can take us in an entirely different direction. We can become so entranced by it, so enmeshed in the legal processes and learning what the Law requires of us, that we ignore or become abstracted from what its aim might be. This is not really an objection to Maimonides, since he understands that this is possible; he talks about a category of people who are skilled in the Law yet who are not really advanced in coming close to the truth since they remain at the legal level without inquiring into what the Law, is really for. It is worth pointing to this danger of the Law, though, that it tends to have an intellectual structure of its own that can be satisfying in itself and people may well stay at that level and not delve any deeper. To go further, the greater the complexity of the Law, the greater the sense of achievement in mastering it, and perhaps the less of a tendency there is to wonder what it represents. It becomes an end in itself. In this sense the Law operates against compassion, since we may do what we ought to do legally without asking any of those more searching questions about what the Law is actually supposed to bring about. What the Law usefully addresses is the idea that people have to be treated in general terms, and that is why, in the Anglo-American tradition, justice is depicted as being blindfolded, so that she does not notice the individuals who come before her, just the details of their cases in general. But compassion applies to individuals, and while we may acknowledge that we ought to be compassionate to everyone who deserves it, it is very difficult to act in this way. If we spread compassion too thinly, there is not enough to go round even to apply to those close to us. Yet at the same time that we are limiting our compassion to only a few, we acknowledge our duty to apply it to everyone, and it is this paradox that the Abrahamic religions are very interested in exploring.

In one of the stories that Buber so much enjoyed, the *tzaddik*, the authentic community leader in the mystical pietistic movement of Hasidism is expected to take thorough responsibility for all that goes on in the neighborhood, not limited to his congregation or the people he knows. Rebbe Mordechai of Neshkhizh said to his son, the Rebbe of Kovel:

> 'He who does not feel the pains of a woman giving birth within a circuit of fifty miles, who does not suffer with her and pray that her suffering may be assuaged, is not worthy to be called a tzaddik.' His younger son Yitzchak, who later succeeded him in his work, was ten years old at the time. He was present when this was said. When he was old he told the story and added, 'I listened well. But it was very long before I understood why he had said it in my presence.' (Buber, 1991, 164)

The degree of empathy and compassion referred to here is evidence that the Hasidic *tzaddik* is supposed to have an almost organic connection with the body of the community as a whole, and there are many such stories. The community in these stories is certainly not limited to that of the Jews, and he is required to be constantly attuned to what is taking place around him.

Yet how is this possible, except in a story that is intended to have as its moral the idea that we should be interested in the welfare of others? If someone is really in tune with all the feelings of even a limited group of people, how will that individual be able to function? Will he or she not be so affected by those sufferings, and also the pleasures, that he or she will be unable to concentrate on his/her own affairs or even carry out his/her basic religious functions on behalf of the community? It would be like trying to have a conversation with one person while carrying on a conversation with lots of others at the same time.

Religions are good at emphasizing the significance of compassion, but they are also excellent at explaining how to maximize compassion while allowing the other aspects of life to continue. In Judaism, the *yetzer ha-ra*, the evil inclination, that leads us to do evil actions, attracts, as one would expect, a lot of abuse, and yet it is also praised as a faculty that also allows for a lot of good things. It is involved in the notion of ambition, of competition and the desire to succeed. Unless we have these desires we shall do very little in life, unless we are saints, and most of us are not. It is the point of religion to direct our evil inclinations in positive directions, and for this to happen, what religion does is to work with who we are, where we are and how we can become better. It does not just tell us to reform and improve; on the contrary, it works with those negative aspects of our personalities and thoughts to direct and transform them into more positive directions. A *tzaddik* is a very unusual person, certainly very different from most members of the community. This leads to another danger, the opposite of feeling dissatisfied if one is not perfectly compassionate to everyone (and everything?) around one, the danger of feeling that since this is an ideal one is unlikely to meet, one does not need to try. As it suggests in the very practical *Pirkei Avot* (Ethics of the Fathers), we may not complete our task in life, but that does not mean we can just give it up. This still does not help us much, since it leaves open precisely how compassionate we ought to be, the level of compassion that is acceptable and compatible with bringing about the appropriate degree of improvement in the world that we are capable of with our ordinary, not especially compassionate, activities.

Another Hasidic story that is often quoted is of a rabbi called Zusya who regretted not being Moses, by which he presumably meant that he regretted not reaching the heights of prophecy and leadership established by Moses. Moses is supposed to have said to him that his role was not to be Moses but to be Zusya, and we are reminded of the passage from the *Pirkei Avot*, where we are told to be both for ourselves, not only for ourselves and to regard the present time as the time when things ought to be done. That is, we should not constantly put off what we know we ought to do because we are waiting for the time to be right. This brings out nicely the sort of balance that is involved in being human, and for different people the amount of compassion their lives encompass will differ. For example, there are people who perhaps would find it easier and more effective to work for a living in some commercial field where they can earn money and then dispose of it in charitable directions, to an extent, and where their improvement of the economic structure of their country is in itself a helpful activity. Their ordinary work creates the context within which compassion can be effective when carried out by others, those who perhaps are more comfortable helping people directly who need to be helped, and who have the interpersonal skills to achieve something significant in this area. Not everyone has these skills. For them to do this, other people need to make resources available to them for their work, and so are perhaps better regarded as indirectly compassionate. There is no general formula that suits everyone and every situation, and again religions are very good at inviting individuals to think about how they can best participate in the project of making the world a better place – what in Hebrew is called *tikkun olam*.

Jews do Not Believe in the Afterlife

Judaism is reticent on the nature of the afterlife, and no doubt this had something to do with its growing unpopularity when it had to compete with Christianity and Islam. When Christianity did pose a challenge, a more robust notion of the afterlife suddenly emerged, and can be seen, for example, in the Mishnah and the Talmud, but it is certainly absent in most of the Bible. There are various under-standings of the afterlife. On some accounts it is part of the messianic era, or comes after it. For Maimonides it is entirely spiritual and exists when we throw off the influence of the body and identify entirely with our intellect. Those who see it as material require this sort of imaginative language to make sense of it in their very limited way of looking at things, and that is acceptable, since it may lead to a further refinement of their thought which will enable them to reach a more sophisticated and spiritual conception of the afterlife. In any case, we have a body, and so for at least part of the afterlife it might seem that we need to be embodied in some form or another. According to Albo, the afterlife will last for a millennium, equivalent to the length of time Adam would have lived after eating the forbidden fruit. For us, the afterlife will not be free of struggle, but it is all internal, since there is nothing physical to confront us. This does not mean that we can relax, though, and just enjoy the life we are given. On the contrary, we are supposed to use this period to perfect ourselves and develop into the sorts of people we need to become. Abraham Isaac Kook took the more spiritual line, that the resurrection occurs with the ending of the illusion that separates this universe from heaven.

What Kook has in mind is a kabbalistic, or mystical, view of the individual, consisting of a body and a soul. When the body dies, if the person deserves it, a small portion of the soul remains with it to retain its connection with the soul's source, waiting for the general revival of the dead at the appointed time. Different parts of the remainder of the soul may go to different places and be reincarnated into new bodies, in an attempt to work on and purify one of its spiritual aspects, for example. One part might go to paradise. Another might go to Gehinnom or hell for a period, to work on the sins of that life and prepare it for a future one. Another part might even have a role in the life, albeit temporarily, of an already living person, to help it develop in the right direction and so improve its moral character.

The descriptions of *olam ha-ba*, the world to come, is sometimes taken to refer to the messianic era, where this is seen as something that is going to come about in our world. Sometimes it is identified with *Gan Edan*, the Garden of Eden, or paradise. On its journey through the afterlife the soul can experience many different phenomena, some very unpleasant, but these have the purpose of refining the soul so that it may eventually reach the more ethereal realms where it can finally attain its proper place. Gehenna, or Gehinnon, is often identified with hell, and it originally refers to a valley outside Jerusalem, one associated with idolatrous practices in the past. Like hell, it is a rather nasty place, but one that is only experienced temporarily, and is there to rid us of our imperfections and to move us up to heaven. Some have speculated that the Valley of Hinnon (Gehinnon) and *Gan Edan* (heaven) are in fact the same place, but evil people experience it as the former and virtuous ones as the latter. Not only our deeds govern our time in Gehenna; we are told that the merit of Abraham will bring about the release of all the Jews in the place and move them up to the next stage, the world to come (*Eruvim* 19a).

Souls are said to originate in the physical realm, *guf* (*Avodah Zarah* 5a, *Nedarim* 13b, *Yevamot* 62a), though originally they are in the *otzar*, a realm of pure spirituality, from which they descend to earth to animate our bodies. After death, their role here is finished, and so these souls return to the *otzar*, or *tzror ha-chayyim* (*Shabbat* 152a; *Pesikta Rabbati* 2.3). There are three parts to the soul:

1 *nefesh* – the lower part, or animal part, of the soul.
2 *ruach* – the middle soul, the spirit. This contains the moral virtues and the ability to distinguish between good and evil.
3 *neshamah* – the higher soul. This is related to the intellect, is least affected by our ordinary lives and is most at home in the afterlife. This is the intermediary point between this world and the next.

These three souls are related to three parts of the body – the liver, heart and brain – in an ascending order of spirituality. The *Zohar* explains that, after death, each part of the soul takes a different route through the afterlife. The lowest elements of the soul are purified and purged of physical and emotional attachments, while the higher levels experience perfect happiness through shaking off the body and finally being able to contemplate in an unconstrained and pure manner. The *nefesh* remains with the dead body in the grave, and there experiences the unpleasant consequences of being part of a dead body. By contrast, the *ruach* will typically spend time in Gehinnon, where it will have the opportunity to refine its mental processes, especially its tendency to depend on the emotions for working out how to act. The *neshamah* remains above the fray throughout, and for it the afterlife is nothing but pleasure, since finally it is able to think about things without the limitations it had been forced to tolerate. Eventually, the different parts of the spirit come together again and go to heaven, but only when the *neshamah* – the finest part of the soul – is in control of the other constituents.

What is the relationship between these developments in thinking about the afterlife and the Bible? They are precisely that – developments – and Judaism was flexible enough to invent a rich concept of the afterlife when it needed one, as it soon did in its confrontations with religions that stressed this notion. As with all religious ideas, though, what is important about it is not the existence of the idea but what it means, and here again we have a range of views that explore different ways of looking at the topic. It certainly remains the case that the Bible includes little or nothing on the topic, but later works made up for this omission in an enthusiastic and detailed manner.

What makes something Jewish?

What makes anything *anything*? If we can point to the principles of an activity, then when the principles exist, we can say that the activity exists. We know what a football game consists of, and if the various principles behind a game obtain, then what we have in front of us is a football game. This won't work when it comes to Judaism, though. There is a tempting trap that defining things as Jewish falls into – the trap of defining Judaism, as though it were a set of discrete and limited principles, and once one falls into that trap, there is no escape. Religion is far more than just a set of basic principles, yet it is that set of principles that fascinate people who like to classify things as Jewish.

But perhaps it is useful to do this if the theological phrases that are selected are basic to the religion? It is precisely because many modern thinkers see Judaism as being based on specific, very general, principles that makes their work rather limited in scope. If they are right, then Jewish thought would in effect be the working out of the implications of those very general principles and so as a result would be restricted to that. Yet is it not true that religions do restrict what can be said to be a way of thinking and working within or about that religion? Is not an appropriate way to understand this, that the religion is based on specific ideas which need to be developed and followed in any explication of the religion? No, the argument is that there are specific ways of working that represent the religion, not specific axioms or conclusions that underpin the religion itself. Provided those ways of working are pursued, one is continuing to operate within the framework of the religion, while if those ways of working

are restricted in some way, because of an insistence that certain principles are more basic than others and define what can be said, say, then
the context within which the discussion takes place becomes immediately questionable. It is worth recalling that the variety of opinions in
the Talmud are accepted with apparent leniency by the rabbis
involved, but what would not be accepted would be a refusal to use
the Talmudic methodology of comparing passages with each other,
and developing in that way some notion of what the general view of
Judaism is on a certain topic.

One of the most interesting thinkers in this tradition is Emmanuel
Levinas (1906–95). Time and again he contrasts what he calls the
Greek (reason) and the Hebrew (religion; i.e. Judaism). Judaism
accords with his view of the ethical life; perhaps not the only ethical
life that can be lived, but an ethical life that makes the kinds of huge
demands on the individual of which Levinas approves. He also
approves of the orthopraxy of Judaism, the emphasis on ritual and the
fact that he finds in the religion not just a relationship between the
individual and God, but that there is always another, a third – in
other words, a society. So whereas the traditional first question in
philosophical ethics is how to link the individual actor with others,
for Levinas the individual is already in society, since otherwise the
notion of choice and decision makes no sense, and within that context he or she has to work out how to act. Normally, we think in the
philosophy of religion that the first issue is how the individual should
relate to God, but according to Levinas there is always a third: the
individual does not only have to relate to God but also to society, and
in fact the relationship to God cannot be carried out except by going
through society. Hence the emphasis in Judaism, and here he means
traditional Judaism, on the Law, ritual, communal prayer, charity and
so on.

What is his method here? It is not that easy to work out, but one
thing is clear about it: it is not a Talmudic method. Levinas uses the
Talmud in the sense that he uses passages from it, but he does not
use them Talmudically, in the way that traditional Talmudic commentators use them. It is tempting to say that he does not employ
the Talmudic method, but that would suggest that there is only one
such method and of course there are a whole variety of approaches,
and we might ask why we are not happy to include Levinas's
approach as a valid Talmudic approach. It would be wrong to rule

out a particular way of understanding the text just because it was new and different from the past, since the fact that Jews still study this text suggests that it is always open to interpretation and reinterpretation, to new methods of inquiry, and we would not want to rule out dogmatically Levinas' approach to the Talmud as just one such new and valid way of looking at the text.

But we can rule out his approach without being dogmatic; this is because he does not consider a range of texts when exploring the Talmud, he just chooses one particular passage and extemporizes from it. This is not a different Talmudic approach; in fact, it is not a Talmudic approach at all. In normal Talmudic exposition a variety of passages are selected and compared with each other, and then a plausible, or implausible, interpretation of one within the context of the others is carried out. It is worth pointing out that this is far from a method that is limited to the Talmud, but applies to almost all texts, with one exception. If you are trying to understand a passage from Shakespeare you do not just take that passage, but you compare it with other passages, not necessarily from the same author, but probably including such passages by him, and in the end arrive at some sort of interpretation of the passage. Everybody follows this approach apart from philosophers, as they have their own approach to texts, an approach based generally on what they take to be rational, or some other set of principles which embody what they think is the deep structure of the activity that is being analyzed. They could then argue that the normal way of weighing texts against each other within a particular form of thought can be superseded by philosophy, with its ability to work with what lies behind the text and explain it. It is always awkward to try to define how one ought to carry out an inquiry for that inquiry to count as Jewish. Why should we carry on comparing passages with each other for the activity to count as Jewish? Is this not to prioritize what has taken place in the past and to refuse to allow for change? Yet there are ways of dealing with an issue that focus on Jewish tradition and the previous ways of treating the issue, and then there are other ways which do not. It is a bit like complaining if one takes a car to be fixed and the mechanic lays his hands on it and prays to God to change the oil and replace the fan belt. The customer would be entitled to complain that his car had not been fixed, even if he shared the religious enthusiasm of the mechanic, since what we call having a car fixed does not involve doing nothing but praying. We can pray, but we have to do other things as well.

This is where Levinas' method falls down. He just ignores the various ways over the millennia that Jews have discussed the issues he discusses when he considers one or two brief passages, which he then extends and develops in very imaginative ways, but not in what we have here called Jewish ways. This is not to criticize in any way what Levinas does, but it is to criticize calling it Jewish. It is not difficult to take a passage from any culture and then play around with it; the difficulty lies in linking what one has done with the culture from which the passage was taken. As Wittgenstein said, using a word of greeting in the middle of a sentence is not to greet someone (1958, 583–4). We have to respect the style of argument in the Jewish commentatorial tradition if we are to contribute to it, and that means we have to follow that style. We need to be careful of those who appear to follow the style, who say they follow the style, and yet who do something very different. This is not at all to criticize what they do philosophically, since it is no doubt interesting and revealing, but it is of questionable relevance to Judaism. Modern Jewish thought, or what that is taken to be, should accordingly be treated with some suspicion.

Why is Judaism Suspicious of Heroes?

One of the standard themes in the Talmud, and rabbinic literature in general, is suspicion of government and leaders. Nimrod is called a hero (*Gen* 10.8), and the comment is made in *Gen Rabbah* 37.3 that when the word is used in the Bible, the positive references equal the negative. Even Abraham is blamed for the period of slavery in Egypt because of his sin (*Nedarim* 32a). The outstanding rabbi Akiva is thoroughly disparaged throughout the text, not only because of his advocacy of Bar Kokhba as the Messiah.

Akiva is acknowledged to be the main creator of rabbinic Judaism (*Sanhedrin* 86a) and yet is often the butt of criticism, much of which he himself accepts. Yet Akiva dies spectacularly *Kiddush ha-shem*, sanctifying the divine name. In fact, not only is he ridiculed throughout the Talmud, this seems to be something of an inside joke because it is so concentrated. He certainly got Bar Kokhba wrong as the Messiah, and Joshua bar Korchah commented, 'Akiva, grass will

Bar Kokhba: Children's book with stories about the hero who fought the Romans

grow through your cheekbones and the Messiah will still not have come' (JT *Ta'anit* 4.5, 68d). Akiva's ability to interpret the Bible is challenged when he reflects on the use of the singular expression 'frog' to describe the plague of frogs in Egypt (*Ex* 8.2). He suggests there was just one frog initially, which produced all the other frogs that covered the land. Rabbi Eleazar ben Azariah suggests that this idea shows that Akiva should stick to *halakhah*, to ritual law, and not discuss *aggadah* (*Sanhedrin* 67b). It is worth noting that Akiva is not even granted the title of rabbi in these conversations. At *Yevamot* 16a,

Akiva is thoroughly beaten in argument and labeled as not even being fit to herd cattle, to which he replies he cannot even herd sheep. In a reference to Psalm 11, the Midrash *Ex Rabbah* 2.2 asks who God tests, and the answer is that he tests the righteous:

> And with what does He test him? With shepherding sheep. He tested David with sheep and found him a good shepherd, as it says 'and He took him from the sheep folds' (*Ps* 78. 70). … He restrained the adult sheep for the sake of the lambs, and would bring out the lambs to graze in order that they would graze on soft grass. Then he brought out the old sheep to graze on moderate grass. Then he brought out the young sheep to graze on the hard grass. Said the Holy One, blessed be He, 'he who knows how to shepherd sheep, each according to their ability, let him come and shepherd my nation, as it is written "from following the ewes that give suck, he brought him to be shepherd of Jacob his [God's] people and Israel his [God's] inheritance"' (*Ps* 78. 71). Similarly, Moses was tested specifically with flocks. Our rabbis say that when Moses shepherded the flock of Jethro in the desert, one of the goats fled from him. He ran after it until he reached a shady place. When he reached the shady place he happened upon a pool of water, where the goat was standing, drinking. When Moses reached it he said 'I didn't realize that you ran because of thirst. You are tired.' He placed the goat on his shoulders and walked. Said the Holy One, blessed be He, 'you have mercy to guide flocks belonging to flesh and blood this way, by your life, you shall shepherd my flock Israel'. This explains why it says: 'And Moses was shepherding' (*Ex* 3.1).

So when Akiva accepts that he cannot shepherd sheep, this means that he is unable to pass the test that God sets him, and it is a serious charge to which to plead guilty. But then, of course, from what we know of the Talmud we do not know how serious he is in his self-criticism here. Is he really admitting to being hopeless as a leader of the community, is he showing how humble he is by accepting something that he knows is not true, or is he so eager to preserve agreement among his peers that he will go along with anything they want him to say? Or is he poking fun at the idea of someone being so wonderful that he is regarded as an outstanding individual during his time and beyond? After all, both Moses and David, who are here praised in the Midrash, are roundly criticized in the Bible for some of their actions. Not only are they criticized, but they are actually punished.

Rabbi Yose the Galilean says that Akiva has robbed God of his holiness (*Chagigah* 14a). R. Judah b. Batira twice threatened to call down divine punishment on him for revealing secrets in his commentary (*Shabbat* 96b–97a) and he is often regarded as being far too free in his interpretation, shocking his colleagues. On the other hand, they did sometimes admit that there was something to be learned from him, as when he laughed on passing the destroyed Temple (*Lamentations Rabbah* 5.18) and startled them into looking at the disaster in a new and enlightening manner.

There is an interesting passage about Akiva and Moses in *Menachot* 29b. Moses visits God in heaven and finds him adding flourishes to the letters of the Torah. (There are such flourishes, or *tagim*, in the written text when done by a *sofer*, or scribe, in the scrolls containing the text.) God says that someone will arise called Akiva ben Yosef, who will derive from these little flourishes a good deal of legal material. Moses asks to see him. The next thing he knows he is sitting, in the eighth row, in Akiva's college and is listening to what is being said, and has no idea what is meant by it all. Akiva is asked by his students where he derives the interpretation he is using (perhaps they were as confused as Moses) and they are told that it comes from a law of Moses from Mount Sinai. This puts Moses' mind at rest. The implication though is that he still does not really understand what Akiva is talking about, and how the Law he was given on Mount Sinai can be interpreted to involve the laws that Akiva is discussing.

This passage can be taken in two ways. It may show how clever Akiva was to be able to derive so many laws from so little, and indeed that is often a criterion defining a skilled Talmudist – someone who can make something relatively simple appear very complicated. On the other hand, it might be a criticism of Akiva, a suggestion that he is going too far, and indulging himself in a display of his own intellectual versatility rather than trying to understand what the text is really about. If he is really deriving laws from the flourishes on the letters, then this is really going too far, but then it is widely accepted that gematria – deriving interpretations of scripture from the numerical value of terms used in it – is valid, so perhaps thinking also of the shape of the written text may be relevant. There are today Jewish yoga enthusiasts who twist their bodies into the shape of Hebrew letters, from which they claim to derive some spiritual benefit, and

בָּרֵאשִׁית בָּרָא אֱלֹהִים אֵת הַשָּׁמַיִם וְאֵת הָאָרֶץ: וְהָאָרֶץ
הָיְתָה תֹהוּ וָבֹהוּ וְחֹשֶׁךְ עַל־פְּנֵי תְהוֹם וְרוּחַ אֱלֹהִים
מְרַחֶפֶת עַל־פְּנֵי הַמָּיִם: וַיֹּאמֶר אֱלֹהִים יְהִי אוֹר וַיְהִי־
אוֹר: וַיַּרְא אֱלֹהִים אֶת־הָאוֹר כִּי־טוֹב וַיַּבְדֵּל אֱלֹהִים בֵּין
הָאוֹר וּבֵין הַחֹשֶׁךְ: וַיִּקְרָא אֱלֹהִים לָאוֹר יוֹם וְלַחֹשֶׁךְ
קָרָא לָיְלָה וַיְהִי־עֶרֶב וַיְהִי־בֹקֶר יוֹם אֶחָד: פ
וַיֹּאמֶר אֱלֹהִים יְהִי רָקִיעַ בְּתוֹךְ הַמָּיִם וִיהִי מַבְדִּיל בֵּין
מַיִם לָמָיִם: וַיַּעַשׂ אֱלֹהִים אֶת־הָרָקִיעַ וַיַּבְדֵּל בֵּין הַמַּיִם
אֲשֶׁר מִתַּחַת לָרָקִיעַ וּבֵין הַמַּיִם אֲשֶׁר מֵעַל לָרָקִיעַ וַיְהִי־
כֵן: וַיִּקְרָא אֱלֹהִים לָרָקִיעַ שָׁמָיִם וַיְהִי־עֶרֶב וַיְהִי־בֹקֶר
יוֹם שֵׁנִי: פ
וַיֹּאמֶר אֱלֹהִים יִקָּווּ הַמַּיִם מִתַּחַת הַשָּׁמַיִם אֶל־מָקוֹם אֶחָד
וְתֵרָאֶה הַיַּבָּשָׁה וַיְהִי־כֵן: וַיִּקְרָא אֱלֹהִים לַיַּבָּשָׁה אֶרֶץ
וּלְמִקְוֵה הַמַּיִם קָרָא יַמִּים וַיַּרְא אֱלֹהִים כִּי־טוֹב: וַיֹּאמֶר
אֱלֹהִים תַּדְשֵׁא הָאָרֶץ דֶּשֶׁא עֵשֶׂב מַזְרִיעַ זֶרַע עֵץ פְּרִי
עֹשֶׂה פְּרִי לְמִינוֹ אֲשֶׁר זַרְעוֹ־בוֹ עַל־הָאָרֶץ וַיְהִי־כֵן: וַתּוֹצֵא
הָאָרֶץ דֶּשֶׁא עֵשֶׂב מַזְרִיעַ זֶרַע לְמִינֵהוּ וְעֵץ עֹשֶׂה־
פְּרִי אֲשֶׁר זַרְעוֹ־בוֹ לְמִינֵהוּ וַיַּרְא אֱלֹהִים כִּי־טוֹב: וַיְהִי־
עֶרֶב וַיְהִי־בֹקֶר יוֹם שְׁלִישִׁי: פ
וַיֹּאמֶר אֱלֹהִים יְהִי מְאֹרֹת בִּרְקִיעַ הַשָּׁמַיִם לְהַבְדִּיל בֵּין
הַיּוֹם וּבֵין הַלָּיְלָה וְהָיוּ לְאֹתֹת וּלְמוֹעֲדִים וּלְיָמִים וְשָׁנִים:
וְהָיוּ לִמְאוֹרֹת בִּרְקִיעַ הַשָּׁמַיִם לְהָאִיר עַל־הָאָרֶץ וַיְהִי־
כֵן: וַיַּעַשׂ אֱלֹהִים אֶת־שְׁנֵי הַמְּאֹרֹת הַגְּדֹלִים אֶת־הַמָּאוֹר
הַגָּדֹל לְמֶמְשֶׁלֶת הַיּוֹם וְאֶת־הַמָּאוֹר הַקָּטֹן לְמֶמְשֶׁלֶת
הַלַּיְלָה וְאֵת הַכּוֹכָבִים: וַיִּתֵּן אֹתָם אֱלֹהִים בִּרְקִיעַ
הַשָּׁמָיִם לְהָאִיר עַל־הָאָרֶץ: וְלִמְשֹׁל בַּיּוֹם וּבַלַּיְלָה
וּלֲהַבְדִּיל בֵּין הָאוֹר וּבֵין הַחֹשֶׁךְ וַיַּרְא אֱלֹהִים כִּי־טוֹב:
וַיְהִי־עֶרֶב וַיְהִי־בֹקֶר יוֹם רְבִיעִי: פ
וַיֹּאמֶר אֱלֹהִים יִשְׁרְצוּ הַמַּיִם שֶׁרֶץ נֶפֶשׁ חַיָּה וְעוֹף יְעוֹפֵף
עַל־הָאָרֶץ עַל־פְּנֵי רְקִיעַ הַשָּׁמָיִם: וַיִּבְרָא אֱלֹהִים אֶת־
הַתַּנִּינִם הַגְּדֹלִים וְאֵת כָּל־נֶפֶשׁ הַחַיָּה הָרֹמֶשֶׂת אֲשֶׁר
שָׁרְצוּ הַמַּיִם לְמִינֵהֶם וְאֵת כָּל־עוֹף כָּנָף לְמִינֵהוּ וַיַּרְא
אֱלֹהִים כִּי־טוֹב: וַיְבָרֶךְ אֹתָם אֱלֹהִים לֵאמֹר פְּרוּ וּרְבוּ
וּמִלְאוּ אֶת־הַמַּיִם בַּיַּמִּים וְהָעוֹף יִרֶב בָּאָרֶץ: וַיְהִי־עֶרֶב
וַיְהִי־בֹקֶר יוֹם חֲמִישִׁי: פ
וַיֹּאמֶר אֱלֹהִים תּוֹצֵא הָאָרֶץ נֶפֶשׁ חַיָּה לְמִינָהּ בְּהֵמָה
וָרֶמֶשׂ וְחַיְתוֹ־אֶרֶץ לְמִינָהּ וַיְהִי־כֵן: וַיַּעַשׂ אֱלֹהִים אֶת־
חַיַּת הָאָרֶץ לְמִינָהּ וְאֶת־הַבְּהֵמָה לְמִינָהּ

First page, sefer Torah *reproduced on left, with modern Hebrew on right*

there is certainly great beauty in the ways in which some of the letters can be represented artistically, or even by a decent scribe. But surely nothing significant may be derived from the flourishes on them, and this passage is either a criticism of the over-free interpretive methods of Akiva, or an example of Talmudic hyperbole, one example among many others. When it comes to Akiva, the Talmud is either very positive or very negative, but rarely undecided, and the reader has to work out what to make of this juxtaposition of contrary views. One point that is being made here is the familiar one we find also throughout the Bible, and that is that the heroes and villains of these Jewish texts are very human, certainly far from perfect, and often it is difficult to say precisely how we are to regard them, in the same way as it is often difficult to sum up a person's life. It is worth noting that the attack on heroes and heroism makes for a complicated ethical life for Jews, who are only able to set out to emulate God, rather than other human beings, in their attempt at living well. Of course, emulating God is hardly the easiest thing to accomplish, since we are finite and the object we are aiming to resemble is infinite and ultimately unknowable by us.

Even Moses is criticized: for being critical of the Israelites he is punished with leprosy, death and not being allowed to enter the Promised Land. Samuel, Elijah and Elisha are all thoroughly attacked, as are Isaiah and Hosea, while Jeremiah and Ezekiel are linked with their disparagement of Israel with their mother, regarding whose honor doubts are raised. These are extraordinary claims, since these prophets were not giving their own views but were preaching on behalf of God and to God's people, and their purpose was to improve behavior so that the people would function better and be deserving of divine assistance and support. David is prevented from building the Temple because of his warlike activities, but who was he fighting for? It is not as though he decided arbitrarily to attack his neighbors. God gave him a mission of conquering certain groups of people, and he did what he was told.

We need to put these points in context, and that context is the attack on Judaism by Christians, and to a degree also by Muslims, for having pointed to the prophets to identify major faults in Jewish life and activities. It was for this reason that the baton was passed, as it were, to the newer religions, and the Jews remained stubbornly in the den of iniquity that the prophets had identified. What the rabbis were trying to do was to support the Jews in their struggle to survive this onslaught, by emphasizing the positive and the continuing role of Israel in the preservation of the world.

God's choice of Abraham is explained only once, when he is told that he will have a child with Sarah, and he is expected to instruct his children and his household to follow the divine path by doing what is right and just (*Gen* 18.19). This is worth noting – that to be instructors or teachers one does not have to be perfect; in fact, quite the contrary. The most important Jewish prayer, if there can be said to be such a thing, is the *shema*, and this calls on the reciter to teach his children, speak to them when sitting at home or walking outside, when lying down and rising up (*Deut* 6.7). It is worth pointing also to the difficulties that the rabbis had when they decided that certain individuals were the Messiah. There is a certain comfort to be derived from the idea that Jewish suffering plays a role in the coming of the Messiah, since for him to come, difficulties must be experienced. We see this theme in the Bible when Isaiah (11.1–9) reflects on the destruction of the Northern Kingdom of Israel and the near-collapse of the Southern Kingdom of Judah by talking about a time of justice and complete peace. Other prophets, such as Jeremiah and Ezekiel, linked the Messiah with the house of David, and the Psalms give a few extra details, along with Daniel, who is particularly graphic on the finality of the messianic age.

Around the time of Jesus there were apparently many messianic movements, and there continued to be in that region, and one might have expected that the failure of Jesus to do anything dramatic in this world would have damaged his messianic credentials among his supporters, but one thing any observer of a religion cannot help but notice is the constant ability of religions to deal with any awkward facts. Many of those involved in revolts against the Romans were no doubt buoyed up by messianic expectations of divine support for their efforts, and their role in the divinely arranged end of the world as they knew it to be. Not only were all these putative messiahs not the genuine article, but they brought huge disasters down on the community as a whole, leading to the virtual elimination of Jewish life in Judah and suspicion about Jews generally, which did not help relationships in the diaspora between the Jews and the other communities. By the time of the Mishnah in the third century CE the rabbis seem to have learned from this sad experience and downplayed the role of the Messiah, though not denying his existence or the desire for his coming. This attitude was nicely summarized by Maimonides in his listing of belief in the Messiah as a defining part of the Jewish faith, while at the same time in his *Mishneh Torah* rather downplaying the sorts of changes that would exist in the messianic age. Around his time 'messiahs' continued to appear and attract support, sometimes even after their total failure, so we should perhaps not be surprised at the continuing enthusiasm of Christians for the messianic status of Jesus. Once one accepts that difficult circumstances could be *chevlei Mashiach*, the birth pangs of the Messiah, then the frequent problems that occurred to Jews fitted in with at least the idea of what preceded the Messiah, and a charismatic character who offered an easy and quick resolution of such difficulties is always a tempting prospect, both within and outside religion, and often holds on to the allegiance of his supporters despite his obvious shortcomings. In the seventeenth century, for example, Shabetai Zvi set off from Izmir at a time of great suffering in Eastern Europe, with huge backing from the world Jewish community, and led his followers on a triumphant journey to the Land of Israel. This journey was rudely interrupted by the authorities threatening him with death unless he converted to Islam (the Ottoman Empire not at this stage living up to its claims of a tolerant attitude to the Jews, perhaps), which he promptly did, yet the conversion and abandonment of his mission did not give all his followers pause for thought. Some maintained their belief in him, arguing that he was dissimulating or following some complex kabbalistic strategy that one had to believe would work out well. In Turkey today, the descendants of his followers, the Dönmeh, are still regarded with some suspicion by the population at large and have unwittingly taken on many of the familiar stereotypes of the Jews, chief among which is a conspiratorial role. For the rabbis, presumably not those in the Sabbatean camp, this enthusiasm for leaders and messiahs is something to be guarded against, hence the warnings in the Talmud against leaders. There are also many warnings in the *Pirkei Avot* against what is broadly labeled 'the government', by which is no doubt meant the civil authorities, but the instructions not to get involved in politics is a potent caution against dealing with power and where power can lead people.

It is worth recalling that many of the heroes of the Jewish Bible are not very heroic. Jacob cheats his brother, fools his father and then runs away. He returns years later, timidly expecting retribution. Abraham lies about his wife being his sister, and both he and that wife are skeptical when God promises them a son. Jonah disobeys God's command to go to Nineveh and prophesy, David and Solomon had problems with limiting their sexual partners, and so on. The underlying theme here is that we should not expect human beings to be perfect, since they are not, nor should we expect them to be indispensable, since God can bring things about by himself quite easily. This has implications for the language dealing with the Messiah. There is a suspicion about candidates for messiahship in Judaism precisely because of the dependence on one person and on his perfection in carrying out that role. In Jewish history, the plethora of false messiahs is not only a warning against trusting people who seem to fit the bill, but also a warning against the whole process of expecting someone or some system of government to appear and solve all the world's problems. Though messianism is predominantly a religious concept, it does not have to be, and we have seen in recent history how people have followed a doctrine that is entirely secular, but which they feel will bring about, eventually, perfect justice, peace and so on, often even when it is quite obvious that this is far from the case. Many Zionists who were not religious nevertheless took seriously the idea of Jewish nationalism, finding in Israel the outlet for their hopes for the future and the linking of those hopes with the experiences of the past, very much a feature of any sort of nationalism. It led to a discussion about whether Israel should be just another ordinary state in the world among many others, or whether it should live up to the biblical demand that it be a light to the nations, and part of a further process through which the whole world is refined and improved, until eventually it achieves a messianic state. A problem with the idea of this greater conception of Israel is that it calls for leaders and heroes to lead the nation in new and exciting directions, which demands very much of those individuals, more perhaps than it is reasonable to expect. It might even involve transforming the State of Israel itself into the Messiah, or as having a messianic character, as some Christian groups interpret it, and that again brings out huge demands on its leaders and citizens, something we might well think goes entirely against the whole tenor of the Hebrew Bible, with its downplaying of individuals and their power to bring about major, or indeed any, changes entirely through their own efforts.

The idea that the State is messianic offends against the idea also that we cannot really know what the messianic age will be like, as Maimonides argued. One of the features of Judaism is its refusal to submit completely to any of the passing enthusiasms of the age, such as Islam, Christianity, Sabbatianism, Marxism and so on, and the belief in a Messiah actually being present would offend against this principle. What is required is the constant hope of a Messiah, not an actual Messiah, and once that figure appears we do indeed have a hero, but at the cost of bringing history to an end. Once the Messiah comes we no longer need to hope for his coming, and once hope disappears we trust entirely in the new state of the world and the people who bring it about, which in the past was always disastrous. There is scope, then, to wonder whether the State of Israel is closely linked with anything messianic, something that those religious Jews who are anti-Zionist often stress. They sometimes argue that the State should not come about except through the Messiah, and what we see now is clearly not messianic, since it does not accord (yet) with the signs of the Messiah. For example, the truth has not emerged from Israel and spread throughout the world, and the lion does not lie down with the lamb, or if he does we do not expect the lamb to survive. These are similar objections that the Jews have always given to the idea of Jesus as a candidate for messiahship, and they are quite relevant. Of course, it could always be argued that the birth pangs of the Messiah are prolonged, and that in the present they can be perceived, if one looks carefully enough. But that is like arguing that Shabetai Zvi or Jacob Frank, a later false messiah, are really the Messiah, and one can see the signs if one looks in the right sort of way. Judaism was often criticized for being too material and literal in its interpretation of the Bible, but we can see some advantages in this strategy here. The signs of the Messiah are quite easy to determine, as the Bible describes them, and perhaps the point is to discourage the Jews from thinking of the issue as very complex and obscure, since that encourages self-deception and fraud. We all like to place our trust in charismatic individuals and submit to the authority of those who seem to be qualified for that position, but unless the object of our enthusiasm is God, we are warned in Judaism to be very wary of behaving in this manner.

The Jewish God is Violent and Jealous

The Jewish Bible is full of revenge and threats of revenge, and it is an extraordinarily violent work, something that is often politely ignored in modern times. Christians and Muslims, of course, can consider this part of the previous revelation that has now been superseded by something much more up to date and accurate. The prophet

Obadiah is distinguished among other things for having the shortest book in the Bible, a mere 21 verses. He was a convert to Judaism from Edom, and like many converts, he turned totally against his previous heritage, thundering against the Edomites that they would be destroyed by the Israelites, provided (and it is a big proviso) that the latter remain faithful to their covenant. After all, Obadiah lived at the time of King Ahab and Queen Jezebel, when idol worship was all the rage and the traditional Jewish practices were in retreat. The Edomites are the descendants of Esau, and Esau is labeled as a sinner. But what did Esau do that was wrong? The poor man was cheated out of his birthright, we are told, for a mess of pottage, a dish of lentils. Jacob seems to have no doubt that he deserved to be punished by Esau, as he ran away immediately after the deed, and when he eventually returned he approached Esau carefully by sending him conciliatory notes and sent away his family from what he assumed would be a bloody confrontation. Esau was indeed on the move toward Jacob with a considerable force. Before they met, however, Jacob wrestled with the angel, and during a long struggle dislocates his hip, but overcomes the angel in the end and is rewarded with the name of Israel, meaning 'he who won in a struggle with God'. The angel is often said to represent Esau, and so while the account of the struggle is physical, in fact Jacob reconciles himself with Esau spiritually; and this reminds us of why Jacob is superior to Esau, because he is capable of doing things without violence and spilling blood, and because he realizes it is better to wrestle with an angel than with one's brother. Therefore, he is in fact the appropriate person to head his community, rather than the very physically oriented hunter, Esau. Levinas comments on violence, that it occurs when one acts as though one were by oneself: 'Violence is to be found in any action in which one acts as if one were alone to act: as if the rest of the universe were there only to receive the action' (Levinas, 1990a, 6), a strange thing to say, but it brings out the way in which it is only really possible, in his view, if the actor entirely discounts the interests of others.

Some Jews concentrate on the references to Amalek (*Ex* 14–17), in which it is said there will always be someone like that trying to kill the Jews, and so we must always be prepared to defend ourselves. On the other hand, that passage also calls on the Jews to blot out his name, which suggests that there is a virtue in forgetting, as well as remembering. In fact, it is a matter of balance – we do need to bear our enemies in mind, since otherwise they can easily overwhelm us, and we need to take precautions to prevent this from happening. We can transform Jewish history into a martyrology, a history of defeat and suffering, with occasional respites. Yet this is far too gloomy, because the bright spots are also significant, and we need to take them into account if we are to be able to appreciate the good things in life as well as the bad. This is not a bad way of classifying different strains in modern Israeli politics – the distinction between those who are willing to gamble on peace whatever the enemy seems to be contemplating, and those who are constantly suspicious of the other side, no matter how amicable they appear to be. After all, like Amalek, the enemy could just be waiting for a moment of weakness in which to strike. During the Holocaust, many Europeans were delighted at the sufferings of their Jewish fellow citizens, enthusiastically joining in with both the murder and the plunder. Just like Amalek, they attacked at the worse possible moment, from behind, when the Germans had done the hard fighting and the Jews were most vulnerable, and entirely defenseless. Yet if we treat the enemy as though he is always just about to strike, we never treat him as anything but an enemy, and that makes him an enemy all the time.

If religions are good at anything at all, it is at trying to develop in their followers a balanced attitude, and at accusing other religions of not getting the balance right. When the Israelites in their own country decide that they want a king, and they come to Samuel (I *Sam* 9.1–11.13) and ask him to arrange it for them, he at first argues against it, saying quite rightly that this would result in all sorts of negative consequences. He complains to God about what they want and God replies that they are not criticizing Samuel but rather God, which is a kind way of putting it. Despite what God says, presumably if they were happy with being ruled by Samuel they would not want a king! So though it is the wrong decision, God is going to go along with it, and he can, of course, work with anything that his creatures do. Right at the start of the Bible, Adam and Eve disobey God and are punished, yet they are not destroyed, though he does destroy people on occasion. They took the wrong decision, but they did not go so wrong that God never wanted to have anything to do with them again. Violence can be justified, and there is a good deal of violence in the Bible, but we might ponder over the parts where God is not violent, as when Abraham persuades him to spare the towns on the plain, or when he pushes Jonah to carry out, however sulkily, his prophetic mission despite his misgivings. In fact, God apparently enjoys turning things round, or trying to get us to turn things around, as we try to resolve a difficult situation.

When God calls on Moses to go to the Pharaoh, Moses is reluctant, but, unlike Jonah, does not actually run away. He says quite reasonably that he is not much of an orator (*Ex* 3.11) and the court is full of ambassadors and diplomats who are gifted at speaking, so he would by comparison do a very poor job, being nothing like a man of words (*ish debarim*) (4.10). According to Midrash *Tanchumah* (*Deut* 1.2), God reminds Moses that it was God who gave humanity a tongue in the first place and so it is hardly difficult for him to help Moses move from not being a man of words to becoming precisely someone who can say 'These are the words' (*ellah debarim*) (*Deut* 1.1) (Bregman, 2003, 114–16). It is reasonable to think that God could do this, and also reasonable for Moses to wonder if he will, and throughout the exodus Moses does things that go against God's direct orders, for which he is eventually prevented from entering the Land of Israel. It might be thought that it was cruel of God to ruin what was after all Moses' lifework, to enter Israel with the Israelites and enjoy the fruits of all his efforts, difficulties and travels. Yet one might also think that to fail to punish Moses would be to fail to respect Moses. If transgressions are forgiven and forgotten, they could not have been that serious at all, yet when God tells his creatures to do something, he expects to be obeyed. Nadav and Avihu certainly found that out when they were destroyed by God for taking strange fire, whatever that might be, for a ritual (*JT* ch. 1).

There are many violent passages in the Bible, and God often seems to be an angry and vengeful individual. But these are not the only passages to be found. The Bible reflects the fact that we live in a violent and vengeful world, something that is explored at some length in *JT*.

Yet people who concentrate on particular verses and say that they encapsulate the religion are wrong. Along with the sad passages are happy ones, along with the aggressive go the gentle and so on, and this is not just a feature of Judaism either. It is in trying to bring these different passages together that so much Jewish commentary takes place, and they do, of course, reflect what from our point of view is

Zarah: A Jewish maiden about to be executed by the Greeks

the highly complex notion of the divinity. They also reflect the mixture of experiences and emotions that we feel when trying to get to grips with the world in which we live, and our views on how we should live in it and treat others.

Modern Jewish thought: Just say No

We often wonder at the discrepancies that are found in the Bible and then establish complex ways of resolving them, which is something I have just been doing. Some argue that since the text is really a collection of texts by a variety of different authors from a number of different periods, it is hardly surprising that there are discrepancies and difficulties. If, however, one sees it as entirely the product of one author, God, then all these apparent problems need to be resolved in so far as we can, since they hide something significant that God means us, or at least some of us, to know. This is the gauntlet that the traditional Jew throws down to his more reform-minded co-religionists. If you do not think the Torah is the product of God, totally and without question, then when you study it you are going to have little interest in finding out what it means as a whole, since it may well not mean anything in particular, it is just parts of it and their various authors that are worth studying, since they will have a meaning that can be assessed. It is rather like a timetable where the different parts of a city have not cooperated in organizing the schedule. The different bits will work efficiently and can be understood, but the whole is beyond understanding as a unitary system, unless by chance everything does fit together. The chances of that are minimal, of course.

But we could interpret the system as unified even if it is not. By dint of clever reasoning, almost anything can be connected to anything else. The question is whether it is worth doing this, and this is very much reliant on the idea that what is being unearthed is something that was originally connected. One of the great difficulties of accepting the traditional account of the Torah is that it includes not only the written Torah, but also the oral teaching of the rabbis as holy and derived directly from God. One can understand why the rabbis would have wanted rabbinic commentary to be identified with God in this way, but its plausibility is seriously dubious, however much one may regard the Bible itself as given by God. Here we have reached a real problem with a great deal of Jewish theology. It could well be an issue with theology as a whole. It relies on the comparison of texts and the use of those texts to explore the religion, but the orientation of the theologians entirely drives the analysis. He or she can surely select the right passages to illustrate almost *any* point, or perhaps any point, since from the Bible, and all the commentatorial materials such as the Mishnah, the Talmud, the Tosefta, the Midrashim, the *baraitot* and so on, a wide variety of views can be found. It is surely not difficult for the more decorous of those views that are easily available to be applied to a particular issue and for that issue then to be 'explained' with respect to those views. The result is an apparently Jewish interpretation of the issue, vouchsafed by the many Jewish texts that have been quoted to establish that view.

Let us take as an example here the argument by Jonathan Sacks on what he regards as revolutionary about the Jewish religion. He quotes the fact that so much emphasis was given in the Bible to the treatment of the stranger among the Israelites. This concern for the other impressed him and he suggests that it is paradigmatic of the religion as a whole. Yet these passages could be taken in a very different way. They might be taken to support the legitimization of those among the Israelites who had accompanied them on their journey as the community organized itself into a political group, since clearly these people were both a valuable resource and had contributed in the past to the success of the exodus mission. In much the same way today in Israel, there is a discussion about what to do with the foreign workers who are not Jewish, but who have contributed to and wish to remain within the State. Should a Jew from Harrisburg, USA, say, be given preference for nationality over a Thai who actually lives in Haifa and who is making a direct contribution to economic life in the State of Israel? At present this is what happens, but the account of how the stranger ought to be treated in the Bible does not really help us, since the original formulation of the issue does not mention citizenship or a comparison between different claims on joining the community. According to Jonathan Sacks (Sacks, 2000, 92), what makes Judaism an especially desirable religion is that it puts the stress on safeguarding the interests of the stranger (mentioned 36 times in the Torah, according to *Bava Metzia* 59b). The injunction to love one's neighbor is easy to follow, since we know who our neighbors are and what they are like, he suggests, so we like the people who resemble us, in many cases, but the stranger is precisely someone who is strange and alien, someone whom we might even fear and find it difficult to accept. Yet we are told on many occasions that the stranger must be considered, and the Israelites should reflect on the fact that they were once strangers in Egypt. This sounds great, and he comments at some length about the high moral standard that is being set here for the Israelites. This is typical of what I have here called the rabbinic method, which is to put together an argument for a conclusion based on reasoning, together with some quotations from Jewish texts.

Should we accept his argument? Perhaps not, if by stranger is meant someone who is traveling with you and who needs to have their relationship with the community as a whole resolved. Reminding the Israelites of life in Egypt is designed to remind them that a minority that does not become integrated with the wider society comes to be seen as a threat to that society and may find itself set up for persecution. It is highly inappropriate to think that these references to the stranger are an early form of toleration of diversity and difference. On the contrary, they could be seen as an attempt to do away with that diversity by enabling alien groups to become integrated into the wider society. There is good reason to think that Judaism is not very open to other groups on the whole, since so much of the Torah is about separating the Jewish community from everyone else; for example, the 613 commandments compared to the seven Noahide rules – the Laws that should be followed by any human being. The very issue of who is a Jew is so fraught because of different definitions, some very restrictive and some quite loose, and it can hardly be said that the distinctions that are made between people are not regarded as significant in Judaism. If Judaism can be described in a single phrase at all, it is the religion that insists on distinctions.

This does not mean, of course, that Jews are to regard themselves as better than anyone else. Non-Jews have just as much opportunity to live a good life as Jews do, and if one believes that salvation is an option then non-Jews will be just as likely to participate in it. But the idea that the Torah does not emphasize the differences between Jews and the rest is ridiculous. It constantly explores this relationship, and commentators have continued to do so. Most of the rules in the Talmud and Mishnah deal with what is incumbent on Jews as Jews, not on what is incumbent on them as human beings. So Sacks' interpretation, heart-warming though it is, is wildly implausible, and demonstrates a real problem with this way of arguing, of which it is an excellent example. One of the problems in the Bible for the Israelites is preventing them from assimilating into communities that were all around them and were in fact rather similar to them, and for whom intermarriage ought to be prevented if at all possible. The

Moabites and the Ammonites, who were contiguous with the Israelites, and very similar to them in a range of ways, were said to be universally the descendants of an incestuous relationship and so all had the status of bastards (*Gen* 19.30–8). The Canaanites are constantly portrayed in negative terms. The Bible rightly perceives that the greater danger comes from assimilation with people who resemble us, not those who are distinct. If Judaism is to continue to exist it has to preserve its unique characteristics, and the Bible sets out to create a distinction between the Israelites and others for this to be possible. The idea that the religion does not distinguish clearly between its adherents and everyone else is difficult to accept.

The main texts of religions are complex documents, with a wide variety of views on a range of topics, and to derive any particular unitary message from them is never easy, though religious teachers often argue otherwise. It is because religions are complex that they have lasted, since they can then fit with the complexity of people's lives. A simple set of standards would be highly inappropriate, though we do often think that religion consists of such a simple set. What religious teachers such as rabbis often do when writing for a general audience is to present their religion in a simplified way, to make it easier for people to understand its basic principles. This works rhetorically, but is quite unsatisfactory as a serious account of the topic. The modern thinker whose method is a perfect example of this is Emanuel Levinas, whose Talmudic commentaries have almost nothing to do with the Talmud, but a great deal to do with his own views and philosophy. And why not – there is no reason why a thinker should not seek inspiration from many sources, and the Talmud is as good a place as any to start, or so it might be suggested. The trouble is, however, that the commentaries that emerge are not really commentaries on the religion or the laws of the religion, but are connected only superficially with it.

We need to be quite clear about what the purpose of this sort of rabbinic commentary is, though it is worth adding that not all of its authors are in fact rabbis. The purpose is to inspire, persuade and motivate an audience, generally a Jewish audience, and so the quotations that would be appropriate are carefully chosen, and the arguments selected to meet the task in mind. There is, of course, nothing wrong with this, but it is important to understand what is going on here, since otherwise the gaps in the argument will seem glaring.

A few quotes from a religious text are never enough to establish what the religion is all about, however impressive they are, or however far they are stretched. This is not a point specifically about Judaism, but applies to religions in general. So those who select a few Qur'anic passages to argue that Islam is aggressive, or passive, or anything at all, are bound to fail to define the religion, as are those who ask what Jesus would do.

On the other hand, some of the theological expressions we find in the main texts of Judaism are heavy with implications for practice and interesting ideas about how we should live. One of the issues the rabbis emphasized was that, since the destruction of the Temple, the tables on which Jews eat and invite people to join them has replaced the altar (*Menachot* 97a, *Chagigah* 27a). The person at their table, even if they know him or her, is a stranger if this is not his/her home, and one of the features of Abraham that we are called on, rightly, to admire, is his extreme attitude to hospitality. R. Yehudah drew from this the principle that hospitality to travelers is more important than welcoming the *Shekhinah* (*Shabbat* 127b). Presumably, he means by this that it is a way of attracting the *Shekhinah*, the divine presence, to one's house. Abraham, after all, interrupted a revelation from heaven itself in order to rush out and bring strangers into his house (*Gen* 18.1–2). God appeared to him but he left to attend to three men, leaving the cool of his tent to go out into the heat and invite them in. He knew nothing about them, except that they would be honoring him if they joined him in his tent and shared his food and drink. This is a remarkable attitude to take to the stranger, yet not so remarkable if one acknowledges the significance of society and companionship, a constant theme in Judaism, something that the modern thinker Levinas appropriately emphasizes in his account of Judaism. Strangers are very helpful to us, since they give us the opportunity to meet new people, to learn from them and to link up with them in some way. Presumably, in the past that is what the Temple did: many people visited it and no doubt socialized among themselves at the same time, but even with it gone this opportunity still remains when we eat with others and invite them into our homes.

Let us take another example of how some modern thought appears to be Jewish, but is not. The philosopher Ken Seeskin (2007) is enthusiastic about the thinker Immanuel Kant, and not unnaturally finds that, on the whole, Judaism is in line with Kant, even where it seems clearly to be different. He suggests that Judaism, like Kant, sees the Law as something it imposes on itself. He certainly accepts that the idea that Kant and Judaism are in broad agreement on the attitude to the Law is highly implausible. After all, religions tend to find a role for God in the Law, and they often argue that the Law is the Law because God orders it for us. Some thinkers, such as Maimonides, certainly argue that laws often have reasons, and that we can even grasp those reasons on occasion. Yet this is very far from arguing that what makes a Law our Law is our coming to it ourselves and agreeing to it. Maimonides, for example, accepts that most people just have to accept the Law, without really understanding the reasons for it, since most people are not able to work these things out for themselves. Here, doing things because God tells us to has a real impact on our lives, and one has to wonder quite generally what point there is to having a deity if we can work out the reasons for the laws ourselves, along with the laws themselves, a conclusion that many Jews have themselves come to if the present parlous condition of the Reform and Conservative movements in the USA are any indication.

Seeskin goes further than arguing that the major moral rules established at Sinai are rules that the people then present agreed to because they expressed the considered judgment of everyone in the group. He even suggests that the Jews agreed to the ritual laws, the *hukkim*, which even Maimonides said had rationales so far back in time that their purpose is obscure to us. Yet Maimonides also said that we could not doubt them and anyone who sought to vary them even by a tiny amount was in danger of upsetting the whole body of the Law. This seems very far indeed from Kant, and the idea of binding ourselves to a ritual body of Law whose rationale is no longer extant gives even Seeskin pause for thought. However, he goes on to argue, rather like Levinas, that the ritual is in fact the practical, physical side of the theoretical moral principles we can see a justification for, the *mishpatim*, and so can also freely consent to them when we take on those rules that have an obvious role in our lives. That is certainly possible, if I freely consent to do what someone tells me to do, on the basis that I think they know better than I do about how I should behave, then I can be said to have freely consented to take on those obligations and all that they entail. We often do this; we take the advice of a physician or a lawyer, perhaps, precisely because we do not understand the complexity of the situation in which we find ourselves, but (we hope) they do. Yet surely we cannot be said to be acting autonomously here, since we literally do not understand why we are being asked to do what we are agreeing to do. We are not forced to do it, but we do it on the basis that someone else knows better than we do how we should behave, and that is not in any sense autonomy. To say that if we understood then we would agree is besides the point, since that is the principle of paternalism, and while there are no doubt many circumstances in which it is in our interests to sacrifice our autonomy for our own best interests, we do sacrifice our autonomy nevertheless. Any reading of Jewish Law that sees this otherwise surely fails to do justice to the nature of that Law.

What, then, are the Jewish ways of doing things? In language it is to hold texts against each other, to use the processes of compare and contrast, and then say something about what emerges. Sometimes the emphasis is on the *peshat*, the direct meaning of the text or word. Often a passage from one part of the Bible is compared, using a commentary that flourished in the past, with a passage from a different part, since it may be a similar text, or it may amplify the meaning, or indicate a contrast that helpfully provides a deeper insight into the meaning. Sometimes the commentators think it is a good idea to go deeper into the *derash*, the more obscure meaning, both deeper and wider; here there is a greater use of creativity, and perhaps a rather more far-fetched interpretation is involved. After all, since the Bible represents the divine guide for human beings, it is reasonable to explore it (which is the literal meaning of *derash*), for any indication of meaning that might have been missed the first time around, including a variety of spelling in the text, the numerical rendering of a term and the other terms that have the same rendering, what happens if we substitute a different letter, or transpose a verse, and so on. The point is to work out an issue of Law, generally, and how the Bible contributes to that issue, and in recent times the connection between this creative approach to the Talmud and postmodernism has not gone unremarked. It does look very much as though anything goes, and the unbridled creativity of the commentator to manipulate the language as he or she sees fit cannot be challenged. In fact, it represents what has always taken place and what takes place today in the writings of modern commentators. When one looks at what can only be called the wildness in interpretation of some Talmudic excurses, it seems invidious to criticize modern commentators for their lack of respect for the tradition. Is it not the case that the tradition itself is based on an extreme form of freedom of interpretation, so that what in fact is being done in modern times is precisely part of the tradition of Jewish commentary.

Yes and no. There are many very strange and improbable uses of language in the Talmud, especially the Babylonian Talmud, which makes full use of *aggadah*, of stories designed to illustrate what are taken to be serious points that need to be made. So, for example, we learn from R. Abbahu that Mordechai not only gave sustenance to Israel in ways that are well known, but also suckled Esther in the absence of a wet nurse, and of course he tells us that we know that according to at least one Tanna that male milk is kosher (*Gen Rabbah* 30.8). On the other hand, there is great concern for appropriate balance and a reconciliation of different views in agreement on the legal position. This balance is nicely illustrated in the story of R. Isaac the Smith who had two students, one of whom was very keen on *aggadah* and the other who preferred *halakhah*. That was fine, but each insisted on a diet consisting only of his preference. R. Isaac compared them to two wives of a man, one older and one younger. The younger wife kept on plucking out his gray hairs, the older one his black hairs, with the result that he ended up almost bald (*Bava Kama* 30b). It is this respect for balance which suffers so much at the hands of modern Jewish philosophers, who are not after all interested in deriving a legal conclusion from their deliberations and so can treat the material at their disposal as though it may be taken in any logical direction at all. They are right, it can, but what they do does not throw light on the Jewish nature of the subject matter they are considering, only on its logical nature. They resemble the modern Jew in Israel Zangwill's *Children of the Ghetto*, rejecting the tradition represented by his embarrassing father, as illustrated on the next page.

There is nothing specifically religious or Jewish about this issue. It is a matter of how one works with texts. To understand a text we need to compare it with other similar and dissimilar texts, and it is not enough just to use one or two texts and then play about with them philosophically as though one was doing something with those texts that relates to the tradition from which they are taken. Some philosophers think they can do this since they are not limited to the actual grammar of the texts, but can explore their deep grammar, as it were, using whatever philosophical methods they favor. But we

"*Levi! A great cry of anguish rent the air*"
Chapter VIII

Zangwill: The emancipated Jew meets his nemesis

need some idea about how to link theological material from the traditional Jewish texts to the philosophical ideas that are being
explained in tandem with those texts, and in modern Jewish philosophy we have a real problem in understanding how this is to work. It

is a bit like someone seeking to condemn, or praise, a particular religion by selecting a few sentences from the religion's tradition and saying that they represent the religion, and so can be used as the basis of an attack, or a vindication, of the religion. Even considerable thinkers such as Levinas and Seeskin fall into the trap of seeing particular passages and interpretations of Judaism as completely defining it, so that the religion falls neatly into the theoretical straitjacket that they have already prepared for it.

Modern Jewish thought is generally taken to be about reconciling religion and reason, and if one likes both, it is natural to try to do this. How one goes about it is crucial to doing anything that is really both Jewish and theoretical. I have concentrated on the former rather than the latter, and have argued that calling just anything Jewish really will not work in the sense of getting us anywhere. A working principle of much modern Jewish thought is that when you are really desperate do not panic, because there will always be a passage that agrees with you somewhere, perhaps in the Midrash, Mishnah and Talmud, and as Ben Bag Bag suggests, you can find anything in the Torah if you look hard enough and are creative enough with what you do with it (*Pirkei Avot* 5.25). It is not difficult to play around with a passage or a phrase that interests you and get a lot out of it, but what is the relevance of that process to Judaism? We end up with the pompous platitudes of the professional religious authorities which tell us nothing new, and which are often far less exciting and challenging than the traditional Jewish sources of commentary.

Illustration, Map and Picture Credits

Bar Kokhba: Children's book with stories about the hero
who fought the Romans 205
  Sh. Sekulsky, *Agadot Bar-Kokhva* (Tel Aviv: Shmuel
  Simson, 1956)

First page, *sefer Torah* 208
  Tikkun l'korim (New York: KTAV, 1946)

Zarah: A Jewish maiden about to be executed by the Greeks 217
  A.L.O.E., *Hebrew Heroes: A Tale Founded on Jewish History*
  (London: Nelson and Sons, 1880)

Zangwill: The emancipated Jew meets his nemesis 226
  Israel Zangwill, *The Grandchildren of the Ghetto*
  (London: Dent, 1914)

Bibliography

Aberbach, Moshe (2009) *Jewish Education and History: Continuity, crisis and change*, ed. and trans. David Aberbach, London: Routledge

Abravanel, Isaac (1982) *Principles of Faith (Rosh Amanah)*, trans. M. Kellner, London: Associated University Press.

Adang, Camilla (1996) *Muslim Writers on Judaism and the Hebrew Bible: From Ibn Rabban to Ibn Hazm*, Leiden: Brill.

Ahad Ha-Am (1946) *Essays, Letters, Memoirs*, ed. Leon Simon, Oxford: East and West Library.

Alba, Richard (2006) 'On the Sociological Significance of the American Jewish Experience: Boundary Blurring, Assimilation, and Pluralism', *Sociology of Religion*, 67: 347–58.

Albo, Joseph (1946) *The Book of Principles (Sefer ha-Ikkarim)*, trans. I. Husik, Philadelphia, PA: The Jewish Publications Society.

Albright, William (2006) *Archaeology and the Religion of Israel*, Louisville, KY: Fons Vitae.

Arendt, Hannah (1978) *The Jew as Pariah*, ed. Ron Feldman, New York: Grove Press.

Baeck, Leo (1936) *The Essence of Judaism*, trans. V. Grubwieser and L. Pearl, London: Macmillan.

—— (1958) *Judaism and Christianity*, trans. W. Kaufman, Philadelphia, PA: Jewish Publication Society of America.

Baer, Marc (2009) *Jewish Converts, Muslim Revolutionaries, and Secular Turks*, Stanford, CA: Stanford University Press.

Bali, Rifat (2008) *A Scapegoat for All Seasons: The Donmes or Crypto-Jews of Turkey*, Istanbul: Isis Press.

Barnavi, Eli (2003) *Historical Atlas of the Jewish People*, New York: Schocken.

Baskin, Judith (2002) *Midrashic Women: Formations of the Feminine in Rabbinic Literature*, Hanover, NH: University Press of New England.

Benvenisti, Meron (1996) *City of Stone: The Hidden History of Jerusalem*, Berkeley, CA: University of California Press.

Berger, David (1979) *The Jewish–Christian Debate in the High Middle Ages*, Philadelphia, PA: Jewish Publication Society.

Berkowitz, Michael (2000) *The Jewish self-image: American and British perspectives, 1881–1939*, London: Reaktion Books.

Berkowitz, Michael and Ruti Ungar (2007) *Fighting Back? Jewish and Black Boxers in England*, London: University College London.

Berman, Lila (2009) *Speaking of Jews: Rabbis, Intellectuals, and the Creation of an American Public Identity*, Berkeley, CA: University of California Press.

Bernstein, Richard (1998) *Freud and the Legacy of Moses*, Cambridge: Cambridge University Press.

Bloom, Maureen (2007) *Jewish Mysticism and Magic: An Anthropological Perspective*, London: Routledge.

Borowitz, Eugene (1991) *Renewing the Covenant: A Theology for the Postmodern Jew*, Philadelphia, PA: Jewish Publications Society.

—— (2006) *The Talmud's Theological Language Game*, Albany, NY: SUNY Press.

Botwinick, Aryeh (1990) *Skepticism and Political Participation*, Philadelphia, PA: Temple University Press.

Boyarin, Daniel (1990) *Intertextuality and the Reading of Midrash*. Bloomington, IN: Indiana University Press.

—— (1993) *Carnal Israel: Reading Sex in Talmudic Culture*, Berkeley, CA: University of California Press.

Boyarin, Jonathan (2010) *The Unconverted Self: Jews, Indians, and the Identity of Christian Europe*, Chicago: University of Chicago Press.

Bregman, Marc (2003) *The Tanhuma-Yalammedenu Literature*, Piscataway, NJ: Gorgias Press.

Browning, Christopher (2010) *Remembering Survival: Inside a Nazi Slave-Labor Camp*, New York: W. W. Norton.

Buber, Martin (1988) *Moses: The Revelation and the Covenant*, Amherst, NY: Prometheus Books.

—— (1991) *Tales of the Hasidim*, New York: Shocken.

—— (2002) *Meetings: Autobiographical Fragments*, London: Routledge.

Castaño Gonzales, Javier (1997) 'Social Networks in a Castilian Jewish Aljama and the Court Jews in the Fifteenth Century: A Preliminary Survey (Madrid 1440–1475)', *En la España Medieval*, 20: 379–92.

Chazan, Robert (1989) *Daggers of Faith: Thirteenth Century Missionizing and the Jewish Response*, Berkeley, CA: University of California Press.

—— (1992) *Barcelona and Beyond: The Disputation of 1263 and Its Aftermath*, Berkeley, CA: University of California Press.

Cixous, Helene (2004) *Portrait of Jacques Derrida as a Young Jewish Saint*, trans. Beverley Brahic, New York: Columbia University Press.

Coggan, R. (ed.) (1998) *The Oxford History of the Biblical World*, Oxford: Oxford University Press.

Cohen, Jeremy (ed.) (1991) *Essential Papers on Judaism and Christianity in Conflict: From Late Antiquity to the Reformation*, New York: New York University Press.

Cohen, Steven and Arnold Eisen (2002) *The Jew Within: Self, Family, and Community in America*, Bloomington, IN: Indiana University Press.

Cohen, Steven and Laurence Kotler-Berkowitz (2004) *The Impact of Childhood Jewish Education on Adult Jewish Identity*, New York: United Jewish Communities.

Cohn-Sherbok, Daniel (2003) *Judaism: History, Belief and Practice*, London: Routledge.

Diner, Hasia (2001) *Hungering for America: Italian, Irish and Jewish Foodways in the Age of Migration*, Cambridge, MA: Harvard University Press.

Dorf, Elliot and Louis Newman (1999*) Contemporary Jewish Theology: A Reader*, New York: Oxford University Press.

Eden, Esin and Nicholas Stavroulakis (1997) *Salonica: A Family Cookbook*, Athens: Talos.

Efron, John, Steven Weitzman, Matthias Lehmann and Joshua Holo (2008) *The Jews: A History*, Harlow: Pearson Education.

Elon, Menachem (1994) *Jewish Law: History, Sources, Principles*, trans. B. Auerbach and M. Sykes, Philadelphia, PA: Jewish Publications Society.

Endelman, Todd (2002) '"Practices of a Low Anthropological Level": A Shehitta Controversy of the 1950s', in A. Kershen (ed.), *Food in the Migrant Experience*, Aldershot: Ashgate.

Engel, David (2010) *Historians of the Jews and the Holocaust*, Stanford, CA: Stanford University Press.

Feldman, Seymour (2003) *Philosophy in a Time of Crisis: Don Isaac Abravanel, Defender of the Faith*, London: Routledge.

Feuerbach, Ludwig (1881) *The Essence of Christianity*, trans. M. Evans, London: Trübner.

Finkel, Avraham (1990) *The Responsa Anthology*, Northvale, NJ: Jason Aronson.

Fisch, Menachem (1997) *Rational Rabbis, Science, and Talmudic Culture*. Bloomington, IN: Indiana University Press.

Fishbane, Michael (2003) *Biblical Myth and Rabbinic Mythmaking*, Oxford: Oxford University Press.

Fraade, Steven (1991) *From Tradition to Commentary: Torah and its Interpretation in the Midrash Sifre to Deuteronomy*, Albany, NY: State University of New York Press.

Frank, Daniel and Oliver Leaman (eds) (1997) *History of Jewish Philosophy*, London: Routledge.

—— (eds) (2003) *Cambridge Companion to Medieval Jewish Philosophy*, Cambridge: Cambridge University Press.

Frank, Daniel, Oliver Leaman and Charles Manekin (eds) (2000) *The Jewish Philosophy Reader*, London: Routledge.

Freud, Sigmund (1964) 'Moses and Monotheism: Three Essays', in *The Standard Edition of the Complete Psychological Works of Sigmund Freud*, Vol. XXIII, trans. James Strachey, London: Hogarth Press, pp. 36–53.

Geller, Jay (2007) *On Freud's Jewish Body: Mitigating Circumcisions*, New York: Fordham University Press.

Gilbert, Martin (1993) *The Atlas of Jewish History*, New York: William Morrow.

—— (2007) *Churchill and the Jews: A Lifelong Friendship*, New York: Henry Holt.

Gilder, George (2009) *The Israel Test*, Minneapolis, MN: Richard Vigilante Books.

Gilman, Sandor (1997) *Smart Jews: The Construction of the Image of Jewish Superior Intelligence*, Lincoln, NE: University of Nebraska Press.

Goitein, S. (1988) *A Mediterranean Society: The Jewish Communities of the Arab World as Portrayed in the Documents of the Cairo Geniza*, Berkeley, CA: University of California Press.

Goldstein, David (trans.) (1971) *The Jewish Poets of Spain*, Harmondsworth: Penguin.

Goldstein, Rebecca (2010) *36 Arguments for the Existence of God*, New York: Pantheon.

Gorenberg, Gershom (2000) *The End of Days: Fundamentalism and the Struggle for the Temple Mount*, Oxford: Oxford University Press.

Grabar, Oleg (1996) *The Shape of the Holy: Early Islamic Jerusalem*, Princeton, NJ: Princeton University Press.

Graham, David (2003) *Secular or Religious? The Outlook of London's Jews*, London: Institute for Jewish Policy Research.

Gürkan, Leyla (2009) *The Jews as a Chosen People: Tradition and Transformation*, London: Routledge.

Halevi, Jehuda (1947) *Kuzari: The Book of Proof and Argument*, trans. I. Heinemann, Oxford: East and West Library.

Halivni, David (1991) *Peshat and Derash: Plain and Applied Meaning in Rabbinic Exegesis,* New York: Oxford University Press.

Hamblin, William and Rolph Seely (2007) *Solomon's Temple: Myth and History*, London: Thames & Hudson.

Handelman, Susan (1982) *The Slayers of Moses: The Emergence of Rabbinic Interpretation in Modern Literary Theory*, Albany, NY: State University of New York Press.

Harlow, Jules (2003) *Pray Tell: A Hadassah Guide to Jewish Prayer*, Woodstock, VT: Jewish Lights.

Harris, Jay (1995) *How Do We Know This? Midrash and the Fragmentation of Modern Judaism*, Albany, NY: State University of New York Press.

Heilman, S. (1992) *Defenders of the Faith: Inside Ultra-Orthodox Jewry*, New York: Penguin.

Herf, J. (2006) (ed.) *Anti-Semitism and anti-Zionism in Historical Perspective*, London: Routledge.

Heschel, Abraham (1996) *Prophetic Inspiration After the Prophets: Maimonides and Other Medieval Authorities*, Hoboken, NJ: KTAV.

Hezser, Catherine (1997) *The Social Structure of the Rabbinic Movement in Roman Palestine*, Tübingen: Siebeck.

Hillenbrand, Robert (2002) *The Architecture of Ottoman Jerusalem*, Louisville, KY: Fons Vitae.

Hirsch, Marianne and Leo Spitzer (2010) *Ghosts of Home: The Afterlife of Czernowitz in Jewish Memory*, Berkeley, CA: University of California Press.

Hollander, Dana (2008) *Exemplarity and Chosenness: Rosenzweig and Derrida on the Nation of Philosophy*, Stanford, CA: Stanford University Press.

Holo, Joshua (2010) *Byzantine Jewry in the Mediterranean Economy*, Cambridge: Cambridge University Press.

Holtz, Barry (1992) *Back to the Sources*, New York: Touchstone.

Hull, Margaret B. (2002) *The Hidden Philosophy of Hannah Arendt*, London: Routledge.

Ish-Shalom, Benjamin (1993) *Rav Avraham Itzhak HaCohen Kook: Between Rationalism and Mysticism*, trans. Ora Elper, Albany, NY: State University of New York Press.

Jaffee, Martin (2001) *Torah in the Mouth: Writing and Oral Tradition in Palestinian Judaism, 200 BCE–400 CE,* New York: Oxford University Press.

Judd, Robin (2007) *Contested Rituals: Circumcision, Kosher Butchering, and Jewish Political Life in Germany, 1843–1933,* Ithaca, NY: Cornell University Press.

Julius, Anthony (2010) *Trials of the Diaspora*, Oxford: Oxford University Press.

Kadushin, Charles and Elizabeth Tighe (2008) 'How Hard Is It to Be a Jew on College Campuses?', *Contemporary Jewry*, 28: 1–20.

Kadushin, Charles, Shaul Kelner, Leonard Saxe, Archie Brodsky, Amy Adamczyk and Rebecca Stern (2000) *Being a Jewish Teenager in America: Trying to Make It*, Waltham, MA: Brandeis University, Cohen Center for Modern Jewish Studies.

Kadushin, Max (2001a) *The Rabbinic Mind*, Binghamton, NY: Global Publications.

—— (2001b) *Worship and Ethics: A Study in Rabbinic Judaism.* Binghamton, NY: Global Publications.

Kalimi, Isaac (1998) 'Zion or Gerizim? The Association of Abraham and the *Aqeda* with Zion/Gerizim in Jewish and Samaritan Sources', in *Boundaries of the Ancient Near Eastern World: A Tribute to Cyrus H. Gordon* (JSOT Sup 273), Sheffield: Sheffield Academic Press, pp. 442–57.

Kamenetz, Rodger (1994), *The Jew in the Lotus*, San Francisco: Harper.

Karsh, Efraim (1999) *Islamic Imperialism: A History*, New Haven, CT: Yale University Press.

Kenyon, Kathleen (1974) *Digging up Jerusalem*, London: Benn.

Koestler, Arthur (1976) *Thirteenth Tribe: The Khazar Empire and its Heritage*, New York: Random House.

Kogman–Appel, Katrin (2004) *Jewish Book Art Between Islam and Christianity: The Decoration of Hebrew Bibles in Medieval Spain*, Leiden: Brill.

—— (2006) *Illuminated Haggadot from Medieval Spain: Biblical Imagery and the Passover Holiday*, University Park, PA: Pennsylvania State University Press.

Konner, Melvin (2009) *The Jewish Body*, New York: Nextbook/Schocken.

Kook, Abraham (1978) *Abraham Isaac Kook: The Lights of Penitence, The Moral Principles, Lights of Holiness, Essays, Letters, and Poems*, trans. Ben Zion Bokser, New York: Paulist Press.

Krauss, Samuel and William Horbury (1996) *The Jewish–Christian Controversy from the Earliest Times to 1789*, Tübingen: Mohr.

Laor, Yitzhak (2010) *The Myths of Liberal Zionism*, London: Verso.

Laquer, Walter (2003) *The History of Zionism*, London: Weidenfeld & Nicolson.

Lasker, Daniel (1977) *Jewish Philosophical Polemics against Christianity in the Middle Ages*, New York: KTAV.

Lavie, Aliza (2008) *A Jewish Woman's Prayer Book*, New York: Spiegel & Grau.

Lazarus-Yafeh, Hava (1992) *Intertwined Worlds: Medieval Islam and Bible Criticism*, Princeton, NJ: Princeton University Press.

Leaman, Oliver (1986) 'Maimonides and Natural Law', *The Jewish Law Annual*, 6: 78–93.

—— (1988) 'Maimonides, Imagination and the Objectivity of Prophecy', *Religion*, 18: 69–80.

—— (1995) 'Is a Jewish Practical Philosophy Possible?', in D. Frank (ed.), *Commandment and Community: New Essays in Jewish Legal and Political Philosophy*, Albany, NY: State University of New York Press, pp. 55–68.

—— (1996) 'Jewish Averroism', in S. Nasr and O. Leaman (eds), *History of Islamic Philosophy*, London: Routledge, pp. 769–82.

—— (1997a) *Evil and Suffering in Jewish Philosophy*, Cambridge: Cambridge University Press.

—— (1997b) *Moses Maimonides*, London: Routledge.

—— (1997c) 'Is There a Concept of Liberty in Medieval Jewish Philosophy?', *Rivista di storia della filosofia*, I: 141–51.

—— (1997d) 'Jewish Existentialism: Buber, Rosenzweig, and Soloveitchik' and, 'The Future of Jewish Philosophy', in D. Frank and O. Leaman (eds), *History of Jewish Philosophy*, London: Routledge, 1996, pp. 799–819, 895–907.

—— (1998) 'Judaism', in R. Chadwick (ed.), *Encyclopedia of Applied Ethics*, Vol. 3, Sussex: Academic Press, pp. 1–8.

—— (2001) 'Job and Suffering in Talmudic and Kabbalistic Judaism', in P. Koslowski (ed.), *The Origin and the Overcoming of Evil and Suffering in the World Religions*, Dordrecht: Kluwer, pp. 80–99.

—— (2002) 'Ideals, Simplicity, and Ethics: The Maimonidean Approach', *American Catholic Philosophical Quarterly*, 76: 107–24.

—— (2003a) '"No Poetry After Auschwitz". How Plausible Is this Idea?', in G. Scarre and E. Garrard (eds), *Philosophical Perspectives on the Holocaust*, Aldershot: Ashgate, pp. 247–56.

—— (2003b) 'Jewish Philosophy', in R. Solomon and K. Higgins (eds), *From Africa to Zen: An Invitation to World Philosophy*, New York: Rowman & Littlefield, pp. 127–42.

—— (2005a) 'Plato's Republic in Jewish Philosophy', in M. Vegetti and P. Pissavino (eds), *I Decembrio e la traduzione della Repubblica di Platone tra medioevo e umanesimo*, Naples: Bibliopolis, pp. 13–30.

—— (2005b) 'Maimonides and the Development of Jewish Thought in an Islamic Structure', in G. Tamer (ed.), *The Trias of Maimonides*, Berlin: de Gruyter, pp. 187–98.

—— (2007a) 'Maimonides and the Special Nature of the Prophecy of Moses', in G. Cerchiai and G. Rota (eds), *Maimonide e il suo tempo*, Milan: FrancoAngeli, pp. 83–94.

—— (2007b) 'Love in the Bible: The Song of Songs', in Leonard J. Greenspoon, Ronald A. Simkins and Jean Cahan (eds), *Studies in Jewish Civilization 18: 'Love – Ideal and Real in the Jewish Tradition'*, Omaha, NE: Creighton University Press.

—— (2008) 'Silence and Its Significance in Jewish Thought', *Meteria giudaica*, XIII/1–2: 91–6.

—— (2009) 'Maimonides, the Soul and the Classical Tradition', in M. Elkaisy-Friemuth and J. Dillon (eds), *The Afterlife of the Platonic Soul. Reflections on Platonic Psychology in the Monotheistic Religions*, Leiden: Brill, pp. 163–75.

Levinas, Emmanuel (1990a) *Difficult Freedom: An Essay on Judaism*, trans. S. Hand, Baltimore, MD: Johns Hopkins University Press.

—— (1990b) *Nine Talmudic Readings*, trans. A. Aronowicz, Bloomington, IN: University of Indiana Press.

Levine, Lee (ed.) (1999) *Jerusalem: Its Sanctity and Centrality to Judaism, Christianity, and Islam*, New York: Continuum.

Lewis, Bernard (1995) *Cultures in Conflict: Christians, Muslims, and Jews in the Age of Discovery*, New York: Oxford University Press.

Liebman, Arthur (1979) *Jews and the Left*, New York: John Wiley.

Litvinoff, Emanuel (ed.) (1979) *The Penguin Book of Jewish Short Stories*, Harmondsworth, Penguin.

Long, Burke (2003) *Imagining the Holy Land: Maps, Models, and Fantasy Travels*, Bloomington, IN: Indiana University Press.

Lowenstein, Steven (2000) *A Jewish Cultural Tapestry*, Oxford: Oxford University Press.

McCallum, Donald (2007) *Maimonides' Guide for the Perplexed: Silence and Salvation*, London: Routledge.

Maccoby, Hyam (2002) *The Philosophy of the Talmud*, London: Routledge.

Magen, Yitzhak (1993) 'Mount Gerizim and the Samaritans', in F. Manns and E. Alliata (eds), *Early Christianity in Context*, Studium Biblicum Franciscanum Collectio Maior 38, Jerusalem: Franciscan Printing, pp. 91–148.

Maimonides, Moses (1963) *The Guide of the Perplexed*, trans. S. Pines, Chicago: University of Chicago Press.

Mayer, Tamar and Mourad, Suleiman (eds) (2008) *Jerusalem: Idea and Reality*, London: Routledge.

Melamed, Abraham (2003) *The Image of the Black in Jewish culture: A History of the Other*, London: Routledge.

Midrash bibliography. Available at: http://huc.edu/midrash/

Morgan, Michael W. (ed.) (1987) 'The 614th Commandment', in Michael W. Morgan, *The Jewish Thought of Emil Fackenheim*, Detroit, MI: Wayne State University Press.

Nadler, Steven (2001) *Spinoza's Heresy: Immortality and the Jewish Mind*, Oxford: Clarendon Press.

Narkiss, Bezalel (1977) *The Golden Haggadah*, London: The British Library.

—— (1969) *Hebrew Illuminated Manuscripts*, Jerusalem: Encyclopedia Judaica.

Neuda, Fanny (2007) *Hours of Devotion*, trans. and int. Dinah Berland, New York: Random House.

Neusner, Jacob (1973) *From Politics to Piety: The Emergence of Pharisaic Judaism*, Englewood Cliffs, NJ: Prentice Hall.

Neusner, Jacob and Bruce Chilton (1997) *The Intellectual Foundations of Christian and Jewish Discourse: The Philosophy of Religious Argument*, London: Routledge.

Neusner, Jacob and William Scott Green (eds) (1999) *Dictionary of Judaism in the Biblical Period*, Peabody, MA: Hendrickson.

Nirenberg, David (1996) *Communities of Violence: Persecution of Minorities in the Middle Ages*, Princeton, NJ: Princeton University Press.

Panayi, Panikos (1999) *Outsiders: A History of European Minorities,* London: Reaktion Books.

Pardes, Ilana (1992) *Countertraditions in the Bible: A Feminist Approach,* Cambridge, MA: Harvard University Press.

Parkes, James (1934) *The Conflict of the Church and Synagogue: A Study in the Origins of Antisemitism,* New York: JPS.

Patterson, David (2005) *Hebrew Language and Jewish Thought,* London: Routledge.

Peters, Francis (1985) *Jerusalem: The Holy City in the Eyes of Chroniclers, Visitors, Pilgrims, and Prophets from the Days of Abraham to the Beginnings of Modern Times,* Princeton, NJ: Princeton University Press.

Philo (1946) *Selections,* ed. Hans Lewy, Oxford: East and West Library.

Pinsky, Dina (2010) *Jewish Feminists: Complex Identities and Activist Lives,* Champaign, IL: University of Illinois Press.

Ram, Uri (2008) *The Globalization of Israel: McWorld in Tel Aviv, Jihad in Jerusalem,* London: Routledge.

Robertson, Ritchie (ed.) (1999) *The German–Jewish Dialogue: An Anthology of Literary Texts 1749–1993,* Oxford: Oxford University Press.

Roden, Claudia (1996) *The Book of Jewish Food: An Odyssey from Samarkand to New York,* New York: Knopf.

Rosenthal, Erwin (1961) *Judaism and Islam,* New York: Thomas Yoseloff.

—— (2005) *Judaism, Philosophy, Culture: Selected Studies of E. I. J. Rosenthal,* London: Routledge.

Rosenzweig, Franz (2000) *Philosophcal and Theological Writings,* ed. P. Franks and Michael Morgan, Indianapolis, IN: Hackett.

Rotenstreich, Nathan (1963) *The Recurring Pattern: Studies in Anti-Judaism in Modern Thought,* London: Weidenfeld & Nicolson.

Ruderman, David (2000) *Jewish Enlightenment in an English Key: Anglo-Jewry's Construction of Modern Jewish Thought,* Princeton, NJ: Princeton University Press.

Saadya Gaon (2002) *The Book of Doctrines and Beliefs,* ed. D. Frank, Indianapolis, IN: Hackett.

Sacks, Jonathan (2000) *Radical Then, Radical Now: On Being Jewish,* London: Continuum.

Sagi, Avi and Zvi Zohar (1995) 'Giyyur, Jewish Identity, and Modernization', *Modern Judaism,* 15: 49–68.

Salter, James (1975) *Light Years,* London: Penguin.

Sand, Shlomo (2009) *The Invention of the Jewish People,* London: Verso.

Sax, David, *Save the Deli: In Search of Perfect Pastrami, Crusty Rye, and the Heart of Jewish Delicatessen,* Orlando, FL: Houghton Mifflin Harcourt. 3

Schwartz, Seth (2001) *Imperialism and Jewish Society, 200 B.C.E. to 640 C.E.,* Princeton, NJ: Princeton University Press.

Sed-Rajna, Gabrielle (1992) *Hebrew Illuminated Manuscripts from the Iberian Peninsula: Jews, Muslims, and Christians in Medieval Spain*, ed. V. Mann *et al.*, New York: George Braziller, pp. 133–55.

Seeskin, Kenneth (2001) *Autonomy in Jewish Philosophy*, Cambridge: Cambridge University Press.

—— (2007) 'Ethics, Authority, and Autonomy', in M. Morgan and P. Gordon (eds), *The Cambridge Companion to Modern Jewish Philosophy*, Cambridge: Cambridge University Press, pp. 192–208.

Segev, Tom (2002) *Elvis in Jerusalem: Post-Zionism and the Americanization of Israel*, trans. H. Watzman, New York: Metropolitan Books.

Senor, Dan and Saul Singer (2009) *Start-up Nation: The Story of Israel's Economic Miracle*, Washington, DC: Council on Foreign Relations.

Seymour, David (2007) *Law, Anti-Semitism and the Holocaust*, New York: Routledge.

Shlaim, Avi (2009) *Israel and Palestine: Reappraisals, Revisions, Refutation*, London: Verso.

Sklare, Marshall and Joseph Greenblum (1979) *Jewish Identity on the Suburban Frontier: A Study of Group Survival in the Open Society*, Chicago: University of Chicago Press.

Spicer, Kevin (ed.) (2007) *Antisemitism, Christian Ambivalence and the Holocaust*, Bloomington, IN: Indiana University Press/United States Holocaust Memorial Museum.

Spinoza, Baruch (1989) *Tractatus Theologico-Politicus*, trans. S. Shirley, Leiden: Brill.

Steinweis, Alan (2009) *Kristallnacht 1938*, Cambridge, MA: Harvard University Press.

Stern, Efraim and Yitzhak Magen (2000) 'Mount Gerizim – A Temple City: Summary of Eighteen Years of Excavations', *Qadmoniot*, 33: 74–118.

Stern, Samuel (1983) *Medieval Arabic and Hebrew Thought*, ed. Fritz Zimmerman, London: Variorum.

Svonkin, Stuart (1997) *Jews Against Prejudice: American Jews and the Fight for Civil Liberties*, New York: Columbia University Press.

Talmage, Frank (ed.) (1975) *Disputation and Dialogue: Readings in the Jewish–Christian Encounter*, New York: KTAV and Anti-Defamation League of B'nai B'rith.

The Zohar: Pritzker Edition (2003–9), trans. and commentary Daniel Matt, Princeton, NJ: Princeton University Press

Toaff, Ariel (2007) *Pasque di sangue*, Bologna: Il Mulino.

Trautner Kromann, Hanne (1993) *Shield and Sword: Jewish Polemics against Christianity and the Christians in France and Spain from 1100 to 1500*, Tübingen: Mohr.

Walzer, Michael (1986) *Exodus and Revolution*, New York: Basic Books.

Warnock, Mary (1976) *Imagination*, London: Faber & Faber.

Wasserstein, Bernard (1988) *The Secret Lives of Trebitsch Lincoln*, New Haven, CT: Yale University Press.

—— (2001) *Divided Jerusalem: The Struggle for the Holy City*, New Haven, CT: Yale University Press.

Whaley, Joachim (1997) *Theodor Herzl and the Origins of Zionism*, ed. R. Robertson and E. Timms, Edinburgh: Edinburgh University Press.

Wiesel, Elie (1970) *One Generation After*, trans. L. Edelman and E. Wiesel, New York: Random House.

Wildavsky, Aaron (2005) *Moses as a Political Leader*, Jerusalem: Shalem.

Wistrich, Robert (2010) *A Lethal Obsession: Anti-Semitism from Antiquity to the Global Jihad*, New York: Random House.

Wittgenstein, L. (1958) *Philosophical Investigations*, trans. E. Anscombe, Oxford: Basil Blackwell.

Wolfson, Elliot (2006) *Alef, Mem, Tau: Kabbalistic Musings on Time, Truth, and Death*, Berkeley, CA: University of California Press.

—— (2010) *Open Secret: Postmessianic Messianism and the Mystical Revision of Menachem Mendel Schneerson*, New York: Columbia University Press.

Yerushalmi, Yosef (1982) *Zakhor: Jewish History and Jewish Memory*, Seattle, WA: University of Washington Press.

Zangwill, Israel (1914) *The Grandchildren of the Ghetto*, London: Dent.

Zornberg, Avivah (2009) *The Murmuring Deep: Reflections on the Biblical Unconscious*, New York: Schocken.

Index

Ubiquitous terms not indexed are God, Hebrew, Jews, Israelites, law and tradition.

I.B.TAURIS INTRODUCTIONS TO RELIGION

Daoism: An Introduction – Ronnie L Littlejohn
HB 9781845116385
PB 9781845116392

Jainism: An Introduction – Jeffery D Long
HB 9781845116255
PB 9781845116262

Judaism: An Introduction – Oliver Leaman
HB 9781848853942
PB 9781848853959

Zoroastrianism: An Introduction – Jenny Rose
HB 9781848850873
PB 9781848850880

Confucianism: An Introduction – Ronnie L Littlejohn
HB 9781848851733
PB 9781848851740

Sikhism: An Introduction – Nikky-Guninder Kaur Singh
HB 9781848853201
PB 9781848853218

Islam: An Introduction – Catharina Raudvere
HB 9781848850835
PB 9781848850842

Christianity: An Introduction – Philip Kennedy
HB 9781848853829
PB 9781848853836

Hinduism: An Introduction – Will Sweetman
HB 9781848853270
PB 9781848853287

Buddhism: An Introduction – Alexander Wynne
HB 9781848853966
PB 9781848853973